MW00586209

How All Politics Became
Reproductive Politics

REPRODUCTIVE JUSTICE: A NEW VISION
FOR THE TWENTY-FIRST CENTURY

*Edited by Rickie Solinger, Khiara M. Bridges,
Zakiya Luna, and Ruby Tapia*

How All Politics Became Reproductive Politics

*From Welfare Reform to
Foreclosure to Trump*

Laura Briggs

UNIVERSITY OF CALIFORNIA PRESS

University of California Press, one of the most distinguished university presses in the United States, enriches lives around the world by advancing scholarship in the humanities, social sciences, and natural sciences. Its activities are supported by the UC Press Foundation and by philanthropic contributions from individuals and institutions. For more information, visit www.ucpress.edu.

University of California Press
Oakland, California

© 2017 by The Regents of the University of California

Library of Congress Cataloging-in-Publication Data

Names: Briggs, Laura, 1964– author.
Title: How all politics became reproductive politics : from welfare reform to foreclosure to Trump / Laura Briggs.
Description: Oakland, California : University of California Press, [2017] | Series: Reproductive justice : a new vision for the twenty-first century ; 2 | Includes bibliographical references and index. |
Identifiers: LCCN 2017007025 (print) | LCCN 2017014266 (ebook) | ISBN 9780520957725 (Epub) | ISBN 9780520281912 (cloth : alk. paper)
Subjects: LCSH: Reproductive rights—United States—History. | Human reproduction—Political aspects—United States.
Classification: LCC HQ766.5.U5 (ebook) | LCC HQ766.5.U5 B73 2017 (print) | DDC 612.6—dc23
LC record available at https://lccn.loc.gov/2017007025

Manufactured in the United States of America

25 24 23 22 21 20 19 18 17
10 9 8 7 6 5 4 3 2 1

For Jackson

CONTENTS

ACKNOWLEDGMENTS

This book emerged out of many conversations, including ones on playgrounds and in doctors' offices, with family and friends. It particularly came from conversations with students in my Politics of Reproduction course at the University of Massachusetts Amherst, who have been invaluable in helping me think through the arguments of this book. They have been every professor's dream students—thoughtful, committed, and curious in ways that have pushed me and taught me. Their research has inspired my own, and our work together is truly represented on every page. I have been exceedingly lucky in my colleagues as well; the scholars and faculty associated with the Five College Reproductive Rights, Health, and Justice Certificate provided an intellectual community that made it possible to conceive and to write this book. If it makes any sense at all, it's because of that smart group of faculty. The book also received a remarkable amount of help from a Facebook community, for which I am quite grateful, particularly since such support was so unlooked for.

I am also indebted to those who read one of the many versions of the manuscript (and some who read two or more), including Dána-ain Davis, Alexandra Stern, Lynn Morgan, Doug Hornstein, Rickie Solinger, Mimi Petro, Angie Willey, and students in WGSS 187, Gender, Sexuality, and Culture. Niels Hooper of University of California Press first persuaded me that there was a book here, one day over many drinks in Puerto Rico. He offered friendship, encouragement, and support in the much-longer-than-expected process of getting this book written. Martha Balaguera was an ideal reader and a brilliant research assistant, who performed heroics with footnotes at the very last minute. Zaynah Shaikh also provided help with research.

Audiences at the National Women's Studies Association, the American Studies Association, Radcliffe Institute, the Boston Seminar on Women and Gender, Vermont Law School, and Yale University offered smart commentary that made this a better book.

I wrote this while being the chair of the Women, Gender, Sexuality Studies Department at UMass Amherst, which meant that everyone I worked with had to live with this book, including my Friday disappearing act and other moments of absence (physical and mental). I've been incredibly fortunate to have colleagues who not only put up with it but actively supported the thinking that produced this book, all brilliant intellectuals in their own right: Banu Subramaniam, Miliann Kang, Svati Shah, Angie Willey, Abbie Boggs, Jacqueline Luce, Lezlie Frye, Alexandra Deschamps, Tanisha Ford, Kirsten Leng, Mecca Jamilah Sullivan, and Kiran Asher, as well as Linda Hillenbrand and Karen Lederer, who kept everything going.

This is a book about households and reproductive labor, and my own nurtured and inspired this book. I am endlessly indebted to my partner, Jennifer Nye, who was the intellectual companion for so much of this book; our work together to figure out reproductive labor and the public policy that surrounds it was both theoretical and practical, from yelling at the newspaper to juggling our own crises of work and home. Jackson has lived with this book nearly his entire six years of life, and has felt the sacrifices it demanded of him acutely in every marble run I didn't help build, even as his invitations to play hooky from it inspired dance parties and window box gardens. It's ruined him permanently, though, as he has started writing books of his own. This book also had nonhuman companions: Toby the dog, who positioned himself under my desk for nearly every minute of its writing, and Ramona, a cat, who sat on my head when she could. Our other resident feline, Sophie, cared not one whit about this book or my labors, feeling that such things were not the affair of cats. I couldn't have done it without all of them.

Introduction

Let me begin with a story. I am in the waiting room at the pediatrician's office with my kid for a routine checkup, helping him with a learn-to-read app on the iPad and feeling frustrated that the doctor is taking so long, because I need to go to work. Every minute spent here tacks time on to how long I will have to stay when I finally get back to my desk. I look around the packed room at people waiting in line with camp physical forms; a dad helping a ten-year-old with her school project on a laptop; two immigrant moms addressing their kids alternately in English and a second language, one in Spanish, the other in Arabic. In an alcove partly separated from the main room, I see a sick kid leaning on her mom and reading *Diary of a Wimpy Kid,* while next to me, a heavily tattooed young couple is hovering nervously over their few-weeks-old baby.

Maybe because my paid job involves teaching and I am helping my little one learn, suddenly the carefully cultivated separation between "working" and "not-working" slips for me. *I am doing work right now, and so are all these other people.* I look around again, noticing how some of us are intensively engaged in cultivating access to the middle class—providing our kids with technology and camps for "enrichment" (and child care while we're at work and school is out). But not all of us in this waiting room are middle-class, and we're all engaged in the reproduction of things we value. For starters, life itself: all of these children's health and continued vitality depend intensely on the care, concern, and material resources we bring them. Even as we wait in the doctor's office, we are engaged in the social reproduction of language, literacy, culture, comfort, sociability. It is such concrete, tangible labor by so many people. When social scientists theorize what is public and what is private, what work is, what the economy is, how does all this reproductive labor just drop out? What makes this a *private* sphere? As anthropologist Sarah Franklin said, "How is the constant, enduring, and world-historical significance of this reproductive labor constantly relegated to near invisibility?"[1]

In calling this work "reproductive labor," Franklin is drawing on a long intellectual tradition in feminism and on the left. Reproductive labor is the work necessary to the reproduction of human life—not only having and raising children but also feeding people; caring for the sick, the elderly, and those who cannot work; creating safety and shelter; building community and kin relationships; and attending to people's psychic and spiritual well-being. Most reproductive labor is done by people understood to be women, and because it is historically unpaid work—critical to the production and maintenance of a labor force but outside the formal system of work, wages, and production—we often think of it as belonging to a private sphere—the opposite of the public, where politics and economics live.

I want to turn this story on its head. Not only is reproductive labor real, concrete, and important, but it's actually crucial—not just to households but to politics. When we think about the major questions that have animated political debate in the United States in the past half century, what comes to mind? Welfare, immigration, policing, schools, abortion, reproductive technology? All of these are reproductive politics questions. Not just abortion, reprotech, and K-12 education, which of course couldn't be anything else, but all these and a great many others—gay marriage, civil rights and the long Black freedom movement, social security and pensions, and the foreclosure crisis have reproductive politics at their core or as a critical component. When we talk about race on the left, we talk about police shooting young people of color, a conversation developed vigorously in recent years in relationship to the Movement for Black Lives. When the right talks about race and poverty, it is about teen pregnancy, fatherless families, and welfare—the great debate in the 1990s about whether some mothers could stay home with their children, or everyone had to go out and get a McJob. When Donald Trump, vying for the Republican presidential nomination, first hit the front page of every paper in 2015 and generated Twitter storms, it was by saying that Mexico was sending "rapists" to the United States. Aside from strumming an old string in US politics by seeming to defend a violated, victimized (white) womanhood from a racialized other (the lynching story, or before that, the Indian captivity narrative), he also got it wrong in an interesting way: the majority of migrants from Mexico to the United States are women, in significant part because changes in reproductive labor in the United States have made the work of caring for the house, the children, the elderly, and people with disabilities something that, increasingly, someone had to be hired to do—and Latinas, in particular, got those jobs.

Our public conversations about race, immigration, and same-sex marriage center around questions of children, households, and families. (Or, to put it the other way, our conversations about reproductive politics are deeply about race, just as they are about sexuality.) When we think about feminism and careers, abortion, and assisted reproduction, it is perhaps more obvious that we are talking about reproduction, but I want to argue that we are thinking as much about the politics of how to *raise* children and the economy at large as we are the simple facts of pregnancy and birth. When we talk about the economy, we are talking about reproductive politics, because families and households are where we live our economic situation. Reproductive politics are, in fact, powerfully central to everything else we talk about in the United States—whether we look to wealth and poverty, schools and policing, financial speculation in the housing market (and single mothers as a particular niche market to be targeted for subprime mortgages), or even foreign policy (think about overpopulation and development, international adoption, the ever-renewable fight about aid funding for birth control and abortion, or burqas and the politics of modest dress and family relations in the Islamic world). In the United States, this book will argue, there is no outside to reproductive politics, even though that fact is sometimes obscured.

Also, I want to pause here and say a word about language. I am struggling with words like "women" and "mothers" in this book. After all, not just women get pregnant; so do transmen. The trans movement has urged us to use gender-neutral language, like "pregnant people" and "parent," or at least mark the ways that women are produced as cisgendered. Perhaps these would have been better choices for this book. But I have not been able to make this language work, tripping over the other sets of meanings they inadvertently generate. First, "pregnant people" and "non-pregnant people" was also a conservative language for denying protections against pregnancy discrimination in the workplace by insisting that it is not a form of sex discrimination that would be illegal under the Equal Protection clause of the Fourteenth Amendment. Instead, as these commentators argued in an important Supreme Court case, *Geduldig v. Aiello,* as long as all "pregnant people" and "non-pregnant people" are treated the same, it's not sex discrimination to refuse benefits to pregnant people.[2] This argument seems like pure sophistry to me, and it's what stops me every time I hear "pregnant people." Second, at no point in the debates I discuss in this book am I certain that the "women" and "mothers" being spoken to or about are, in fact, exclusively cisgendered. However grotesquely misnamed or mischaracterized, transmen are woven through these stories. Much of what interests me in this book is the ways the category of woman is being enacted or broken apart into unstable pieces, particularly in and through race. What is indispensable to my thinking and borrowed from transgender studies scholarship is that gender is being produced and maintained as a site of inequity in part through trans-specific oppression, and that a binary understanding of gender is an indispensable part of the infra- [*Gender binary*] structure of policy and economy, households and reproductive labor. In fact, this book could not exist without that thought.

Another story. I am standing on the playground years earlier. My kid is still in diapers, and I am talking to other parents of small children. We're comparing notes about how we are managing the work/child care/money problem that is somehow much worse than any of us expected. Day care costs upwards of $16,000 a year per kid, even when we could find a slot and figure out how to have a job with the 9-to-3 hours (or even 9-to-12, someone points out. What do they think? We're trying to go to *yoga?*). Most of us have decided to have one parent at least partly out of the formal workforce, home doing reproductive labor instead of making money to support our household. As far as I can tell, we're all thrilled that we have our kids, but we didn't realize how serious the career and financial ding was going to be. Nobody really anticipates that in five or ten years the parents who opted for less money and less ("real") work will readily go back to their chosen field, or if they were never exactly in a career before, even a job as good as the one they left. A professional career, or even just earning a steady income, is something you go at full tilt or accept the consequences. Given the high cost of day care, we swallow hard and live with it.

This book narrates how we got to this point—how did it get so hard to figure out how to both earn enough to eat and take care of children, elders, neighborhoods, and communities? In the last half century, reproductive labor has become simultaneously more important than ever (as public support is reduced) and harder to find the time and the space to do. Even the irritatingly individualizing corporate phrase "work-life balance" (oh, I see, the problem is just that I have to have better balance … yeah, right) implicitly acknowledges that it's a high-wire act. Declining real wages, longer work hours, and reduced government support for children, mothers, and elders have made families and households in their many configurations more important to the well-being of those who can't care for and support themselves independently—which is to say, all of us, at some points in our lives. Since the late 1970s, real wages have stagnated for nearly all workers (90 percent) and incomes have declined for men as a group,[3] forcing households to put ever more people in the workplace to maintain standards of living even as we have to figure out how to do all that care work. In heterosexual families, this means women—mothers, the caretakers for elders and people who have disabilities that keep them out of the formal labor force and/or need support for tasks of daily living—work. It also means that households use debt as a way to leverage standards of living—credit cards, then second mortgages and home equity loans, and especially as access to unsecured credit has declined since 2008, student loans being leveraged to support family members. You could say that as real wages have stagnated or declined since 1980, families have thrown everything they have at the problem of staying in the middle class: first mothers, then the house, then college students.

The same forces that have eroded wages have also taken away a lot of the "free" reproductive labor—housewives or elders who used to have pensions, for example, are much more likely to be in the work force than they were in the middle of the twentieth century. Everyone is in the formal labor force if they possibly can be, whatever that means about cramming reproductive labor into leftover time around the edges. Leisure time is evaporating, and most middle-class households are relying heavily on credit markets. In 1960, 20 percent of mothers worked. Today, 70 percent of US children live in households where all the adults are employed.[4] In 2008, US Americans reported, on average, just 16 hours of leisure time a week, 10 hours less than when Harris started tracking that number in 1973. If you eliminate those older than forty-three, adults work an average of 50–55 hours a week.[5] Even early in the shift to longer work days—before the delirious 1990s—parents began to report having less and less time to spend with their children; that time declined by 10 hours between 1960 and 1986.[6]

There is a reason we have talked so endlessly in the United States about reproductive politics over the past half century: the time to do reproductive labor is being shut down as a result of broad political and economic changes that have transformed the relationship of business, government, and households. That's what we were talking about on the playground that day. Care labor has been intensely privatized—there's not even a pretense anymore that businesses should pay a "family wage" or protect workers' reproductive health or that government ought to be concerned about the well-being of communities, families, children, or elders. The idea that there should be a federal Children's Bureau seems decidedly archaic. Instead, every family and household has the private responsibility to figure out how to support dependents and enable them to survive and thrive, even as they do so on an uneven playing field constructed by both business and government.

Since the 1970s, the United States and much of the rest of the world have been having a significant political fight about privatization of all kinds. It is about a political-economic system that Latin Americans and Europeans call "neoliberalism" and we used to call "Reaganomics" and now just call the "free market." Another version—the one that animated Donald Trump's 2016 political campaign—is "globalization," the concern about free trade agreements and immigrants, but that is an oversimplification of what has changed in the last half century. (The word "globalization" was also chosen by that campaign to gesture toward the anti-globalism of the white nationalist right—the a fear of world government that reaches back to the John Birch Society's opposition to membership in the United Nations and beyond.) The problem, I argue, is not so much free trade per se, much less immigration, but rather the broader neoliberal system in which they are embedded. As I will discuss in chapter 1—and actually throughout the book—neoliberalism is a political revolution that began in the late 1970s in the United States, in which corporate America and Wall Street have reset government priorities to shrink spending on the well-being of actual humans—from schools to housing to child welfare programs like AFDC—in order to keep corporate taxes low and profits high. Tax cutting and budget cuts are the result of a struggle to make government smaller and to devolve its responsibilities onto families and other civic institutions. Conservatives began during the Reagan administration to succeed in privatizing dependency, making children, elders, and the well-being of households and communities into individual problems.

One of the stunning moral low points of neoliberalism was in 2005, when Fox News network's Bill O'Reilly went off about people trapped on their roofs after Hurricane Katrina, saying that they were the perfect example of bad personal and educational choices—people trapped between the disaster of the Army Corps of Engineers' failed levees and Mayor Ray Nagin's refusal to commit the money to enact the evacuation plans for those without cars or credit cards, who could not just leave and check into a hotel. O'Reilly called it a "teachable moment"—and suggested showing videos of trapped and dead people floating in the water in New Orleans to school-aged children with the question "Do you want to be poor?" as if poverty were just a foolish decision.[7] Welfare reform was a key early issue for neoliberalism's inauguration as state policy in the United States, because only by making the case that supporting the care of small impoverished children was a state responsibility could one argue for privatizing everything else—pensions and social security, health care, education, even public safety (by putting guns in the hands of every individual).

While many scholars and activists have told the story of how neoliberalism has changed our political and economic system, this book tells that story from inside families. Although large-scale changes in the economy or politics often seem abstract (at least until your manufacturing job moves from the United States

to Mexico), they touch us every day. It's not (just) that your partner is a jerk and didn't start the laundry last night, or your kid
dawdles horribly about getting his coat on to go to school, or
that your mother fell again but is being ridiculously stubborn
about even thinking about moving, it's that these little things
have become impossible stress storms because only a very few of
us any longer have the time or resources to do reproductive
labor while also earning the wages it takes to keep us all alive,
never mind thriving. These seemingly trivial household fights
over reproductive labor are where neoliberalism lives in our
daily lives. And, at a slightly larger scale, these changes and sites
of seemingly very personal strife drive the policy debates that
this book explores: feminism, racial justice movements, and the
stagnant real wages that drove us all into the workforce; welfare
and McJobs; immigration, nannies, and housecleaners; in vitro
fertilization (IVF), later childbearing, and rising racial disparities in infant mortality; gay marriage; and Black and Latinx single moms, subprime mortgages, and the foreclosure crisis. It's
not us. It's the economy (stupid).

In analyzing large-scale economic change from inside households, I am drawing on a long feminist political and economic
tradition that has grappled with economic shifts in precisely this
way. The concept itself comes from Marx, writing at the height
of the long workday in the nineteenth century, who realized that
the industrial revolution had taken the working class perilously
close to the limits of how many hours one could work for wages
(and for how little money) and still provide space for the production of "workers' replacements"—that is, the next generation
required even by the capitalist class as workers were dying in
their twenties of sheer overwork. From Cuba to China to European socialism, feminists have described reproductive labor as

particularly *women's* work and built political movements that center its crucial significance to all economies.

The changes in the United States that have brought our households to a new point of crisis didn't happen overnight. They were the result of a long political campaign on the right. The central components of shrinking the state were reproductive politics and race, or better, a specifically racialized account of families and reproductive labor. In the welfare reform debate, conservatives painted families that needed public benefits as Black, Latinx, immigrant, or Native. The more successful they were in demonizing people of color and welfare, the less public support there was for anyone's household, even if it was middle-class and white. Our current time/wages/reproductive labor crisis represents the defeat of a particular version of feminist and racial justice politics, which demanded survival resources for communities and their reproduction—an end to forced sterilization, enough work or public benefits that kids and communities get enough to eat, relief from state violence or neglect that results in lower life expectancy and high rates of infant mortality—and a 40-hour workweek that enables people to get paid and still have time to do essential care work. These movements prioritized reproductive labor as real and important, insisted on the value of people of color and their reproduction, asked for affordable, high-quality child care and wages for housework, embraced many different kinds of households and kinship, and demanded support for and affirmation of gay dads and lesbian mothers, single mothers, working mothers, and those who didn't want to be any kind of parent at all.

Beginning in the late 1980s, as part of its campaign for lower taxes and a smaller (or nonexistent) social safety net, conservatives argued for "traditional" families and their "family values," (which meant heterosexuality, women at home, the privatization of care work and domestic violence, and church as support if families got in bad trouble economically or otherwise). This book shows how "welfare queens" became the target of this Reagan-era crusade for family values, resting on the shaming of Black, Latinx, and Native women as lazy, sexually loose, single mothers who were all "welfare cheats." This campaign went hand in hand with the related invention of the "crack mother"/"crack baby" (despite little evidence that crack has much effect on pregnancies or their outcomes[8]) to describe the kind of government conservatives saw as desirable: no benefits to families or households but a lot of policing (and incarceration—the number of women in prison rose 800 percent between 1980 and 2002).[9] This, despite the fact that the use of AFDC, cocaine, and alcohol are all more common among white mothers.[10]

As anyone who hasn't been living under a rock for the past forty years knows, parenting and other kinds of reproductive labor are intensely racialized. Some people's social reproduction—Black folks, Latin Americans and Latinxs, Native communities, immigrants—not only doesn't count as much as white social reproduction but can be shamed and denigrated. When unarmed teenagers Mike Brown and Trayvon Martin were shot—in Ferguson, Missouri, and Sanford, Florida, respectively—some (white) people actively campaigned to portray them as thugs and suggest that the shootings were justified because, well, they were criminals and their lives simply didn't matter. Anti-immigration activists have sought measures to ensure that some Latinx babies can't get birth certificates ("anchor babies"), that as children they can't go to school or get vaccinations (Prop. 187), that as young adults they can't go to college (state bans on their presence at public universities in Georgia, Alabama, and South Carolina), and that as adults they can't get jobs—all by insisting that they are "illegal." Since the nineteenth century, when Indian boarding schools were founded to "kill the Indian to save the man" by cutting boys' hair and extinguishing kids' use of indigenous languages, the U.S. project with Native kids has been, so far as possible, to eliminate their Nations' social reproduction altogether—sponsoring adoption programs by non-Native people and vigorously pursuing reasons to put them into foster care. Since 2015, the Goldwater Institute, a conservative legal organization, has actively been working to destroy the Indian Child Welfare Act, designed to protect the rights of parents, extended family, and community for children eligible for tribal enrollment.

This book argues that racializing reproductive labor and pretending it doesn't exist or doesn't matter have worked in and through each other to produce a particularly taut and tense politics of families and households across the past forty years: it's incredibly difficult to survive without one (because you can't even get through the flu without someone to care for you, never mind go through any extended period of joblessness or disability, childhood, or aged years), but not all families count. The campaign to shame the welfare queen—begun long before Reagan but intensifying with his campaign for the presidency and subsequent election—produced both these effects: the illegitimacy of some families and the elimination of benefits to support them. "Welfare reform" was both a symptom and a cause of changes in the middle-class family: nobody could stay home with the kids anymore and there could be no expectation of public support. The anti-welfare campaign, more than any other single thing, ushered in the neoliberal moment.

The massive disinvestment in families and communities that neoliberalism represented should have generated more opposition than it did (and, of course, it may yet). As the Occupy movement pointed out, citing economist Joseph Stiglitz, 99 percent of us suffered as a result.[11] However, its racial politics forestalled much of that criticism. That is, the peculiar genius of US conservative politics across centuries has been to compensate white folks for their impoverishment with a belief that whites are morally superior. However down and out they may be, white families could always think themselves better than someone. As social theorists from W. E. B. DuBois to George Lipsitz have argued, this compensatory function of whiteness may have been a bad bargain in that it gave the elite classes virtually unchecked power and a free hand to loot the fruits of other people's labor, but it was not without compensations: it allowed middle and even working-class whites access to better schools, roads, and housing; freedom to use parks, pools, and other public spaces; few restrictions on voting; and relative freedom from surveillance and policing.[12] With the election of Donald Trump in 2016, the United States saw the next iteration of the precipitous drop in wages, health, and family well-being across the middle and working classes begun under Reagan: an authoritarian state that only vaguely promises economic well-being but enthusiastically champions white supremacy.

This book narrates how reproductive politics have been transformed by neoliberalism and how the "culture wars" that were supposedly about God and gays (which is to say, the proper form of the family and reproductive labor) have been the backbone of a campaign to shift the relationship of government, personal responsibility, and economy. That is to say, it shows how all politics became reproductive politics, and remained so. Households are where we have most acutely felt the changes of neoliberalism, its shocks and disruptions. The first two chapters describe feminist and racial justice movements' expansive vision of ways to share care and survival work across family, communities, and government in the middle decades of the twentieth century and the racist welfare reform campaign that crushed it.

The third chapter looks at immigration—the crackdown on immigrants in the United States and the global restructuring that forced a majority female migrant labor force to leave their children behind in home countries as they came to the United States (among a host of other places) to do, for the most part, reproductive labor for other people's families—as nannies, housekeepers, gardeners, and elder care and attendant care workers. They took over the work that had previously been done by women and families who now had everyone in the formal labor force, first in global cities like Los Angeles and New York among the wealthy, and then spiraling down to the middle class all over the country. It's a story about offshoring reproductive labor. This wasn't just a privilege of the wealthy; it was also a survival strategy of those most disadvantaged by the massive impoverishment of that era (think of the Mexican peso collapse of 1994 or the Guatemalan civil war), who were also shifting people in need of care away from those who could work for wages—dramatically so. As these macroeconomic shifts put a migratory workforce in motion, families were often shredded, with elders, children, and those with disabilities that prevented them from holding jobs (and those disabled while trying to migrate, working in unsafe jobs, or doing the militarized labor of imperial expansion, policing borders and waging wars on drugs) staying "home" while the working-age, able-bodied population moved to wherever they could sell their labor.

These raced and gendered changes also resulted in dramatic demographic shifts within the United States, including the rise of what some called neo-eugenics in the form of assisted reproductive technologies (ARTs), which I turn to in the fourth chapter. People started to have kids later, as women in particular delayed

(margin note, handwritten: "childbearing to the futurity transition")

childbearing until after a long period in higher education and getting established in a career. This in turn led to a growing prevalence of "structural infertility"—infertility resulting from women who weren't able to start trying to get pregnant until their thirties, after their peak period of fertility had passed. A new industry, selling ARTs—assisted reproduction technologies (like IVF)—stepped into the breach, promising that this was a problem you could buy your way out of, and offering new options for queer families and transgender folk, too. Unfortunately, its success rates were low—around 40 percent at best; its costs, astronomical. Only under exceptional circumstances was access to it even, as in the military, which had a great welfare system—worthy of socialism—from universal health care to high-quality child care. The privatized cost of ARTs for those outside the military, however, was particularly unfortunate since the effects of growing economic inequality were most strongly felt by people of color, whether as poverty, the grinding stress of staying in the middle class, or the conflicts of work, dependent care, and community. Black women in particular were about twice as likely as white women to experience infertility and about half as likely to use ARTs. African American women were also more than twice as likely as white women of matched economic class or age to lose a child in its first year of life, an epidemic of infant mortality increasingly documented by public health experts as an effect of racism, exacerbated by the decline in survival resources of public benefits and the labor of communities and households and the sharp growth of racial disparities in the period between Reagan-era welfare reform and the Trump administration.

For queer and trans families and households, the contradictions of this situation were intensified as their right to even be considered a family was explicitly challenged in the rhetoric of "family values," which I explore in chapter 5. Neoliberal privatization is the context in which gay marriage became an issue, despite the decided ambivalence of queer activists and communities. Family ties—of a particularly matrimonial sort—were not only the only way to get health insurance or pensions but also to visit your dying lover in the hospital, hang on to custody or visitation of your kids, or stay in relation to the people you love in the event of illness or serious disability. After forty years of changes in the workplace and government, the critical necessity of family to support dependency was the new normal, and the push for same-sex marriage revealed exactly how limited our concept of family and household had become.

In short, the sharply divisive issues of the last forty years—feminism and stay-at-home moms, welfare reform, family values, immigration, crack babies, IVF and surrogacy, disproportionate Black infant mortality rates, gay marriage—have all been organized along a single economic and political fault line: the ballooning importance of households and their private care labor in the face of a disappearing safety net, work lives that make no accommodation to the reproductive work of households and communities, and the shaming of those single mothers, queers, trans folk, feminists, and others not organizing their households into a "traditional" family. The final pages of the book look at the economic meltdown of 2007–2008 and the central role of someone who looks suspiciously like the reincarnation of the welfare queen with a twist: the "subprime" borrower. Disproportionately, Black, Latinx, and single mothers were aggressively targeted by banks and mortgage companies for deceptively marketed loans that often couldn't be paid once the job market and housing markets began to get soft. Or they were sometimes defrauded of their homes and money by the mortgage service industry and robo-signers even if they did pay. And an intensified form of Reaganomics gave rise to the Tea Party, born in a rant against the (false) idea that President Obama was going to bail out "losers' mortgages," apparently held disproportionately by illegal immigrants and African Americans. However much they may have deserved a bailout, the Obama administration in its alliances with Wall Street was never going to deliver it.

In the United States, all politics are reproductive politics. It's not just that our public conversations about feminism, race, immigration, trans and gay liberation have centered around questions of children, households, and families. Wealth and poverty issues center around how many children people can afford, drug use during pregnancy, charter schools and school discipline, foster care, and policing. While the overwhelming majority of people in poverty are women and children, our political conversation about the growing gap between rich and poor and the decline in class mobility seems to take no account of how very gendered this problem is, notwithstanding the brief prominence of a conversation about the feminization of poverty in the early 1980s.[13]

The current state of reproductive labor is marked by crisis. We don't have the time or resources to care for those who cannot work because by keeping wages depressed, business can command that everyone is supposed to work. Government has been artificially and deliberately thrown into crisis by tax cuts that lead to debt and austerity. Crises of care labor are problems that particularly affect those understood to be women, and even more so impoverished women, but they also reach men and stretch up the class ladder: we have built a society and an economic system that makes it very difficult to have dependents and an adequate income unless you are independently wealthy. And this is not, actually, good for anyone.

CHAPTER ONE

"Radical Feminism's Misogynistic Crusade" or the Conservative Tax Revolt?

An account of feminism and reproductive labor has been conspicuously important to the conservative right in the United States, but in the opposite direction of what I have described: the right accuses feminists and feminism of not doing or caring about reproductive labor. For example, Stephen Bannon, President Donald Trump's chief strategist and long the head of Breitbart News, famously described feminists "as a bunch of dykes from seven sisters schools." He contrast them with conservative women "who would be pro-family, they would have husbands, they would love their children."[1] Feminists, in this account, are those who don't do reproductive labor (or love their children)—only conservative women do. In 2012, Rick Santorum, running for the Republican Party's presidential nomination, made the same point (even as gay sex columnist Dan Savage was trying to make Santorum's name synonymous with that "frothy mixture of lube and fecal matter that is sometimes the product of anal sex"[2]). Said Santorum, "Respect for stay-at-home mothers has been poisoned by ... radical feminism's misogynistic crusade to make working outside the home the only marker of social value and self-respect."[3] Not employers, as Marx had it, but *feminists* think that only productive labor is worthy of value. In 2015 Fox News guest Gavin McInnes, founder of Vice Media, turned to a startled program host, Tamara Holder, and explained to her, "Look, you're miserable. You would be so much happier with kids around you tonight.... Feminism has made women miserable. Women were much happier when housewives were glorified."[4] Here, at least, he gets the narrative right—anti-feminism has offered a compensatory "glorification" of household labor (though not wages, support, or help), while feminists have offered an analysis of the exploitation or at least exhaustion inherent in the "double day" that suggests why an attorney and analyst like Holder might have to hold off on or decide not to have children.

This chapter argues that if we want to figure out who's to blame for the kind of stress storm that reproductive labor has become, we would not look to feminists. On the contrary, the politics represented by Trump's administration, Fox News, and Santorum (the man, not the gooey sex by-product)—the wing of the Republican coalition that has relentlessly pushed for lower wages and lower taxes—has a great deal more to answer for than feminism does about why it's become unimaginable for most caregivers to stay home with children or other dependents, or even be able to find a humane enough workplace where they can deal with family or community responsibilities without being afraid of being fired (or at the very least, expect they can successfully file a complaint if they are fired for being pregnant[5]). The capacity for any household (except for those with the highest-paid executives or inherited wealth) to afford a house, a car, food, and some middle-class consumer goods on a single income has all but disappeared, and the problem of who is watching the kids is only a snow day or summer vacation away from near-crisis.[6]

The argument that "stay-at-home moms" are disappearing because of "working mothers" is structured by the same kind of magical thinking as the conservative gay marriage argument—if gay people marry, something bad will happen to heterosexual marriages—or the anti-immigrant one—if they have jobs, you won't—and is just as flawed. Working mothers don't actually *do* anything to those who would prefer to stay out of the workforce to do reproductive labor; the economy does. In fact, all reproductive labor—from caring for elders to building relationships across communities—is under severe pressure from the massive upward redistribution of wealth that began in the 1980s. By the 1990s, these politics had become the mainstream of the Democratic Party as well, especially under Bill Clinton and the South's Democratic Leadership Council, which called for making the Democrats the party of business and white men again.[7] It's not feminists. It's business and politicians. Rising conservatism in both parties and "business friendly" lower taxes in the eighties turned back feminist, labor, and racial justice activism for public benefits, affordable, high-quality day care, education, and decent workplaces that were safe and compatible with human reproduction. This was the real "war on women"—except it wasn't just on women, or even those whose boring, repetitive, insecure jobs made them like women in the labor force. It was on impoverished people, the working class, and the middle class generally as they scrambled to figure out how to reproduce the species, care for those who couldn't care for themselves, and enjoy their lives and leisure—while greedy jobs and stingy public support steadily eroded their ability to have those things.

This chapter explores how the activist movements on the left in the twentieth century fought for the time and space for reproductive labor. From the Popular Front and radical labor in the first third of the century to racial justice movements at midcentury and feminism in the late sixties and seventies, reproductive politics was crucial to left activism throughout the century, even if the only part of it that we seem to remember is the fights over abortion and birth control. Because this kind of activism made demands on business and government to give people time, sufficient wages, and, in a pinch, public support to keep their households afloat, Milton Friedmanesque, hard-right conservatives foundationally opposed these efforts. Instead, movements on the right to turn the mainstream of politics toward reducing the size of government was fundamentally about how far they could push the privatization of reproductive labor. The battles over this question had many names, including the forty-hour workweek (known on the right as the fight against paid overtime or raising the minimum wage); the Black Panther Party's free breakfast programs for children, wages for housework, and subsidized early childhood education (or, as conservative think tanks like the Heritage Foundation preferred, "welfare,"), and workplaces that minimized people's exposure to lead and other toxic substances (aka "excessive regulation."). Some of the headline-grabbing names for these fights were welfare "reform," immigration, gay marriage, and the politics of foreclosure, but we will turn to those in other chapters. This chapter will set the stage for the fights that began in the 1980s and '90s over reproductive politics and neoliberalism by sketching, in broad strokes, the struggles over family, households, workplaces, and community survival that came before—and might provide some ideas for how we could organize for them again.

The left demands for the time and resources for reproductive labor have been taken up again in recent years, powerfully transformed, as an activist politics of reproductive justice—an "approach that links sexuality, health, and human rights to social justice movements," as Black women's health activist Loretta Ross has written, "by placing abortion and reproductive health issues in the larger context of the well-being and health of women, families, and communities," particularly racially and economically marginalized communities, by insisting on the right not only to prevent unwanted pregnancies but also to parent children "with the necessary social supports in safe environments and healthy communities, and without fear of violence from individuals or the government."[8] This approach is exemplified by calling the police shooting of Black youth a reproductive justice issue.[9] These movements link the legacies of the Black Panther Party to the history of feminism in a powerful synthesis that builds out the often invisible legacies of the Black freedom movement's reproductive politics and feminism's antiracism and workplace activism. But that's a long story, one that requires us to look at what activists argued about in the 1970s—and even the 1940s—and a reading of the conservative revolt against a redistributive economy and government that launched the current crisis of reproductive labor.

EIGHT HOURS FOR WHAT WE WILL:
LABOR FEMINISM

Labor feminists fought for an eight-hour day and the health and safety of women and children in an important struggle that began decades before what we usually think of as feminism's "second wave" in the 1960s and '70s. Historian Dorothy Sue Cobble has called it "the other feminist movement" and argues that these activists were foundational to the wave of (often young) women's activism that came afterward.[10] A surprising number of women were in labor unions by the 1950s—about three million, with another two million in auxiliaries. Even in the 1950s and '60s, when "stay-at-home" was considered an unnecessary modifier for "mother" (because women's place was in the home), it was nevertheless true that a quarter of married women with children worked, a percentage that was conspicuously higher for African American women. Many women entered the workforce during World War II, and that number continued to grow throughout the twentieth century, the Ozzie-and-Harriet ideology of the 1950s notwithstanding.[11] It was labor feminists who called for and won what became John F. Kennedy's Commission on the Status of Women, founded in 1961 to combat discrimination against women in employment, subsequently empowered with new tools after Title VII of the 1964 Civil Rights Act legislated against sex discrimination.

Mid-century labor feminists drew on much older traditions of labor militancy by and for women that stretched back into the nineteenth century. They organized and advocated for a 40-hour workweek that would give women time to care for their children. Trade unionists had long demanded "Eight hours for work, eight hours for rest, eight hours for what we will!"[12] Labor feminists organized for protectionist legislation, which required shorter work hours for women workers and specified things like maternity leave, not working nights (because children and the dangers of the streets), avoiding heavy lifting and prolonged periods of standing (thought crucial to protecting pregnant women), and avoiding certain dangerous jobs. Labor feminists argued for equality in the workplace *and* protectionism; they did not see these as contradictory. As Dorothy Sue Cobble writes, "they refused to privilege breadwinning over caregiving."[13] Labor feminists argued that at least *women* needed an eight-hour day, conceding maybe more than they should have to the protectionist idea that women had delicate constitutions. As much as anything, though, in the pre-1970s era when reproduction was often difficult to control, they were thinking about the need to provide accommodations for younger women who (always) might be pregnant. The New Deal's ending of child labor created a new crisis for industrial workers—if childhood was to be understood as an extended period of dependency and children could not enter the workplace, how were parents (mothers) to care for them? The eight-hour day and protectionist legislation took on a new importance.

Myra Wolfgang was a typical labor-feminist figure. She organized her first sit-down strike of sales clerks and waitresses at a Woolworth's five-and-dime in the 1930s; in later years she organized the "bunnies" at a Detroit Playboy club, demanding longer bunny suits that covered more of their bodies, rules that prevented customers from touching the waitresses, and job protection as food servers aged and their "bunny image" declined. They also demanded pay in wages, not just tips. Wolfgang objected to the entire Playboy philosophy, which, she said, was a "gross perpetuation of the idea that women should be obscene and not heard." What began in the labor bastion of Detroit under Wolfgang's charismatic leadership spread across the country, and ultimately all the Playboy clubs were unionized.[14]

While the fight for an Equal Rights Amendment (ERA) became synonymous with liberal feminism in the 1970s, it's important to listen carefully to the labor feminists' arguments against it, particularly that the ERA would end workplace protections for women's health and reproduction. In fact, even

Betty Friedan, who by the 1970s was virtually a symbol of the ERA (Wolfgang called her "the Chamber of Commerce's Aunt Tom"[15]), had in the 1950s fought for a different kind of feminism, based in the most radical of labor unions. Historian Daniel Horowitz has told us about Friedan's clandestine past working in the labor movement in the forties and early fifties in the United Electrical, Radio, and Machine Workers Union (UE), which had ties to the Communist Party (CP) and was not welcome in the mainstream of the AFL-CIO in the McCarthyite, anti-Communist decades from 1950 to 1980.[16] There, as the young Betty Naomi Goldstein, child of Russian immigrants, Betty Friedan had worked as a labor journalist and in fact had written a thirty-nine-page pamphlet, "The UE Fights for Women Workers," in 1952 that argued for equal pay for equal work and described the appalling conditions of Black and Latina factory workers. She wrote for *UE News* about food prices, housewives' boycotts, and the "double task of housework as well as shop work."[17] She was, in short, part of the lively crowd of writers and artists of the Popular Front, many of them Jewish, who, in the first half of the twentieth century, kept company with the CP and wrote in the context of an important radical tradition about the entwined issues of race, gender, and labor.[18]

This longer tradition of feminism and labor on the left was what gave birth to what some went on to call second-wave feminism. The birth control movement and Margaret Sanger came out of the Socialist Party and her arrests, exile, and radical insistence on birth control as a strategy for the working class's liberation from wage slavery in the years before World War I. While McCarthyism forced people like Sanger and Friedan to choose between continuing their work in explicitly left movements or working through an autonomous feminist movement, we lose a lot when we forget that feminism was foundationally bound up with radical labor and the 40-hour workweek. Especially after the past half century of conservative, pro-business activism that has eviscerated the time and wages necessary to support households with dependents, it might be time to reactivate that memory.

SURVIVAL PENDING REVOLUTION

The racial justice movements of the twentieth century were also concerned with what we might call reproductive politics, concerned as they were with the well-being of children and households: issues of community survival, stopping sexual predators, and demanding an end to unjust policing and imprisonment. The Harlem Renaissance, Black colleges and churches, the Popular Front, and the Communist Party fostered a specifically Black radical tradition with respect to reproduction and reproductive labor throughout the early twentieth century.[19] For example, in the 1940s, iconic civil rights figure Rosa Parks was engaged in an anti-rape campaign with the Popular Front, demanding respect for Black women and an end to white men's sexual assault and racial-sexual terrorism.[20] Ella Baker, who in the 1960s would found the Student Nonviolent Coordinating Committee (SNCC) and support the activism of women and young people in a civil rights movement that often valorized messianic male leaders like Martin Luther King Jr., spent the 1930s and '40s teaching workers about Black and labor history, leading the Young Negroes Cooperative League and building black economic security through co-ops, and working with the Popular Front's campaign to defend the Scottsboro Boys from unjust charges of raping two white women. Baker, who has sometimes been heralded as one of the key people who midwifed women's liberation out of SNCC,

brought to her activism a fundamental commitment to the reproductive labor of building strong Black communities.[21]

By the 1950s, the Black freedom movement was organizing
explicitly for reproductive justice. SNCC fought bills in the Mississippi state legislature calling for the sterilization of Black
women, which were proposed every year from 1958 to 1964.
Desegregating public schools was also central to the movement
and its opposition; in fact, it can be argued that civil rights was
above all a fight over children, from the children's crusade that
brought down Bull Connor in Birmingham to the legal case that
ended the lawfulness of segregation in public accommodations,
Brown v. Board of Education.[22] Fannie Lou Hamer, a delegate to the
Mississippi Freedom Democratic Party that sought to run white
supremacists out of the state Democratic Party, spoke often about
the sterilization of Black women in Mississippi, including on
national television at the 1964 Democratic National Convention.
In 1973, the Southern Poverty Law Center and National Welfare
Rights Organization brought a lawsuit on behalf of Minnie and
Mary Alice Relf, 12- and 14-year-old Black sisters who were ster-
ilized without their or their family's consent under a federal
Health, Education, and Welfare (HEW) program.[23]

Although few remember the Black Panthers as having anything but a negative relationship to feminism, their community
survival programs were fundamentally about a vision of how a
just society would treat communities, families, and children.
They provided clothing, health clinics, and the free breakfast
program that eventually shamed states into feeding children in
the morning in schools and day care programs and gave rise to
the only substantial and long-lasting free early childhood education program in the United States, Head Start.[24] The breakfast
program was designed to demonstrate to children what the Pan-

thers were fighting for: Black people's legitimate demands for survival by virtue of their simple humanity. One activist recalled a transformative moment for a hungry child found filling his pockets with food. She told him he wasn't stealing, that the food was his—did he want a bag? Joan Kelley, national coordinator of the Panthers' breakfast program said, "We try to teach the children not so much through indoctrination but through our practice and example about sharing and socialism."[25] While they are remembered for their advocacy of armed resistance and responses to police violence (and the police and FBI surveillance of them through COINTELPRO, including infiltration and harassment up to and including murder),[26] a local group had to do only two things to become a chapter of the Black Panther Party, neither of which had to do with police or guns: they had to provide a breakfast program for children and a health clinic.[27]

Latinx and Native communities also organized around reproductive politics. Mexican American women organized against coerced sterilization in the 1960s and '70s, culminating in a suit against the Los Angeles County Medical Center–USC in *Madrigal v. Quillian*.[28] Puerto Rican women on the East Coast organized even earlier against sterilization, forming CESA, the Coalition to End Sterilization Abuse, under Helen Rodriguez-Trías, while the militants of the Young Lords Party also called for abortions under community control.[29] Native people and communities fought the taking of children to Indian Boarding Schools and in adoptions, and involuntary sterilization in Bureau of Indian Affairs hospitals.[30]

Racial justice movements, feminism, and labor have long, deep, and intimate links—including failure and betrayal but also support, solidarity, and, especially because of the many people who worked simultaneously in all of them, inextricable interconnection. Above all, what I want to call to our attention is the ways they were all about reproductive politics—imagining a just society that would see that children were fed, fighting to limit the overreach of business and the long workday, trying to halt involuntary sterilization and sexual assault, and ensuring communities, families, and households had the resources to safely raise healthy children and care for others who could not work. We're good at naming the ways that feminism was embedded in reproductive politics when that movement demanded birth control and abortion rights, but it was much broader than that.

FROM WAGES FOR HOUSEWORK
TO WELFARE RIGHTS

In the 1970s, feminists inaugurated a Wages for Housework movement that focused on demanding support for reproduction and reproductive labor and acknowledging it as equally significant as and necessary to production. Activists sought free birth control, abortion on demand, and free day care as unwanted pregnancy, childbirth, and child rearing were increasingly being identified as sources of women's oppression. Indeed, they came closer than most of us remember to winning affordable, high-quality day care. In 1971, in the wake of feminists' campaign for 24-hour-a-day child care centers to meet the needs of working mothers, no matter what shift they worked, Congress passed the Child Development Act, which would have established a federally subsidized network of community child care centers, with the initial support of President Nixon. These would have been available to families on a sliding scale of payment, enabling low-income people to afford high-quality child care (which wasn't all that unimaginable in the 1970s—only thirty years earlier, during World War II, the

Lanham Act actually had established on-site day care centers at defense plants[31]). While President Nixon initially said that the bill had his full support, a coalition of evangelical Protestants and John Birchers mobilized against it, calling it an attack on the family. Conservative columnist James Kilpatrick argued that it was a plan "to Sovietize our youth.... This bill contains the seeds for destruction of Middle America."[32] Nixon vetoed the bill. (Here's what happened instead: in the decade after 2010, care for an infant in a day care center was more expensive than tuition and fees at a public university in half the states in the United States, yet day care workers were still severely underpaid—on average, they would have to pay more than 80 percent of their wages to put their own child in a day care center.[33])

Wages for Housework groups also demanded an end to forced sterilization, as awareness was growing about the HEW program that sterilized the Relf sisters. The New York Wages for Housework Committee also demanded the right of women to stay home with their children, framing it as "the power to refuse the double shift of a second job," following the feminists of the decade from 1910 to 1920, who had demanded and mostly won "mothers' pensions" for widows, laying the groundwork for ADC (Aid to Dependent Children) and AFDC (Aid to Families with Dependent Children).[34]

Meanwhile, other socialist feminists were theorizing the ways that "leisure time" for women was anything but, and they demanded that men in heterosexual families do more housework. A widely circulated pamphlet from the New York women's liberation group Redstockings was called "The Politics of Housework." Written by Pat Mainardi, it detailed the arguments between her and her husband about his doing half the housework. He agreed in principle but dragged his feet in fact, a dynamic others described over and over. She concluded:

Participatory democracy begins at home. If you are planning to implement your politics, there are certain things to remember. (1) He is feeling it more than you. He's losing some leisure and you're gaining it. The measure of your oppression is his resistance. (2) A great many American men are not accustomed to doing monotonous, repetitive work which never issues in any lasting, let alone important, achievement. This is why they would rather repair a cabinet than wash dishes. If human endeavors are like a pyramid with man's highest achievements at the top, then keeping oneself alive is at the bottom. Men have always had servants (us) to take care of this bottom stratum of life while they have confined their efforts to the rarefied upper regions.[35]

This was also a period when there was a lot more housework than most of us do now. Most people ironed sheets and vacuumed curtains. Birth rates were rising, reversing a long trend, and mothers were caring for three, four, five, and more children. White women—including the newly "whitened" Jews, Poles, Italians and other "ethnics"—were increasingly likely to be in the newly built suburbs, far from family and the old neighborhood, and mothers were having their first child at younger ages.[36] Husbands were gone for long hours, taking the family car on their long commutes from the suburbs to the city. Mothers kept up with passels of little ones alone and isolated; doctors spoke of "tired-mother syndrome."[37] The laundry was ever-present, and in the era when most clothing was cotton, everything had to be ironed. Floors needed to be washed and waxed. Fast food or prepared food meant canned vegetables; everything else had to be cooked from scratch, and eating out was rare for all but the very wealthy. Rising consumer prices in the seventies meant working hard to stretch food budgets, clipping coupons, watching for sales, collecting Green Stamps, wishing children didn't grow out of shoes and clothing so fast. Bills had to be paid and yards tended. Sick elders and family members were mostly cared for at home. Labor-saving devices like washing machines and dishwashers notwithstanding, housework was hard labor, and women in heterosexual families did nearly all of it.

Of course, much of the conversation about "wages for housework" and "leisure" time skirted another real issue: in the United States, as in Europe's colonies, there had long been a reservoir of unfree women who did reproductive labor for others. Housework was not just unpaid because women did it or because family was a category of "private" work—but also because there was a group of racially minoritized women who could be forced to do it for very low pay or no pay. Black women tended white children and households during and after slavery (which, it bears remembering, is still a longer period of U.S. history than freedom). Native girls were trained in boarding schools to do housework and often spent their summers—and more—in nearby towns doing that work for free. In Phoenix, for example, where Indian School Road is still part of the morning traffic report, many older residents recall when having an "Indian girl" to do the housework was common. For immigrant girls and women, household labor was often the only work available, often live-in, with all that suggested about vulnerability to rape and other sorts of abuse, and the wages were slight indeed (a situation that has changed little for many immigrant women now).[38]

The movements to change the gender politics of housework and waged labor in households and in the United States at large had mixed success. One snapshot of families in Berkeley, California—surveys conducted across the 1980s and published as a book, Arlie Hochschild's *The Second Shift*—found limited change. Men in heterosexual families were still fighting to do less housework, just as Pat Mainardi had recorded in 1970. Women were still coming home from work and putting in a "second shift," primarily responsible for children, food, and housekeeping. In one particularly poignant vignette, "Evan" and "Nancy," after years of negotiation in which his share of domestic chores somehow never got done, settled into a bargain where she was responsible for the "upstairs"—cooking, cleaning, laundry, bills, shopping, and most of the child care—and he was responsible for downstairs—car, garage, his workshop, and the dog. They seem to believe that this was a fair and even division of labor. "Evan won on the reality of the situation; Nancy won on the cover story," writes Hochschild.[39] One of Hochschild's intriguing and suggestive findings is that working-class households seemed to fare better, often with less egalitarian gender ideologies composing their "cover stories" but with more shared housework in reality. While her study is too small and local to draw broad conclusions from, it's intriguing to think of this finding in light of the feminist labor movement leaders who fought for maternity leave and shorter workdays to care for children. Perhaps the ideology of the home not as a site of work but also a respite from hard and alienating jobs persuaded men as much as women that this work was sweeter, even if it was the responsibility of women. Or perhaps, as Mainardi's account might imply, some men were less likely to think that boring, repetitive, and never-finished work was beneath them because that's what their paid jobs were like, too.

The most interesting account of household labor and remuneration in the United States in the early 1970s came out of the Black freedom movement in the form of a welfare rights movement—welfare being the only time that anybody really did pay wages for housework (and child care), although on the most hostile and stingiest terms imaginable. Johnnie Tillmon, a former labor union leader who was forced onto welfare by a back injury, wrote a famous manifesto for the first issue of *Ms. Magazine* in 1972, "Welfare is a Women's Issue." Tillmon's group, the National Welfare Rights Organization (NWRO), emerged out of the feminist wing of the long Black freedom movement. Wrote Tillmon: "Welfare's like a traffic accident. It can happen to anyone, but especially it happens to women." She wrote about the stigma attached to welfare (AFDC) and argued that it was this stigma that kept some women in bad marriages and others working for ninety cents an hour.

> Welfare is like a super-sexist marriage. You trade in a man for The Man. But you can't divorce him if he treats you bad. He can divorce you, of course, cut you off anytime he wants. But in that case, he keeps the kids, not you. The man runs everything. In ordinary marriage, sex is supposed to be for your husband. On A.F.D.C., you're not supposed to have any sex at all. You give up control of your own body. It's a condition of aid. You may even have to agree to get your tubes tied so you can never have more children just to avoid being cut off welfare. The man, the welfare system, controls your money. He tells you what to buy, what not to buy, where to buy it, and how much things cost. If things—rent, for instance—really cost more than he says they do, it's just too bad for you. He's always right. If I were president ... I'd start paying women a living wage for doing the work we are already doing—child-raising and housekeeping. And the welfare crisis would be over, just like that. Housewives would be getting wages, too—a legally determined percentage of their husband's salary—instead of having to ask for and account for money they've already earned.[40]

In the 1970s, Black women like Tillmon asked why AFDC was organized and funded in unfair and unequal ways and dependent on racial exclusions, ensuring that some of those who were entitled to benefits were not getting them.[41] One of the ways Southern and Western politicians denied women welfare was by creating enforcement rules that encouraged child welfare workers to take children—Black and Native children in particular—and put them in foster care.[42] The NWRO and similar groups worked closely with lawyers to demand fair treatment and receive the benefits they were entitled to (everything from getting benefits at all and keeping their children to filing lawsuits to prevent social workers from trying to catch a man in the house). As we will see in chapter 2, by the 1990s, destroying welfare became the linchpin of the conservative effort to destroy state support for reproductive labor. First, though, we need an account of the rise of conservatism, how "free markets" became common sense, and how this was a movement to make reproductive labor so much more difficult.

THE CONSERVATIVE BACKLASH AND THE RISE OF NEOLIBERALISM

Unfortunately, the 1970s feminist and racial justice movements' agitation ultimately failed to ease the burden of women's double day because the economy pushed mothers into the workplace and the business sector refused to treat reproductive labor as more than an annoyance and a problem. By 1980, the majority of mothers worked. Despite limited experiments with subsidized day care, overwhelmingly, parents of children under six either relied on family or other informal caregivers or they paid (a lot) for day care. Parents of school-aged children fared only somewhat better, dealing with a 180-day school year and a 250-day work year (if you had a 5-day-a-week job); school days that ran from 9 to 3 when they weren't half days; and programs for kids with disabilities that were even shorter (or, before 1975, often nonexistent). Despite societal condemnation of the mothers of latchkey children (those who came home before their parents did and had to let themselves into the house), there were few all-day school programs or affordable, high-quality after-school programs.

Neoliberalism was a social movement that arrived with a vengeance in the United States in the late 1970s and early 1980s. Although its major ideas had been kicking around for generations—that government support was the road to serfdom and people just wanted to be free from state interference, to paraphrase Friedrich von Hayek, one of its intellectual architects—it had to wait for a crisis to capture the imagination of those who operated economic policy institutions in the United States.[43] The palpable concerns about inflation that ran through feminist writings globally in the 1970s represented the early traces of the profound changes that were to come, but in the opposite directions from those that feminists sought. Inflation was to provide a rationale for the brewing conservative revolt against taxes on the wealthy and business. The Keynesian consensus of the postwar period—that large-scale government spending and investment in human capital like education and health care provided steady growth and stabilized the economy—was collapsing. The "stagflation"—or rising prices (inflation), stagnant consumer demand, and declining employment—of the early 1970s provided the proximate cause. Few could claim in the early 1970s that Keynesian economic policies provided any recipes for repairing the economy—lowering unemployment rates suggested an expansion of government spending, while inflation demanded its reduction.

Advocates of a renewed, intensified ("neo")liberalism, including libertarians and other conservatives, had never liked Keynesian liberalism, with its support for governmental investment in communities, including impoverished ones, and they seized the moment to break the power of unions and transform government. These were not people who liked civil rights or feminism, either. This was a radical conservativism by those who felt that public schools were socialism, to paraphrase one of the beacons of the new economics, Milton Friedman. In the United States and globally, the conservative backlash had begun. Although there was a strong argument that much of the economic misery in the United States could be laid at the feet of conservatives—Nixon's decision to go off the gold standard in 1971, the massive cost of the Vietnam War, and conservatives' political support for Israel during the 1973 Arab-Israeli War to prevent Syria and Egypt from retaking the occupied territories, resulting in retribution in the form of an OPEC oil embargo that stalled the economy—"tax and spend liberalism" was cast as the villain. Conservatives—including an unruly mix of economists associated with the Mont Pèlerin society; intellectual fans of Ayn Rand; evangelical anti-Communists, whose forces were symbolized by the rapid political rise of Billy Graham; racist John Birchers; white suburbanites in California who loathed property taxes and school desegregation; and especially big business lobbies—advocated for lower taxes and more laissez-faire, less government, and neoliberalism: a free market fundamentalism and the crushing of the power of organized labor.

At least three measures rapidly and dramatically ended stagflation and ushered in the current conservatism and neoliberalism that have crushed the "family wage," which had enabled some people to stay out of the labor force and gave others 8-hour workdays. These measures were carried out by Democrats as well as Republicans, and they sharply increased the misery felt by those at the bottom. First, Jimmy Carter's Federal Reserve board chair, the cigar-chomping Wall Street insider Paul Volcker, promised to end stagflation by sharply tightening the money supply. The "Volcker shock," as it was known, stabilized the business climate but tripled interest rates, crashing employment in whole sectors of the economy—small farmers, for example, who relied on borrowing for seed to stay afloat. In a massive public protest, farmers drove their tractors to Washington, DC, to blockade the Eccles Building, the home of the Federal Reserve. (The protest was fruitless; a massive wave of farm foreclosures ensued, giving rise to the current consolidation of factory farming.) The Third World, which had been encouraged by the United States and Europe to borrow heavily to finance Western-orchestrated development, went into economic convulsions as its debt load doubled and tripled overnight.

The second measure devastated efforts for racial equality. In California, conservatives strangled redistributive government itself: Proposition 13, designed to limit property taxes, passed as a ballot measure in 1978. A response to rising taxes in the state, it followed a state supreme court decision that for the first time had promised equality of opportunity to all children—Black, white, Latinx, and Native. The court had found that it was unconstitutional to fund public schools with property taxes from a single community, which ensured that those living in wealthy suburbs would always have a better education; instead, it required that property taxes be distributed across the whole state. In a fiercely contested campaign, white suburbanites and business revolted and sharply reduced property taxes, succeeding in maintaining separate and unequal school systems in California, in contrast to the East Coast, where southern (and northern) protests against busing had failed. Within two decades, the California public school system had gone from the best in the nation to one of the worst.

The third measure was directed at organized labor, which had been the unacknowledged but real partner in the feminist movement: in 1980, in one of his first acts as president, Ronald Reagan fired striking members of PATCO, the air traffic controllers' union, risking public air safety to break the back of unions.[44] Two decades later, it was clear that this effort too had succeeded: union membership was at historic lows; real wages had stagnated at pre-1980 levels, forcing more people (including, conspicuously, women) into the workforce to keep households afloat and fueling a massive expansion of consumer debt to keep standards of living up; and work had bifurcated between part-time underemployment and unemployment on the one hand and jobs that required brutally long workweeks on the other. Between 1979 and 2000, the proportion of men who worked more than 50 hours a week rose from 21 to 27 percent, and for women, from 5 to 11 percent.[45]

For feminists and racial justice activists, these three neoliberal moves—the changes in financial policy, taxation, and the sudden, sharp decline of the power of labor—meant not only an explicit defense of better schools for white children but also the crushing of the revolt against the second shift and the absence of resources for reproductive labor that I've been discussing. The wages-for-motherhood welfare rights movement stumbled into an emerging sector of angry white men: neoconservatives, former Democrats who had bailed from the civil rights movement, who hailed the emergence of a Nixonian call for "law and order," and blamed Black women—"matriarchy" and single mothers—for the crime and lawlessness that the Black community was increasingly being tagged with. The redistributive state imagined by the socialist wages-for-housework campaigns, or even that envisioned by liberal feminism's more limited but still crucial demands for free birth control and day care, was increasingly being beaten back. The labor movement was brought down as a policy-setting voice for the working class, further marginalizing the demands of labor feminists. (More than a decade later, Bill Clinton sponsored and signed the Family Medical Leave Act, which enacted the stingiest possible version of labor feminists' demand for parental leave, along with leaves to care for an elderly parent or a gravely ill family member.) In the 1970s and '80s, businesses welcomed mothers' labor—especially because they could pay women less—but they were not about to pay higher taxes to subsidize day care and preschool or, except in limited experiments, to fund day care centers of their own (fewer than 1 percent of employers had on-site child care in 2015).[46]

PRIVATIZING DEPENDENCY: JOHNSON CONTROLS

In the 1980s, a legal case answered any remaining questions about whether business had a responsibility for being "family friendly" in the emerging neoliberal order. Johnson Controls, an automobile battery manufacturer, began in 1982 to tell women that they weren't eligible for any jobs producing batteries unless they could show medical certification of sterility. These were good, high-paying union jobs; the exclusion of women was not trivial. The jobs also exposed workers to high levels of lead, known to cause harm to fetuses at low levels and to be stored in body tissues for a long time after exposure. A woman who became pregnant even months after holding the job could still have a dangerous lead level in her system. Prior to the Civil Rights Act of 1964, Johnson Controls had simply not hired any women at all. From 1977 to 1982, after such overt discrimination became illegal, Johnson Controls had not excluded women from battery production—they had advised women of the danger to fetuses, asked them to sign a release from legal liability, and had monitored blood-lead levels of both male and female employees for poisoning. A worker whose lead level rose too high was supposed to be transferred to other jobs, with wages and benefits partially protected.[47]

The real insult of the 1982 Johnson Controls policy was that it reduced women to their fertility status—and it considered women potentially pregnant up to the age of seventy. Having to discuss your fertility or infertility with your employer or potential employer is humiliating, but being denied access to a job because you are (always) potentially pregnant is something else again. On its face, it seemed that the policy should be illegal—Title VII of the Civil Rights Act prohibits discrimination based on sex (as well as race, religion, or national origin). After 1978, it also prohibited discrimination based on pregnancy or pregnancy-related conditions. Women who said they were not intending to have children were still banned from the lead-using parts of production.

Labor and feminist critics alike insisted that the policy was never in fact about children's health. The United Automobile Workers union (UAW) charged that what the company was really concerned about was *liability:* while workers are generally prohibited from suing companies over unsafe conditions, a growing antiabortion movement was pushing judges and lawmakers to consider a fetus as a third party who could take a company to court. The UAW insisted that levels of lead that are dangerous to fetuses are dangerous to adults as well—women and men—and that the company was concerned only because of the possibility of stronger protections for fetuses than for workers. While by the 1980s the company had installed air systems that were supposed to draw lead-saturated air away from workspaces, and some workers had masks that blew air into their nose and mouth, nevertheless, fine particles of lead were everywhere.

Many workers suffered symptoms of lead poisoning. Some were sent home with pay for five months until their lead level declined as the law required; others were just laid off and called back five months later when their lead level was lower. These were dirty, dangerous jobs, and the union believed that Johnson Controls would keep workplaces only as clean as federal regulation or the fear of liability (to fetuses) made them. Furthermore, the UAW brief argued, "fetal protection" policies were implemented only when women were a minority of a workforce; nurses in hospitals and farmworkers were also exposed to chemicals dangerous to a pregnancy, but there was no talk of protecting the fetuses of women farmworkers, nurses, or nurse's aides.[48]

The parties to the suit had come a long way since the 1950s, 1960s, and 1970s. The union was using an argument for protective legislation for women *and men* alike. It insisted that while the science was underdeveloped, it clearly indicated that men experienced reproductive harm from lead—that sperm was also susceptible to damage from toxic substances.[49] Feminists in NOW and labor leaders had come around to the same position: that "women-only" protective policies and laws were not a social good. NOW president Kim Gandy explained, "They protect women right out of the good jobs."[50]

In 1991, the Supreme Court held that Johnson Controls' fetal protection policies were illegal. "Decisions about the welfare of future children must be left to the parents who conceive, bear, support and raise them rather than to the employers who hire those parents," wrote Justice Harry Blackmun for the majority.[51] "The bias in the Johnson Controls' policy is obvious. Fertile men, but not fertile women are given a choice as to whether they wish to risk their reproductive health for a particular job."[52] This was a sad victory for labor, feminist, and civil liberties groups that a decade earlier had argued for a shared social responsibility for the work of home and children. Six of the nine justices, those who signed the Blackmun opinion, also suggested that there was no tort liability—that fetuses harmed by lead in the workplaces could not later sue the company if they became people who had been born with disabilities. The justices suggested instead that mothers would be negligent if they either became pregnant or kept a pregnancy while working at a job like that. So, as the *New York Times* headline had it, "Court Backs Right of Women to Jobs with Health Risks." The case was anything but a mandate to clean up the workplace.[53] It just gave women (and men) a "free market" right to enter into a terrible bargain with employers, to work in an environment dangerous to them and any future generations of their children.[54]

The *United Automobile Workers v. Johnsons Controls* case made it clear just how privatized responsibility for pregnancy and children was going to be in the context of the neoliberal revolution, as labor and feminists were pushed into ever more defensive positions. It stands in striking contrast to *Muller v. Oregon*, a 1908 Supreme Court that said: "[By] abundant testimony of the medical fraternity continuance for a long time on her feet at work, repeating this from day to day, tends to injurious effects upon [a woman's] body, and as healthy mothers are essential to vigorous offspring, the physical well-being of woman becomes an object of public interest and care in order to preserve the strength and vigor of the [species]."[55] While *Muller* insisted that there was a public interest in reproduction that government and business were bound to respect, *Johnson Controls* put the responsibility for healthy people and healthy pregnancies on individuals. It may have been better for workplace gender equity that fetal protection policies were defeated, but it is still true that parents, children, and all workers lost in that case. Cleaning up the workplace to make it compatible with human life and its reproduction was not what courts demanded, and it reminds us, painfully, of what was lost. The idea that we have a shared responsibility, as feminists argued in the 70s, to provide day care for parents who work or support for those who stay home with their dependents was pretty much off the table. The courts had found, in effect, that industrial workplaces were free to poison fetuses, children, women, and men. From a position like that, how would you argue that workplaces had to change to make them compatible with reproduction? You can't. But for some reason, through the nineties and the new millennium, it was *feminists* who were tagged as not caring about mothers, households, reproductive labor, and children.

A long feminist and racial justice tradition had sought a different approach to reproductive politics for much of the twentieth century—an insistence on public support for children and elders, households, families, and communities. It tried to make household labor more egalitarian. Because a lot of things that are typically public benefits in the social democratic tradition of Western Europe are employee benefits in the United States (like health insurance and parental leave), the feminist movement in particular sought to challenge workplace benefits and the space for reproductive labor. Despite decades of gains, by the 1990s, a great deal had been lost, and *Johnson Controls* was typical. Not only were workplaces never going to provide on-site day care, shorter workdays, and pay the taxes necessary to ensure a robust system of public benefits, they couldn't even be legally compelled to make the workplace safe from poisoning human bodies—fetal or adult—with lead. While feminist and racial justice activism for reproductive freedom never went away, and indeed has continued to be a significant voice, these movements slammed into a wall of organized opposition in the neoliberal moment. It was never "radical feminism's misogynistic crusade," but business's and government's that made it impossible for any member of a household to stay home and do reproductive labor, much less do paid work and still have the time, space, and resources to care for dependents, households, and communities.

CHAPTER TWO

Welfare Reform

The Vicious Campaign to Reform
1 Percent of the Budget

Johnson Controls and the business sector were not alone in seeking to limit their responsibility for and the time they gave employees for reproductive labor. In the 1980s, the government was also seeking to sharply curtail its responsibility for children and dependents. Decades of activism to expand the time and resources communities had for reproductive labor had given way to a conservative movement to reduce support for it by privatizing wealth and care.[1] The Reagan administration cut programs for children and elders and dramatically reduced the availability of low-income housing. While much of that happened quietly, backstage, there was one big, explosive narrative about care work and the evil things that happened when government supported it: "welfare queens." Black feminist scholar Wahneema Lubiano has pointed out that the welfare queen was a cover story for reducing government programs in general.[2] It was remarkably effective. Newspapers, pundits, and policy makers caricatured welfare recipients as lazy, sexually promiscuous, and scamming the government. It became more difficult for anyone to even want to apply for benefits, no matter how hard up they were—and easy for others to have contempt for them. In the nineties, under Bill Clinton, the conservative wing of the Democratic Party (the Democratic Leadership Council) piled on. Through "welfare reform," both major US political parties began to roll back support for family security and time to care for others. "Dependency" was a key word in welfare reform but was used to refer to *caregivers,* not to children, elders, or others who needed to be cared for. President Clinton claimed that welfare reform would "transform a broken system that traps too many people in a cycle of dependence to one that emphasizes work and independence."[3] If you were, say, a child and couldn't work, oh well. "The exclusion from the mainstream debate of any consideration of *enhancing* public assistance to the poor signal[ed] the resounding defeat of a progressive welfare ideal," Dorothy Roberts observed.[4] Given our long and tortured racial history, it was not surprising that the political move that ultimately ensured that work hours would expand, wages stagnate, and time for care work evaporate was one that painted care work Black (or to a lesser extent Latinx or Native, depending on the region of the country). Although people of color were never the majority of welfare recipients (white children were—62 percent of recipients were white), welfare was made into a Black-women thing.[5] Although white women as a group lost the most in welfare reform, they got the one bone that's always been thrown to white working- and middle-class people in the United States: the opportunity to feel they were morally superior to people of color.

When welfare was "reformed," the big winners were the companies that created McJobs: the fast-food industry, Walmart, and other low-wage employers (including state governments that paid starvation wages to attendant care workers for people with disabilities and to family day care providers[6]). Welfare reform also pushed mothers into low-wage work at a time when the value of the minimum wage was declining steeply. In constant dollars, the minimum wage hit its high point in 1968; by 1989, it was worth 40 percent less.[7] It became more and more impossible for mothers to support themselves and their children on low-wage work—40 hours a week of minimum wage didn't pay rent and groceries, never mind health care and child care.[8] It became clear that if business was going to get the most it could out of the potential workforce in the United States without raising wages, it was going to have to eliminate welfare and force impoverished mothers into jobs. The result? In 1997, the year legislation "to end welfare as we know it" went into effect, Walmart became the largest employer in the United States, and three-quarters of its workforce was female.[9] The irony is that only by a particularly narrow definition does a Walmart job get you off welfare—as a matter of policy, Walmart encourages its employees to apply for government benefits. Indeed, Walmart and other minimum-wage workers at McDonald's and similar McJobs are the largest group of Medicaid and food stamps recipients in the United States.[10] That is to say, US taxpayers subsidize Walmart paychecks (and corporate profits) by paying welfare benefits to its workers and their children. Welfare reform eliminated virtually all education and job-training benefits beyond "work readiness" classes that taught women to dress nicely and get their kids up early. The result: women couldn't get the education to get a good job and they were still receiving welfare benefits, but they could be counted on to clock regular hours and make profits for their low-paying employers.[11] From welfare reform to Walmart, it was all reproductive politics.

WELFARE QUEENS AND
WORKING MOTHERS

The Reagan administration used the welfare queen story to great effect, redirecting people's attention from business- and politician-led neoliberal changes in the economy that were affecting working people's lives to blame the most impoverished women and children for their struggles. The welfare queen story told people two important things. First, the reason working mothers (and families and those caring for elderly parents or other dependents) were stressed out was not stagnant wages, unpaid reproductive labor, and the second shift, but those *other* mothers, probably not-white, who were not doing their share of work, and this was raising taxes. *They* were responsible for driving mothers into the work force—not neoliberalism or Reaganomics. Meanwhile, conservatives were shredding the social safety net. The Reagan administration eliminated federal support for elder day programs, shifted funds for Section 8 housing subsidies to wealthy developers, and deinstitutionalized people with severe mental illness without providing the promised community supports, driving some into homelessness and making others' care the life-long responsibility of families, usually mothers.[12] It wasn't that educational opportunities were declining, or that business was driving down wages in the name of ever-greater profits, or that the labor-market deck was stacked against people who were Black, Latinx, suffering from an emotional or physical disability, and/or female—it was that their intimate relationships and character were a mess.

Earlier, in the 1970s, then-governor Ronald Reagan began telling the story about a "welfare queen" who had multiple addresses, claimed fraudulent children, and was making $150,000 a year. Although Richard Nixon had told his own stories of despicable welfare recipients in that decade, Reagan's particular brilliance was to change the pronouns—he made the symbol of welfare fraud a woman and a mother.[13] Reagan made no secret of the race of his imagined welfare recipients, either. His welfare queen with the pink Cadillac, who cashed her checks at the liquor store, was clearly Black.[14]

Although many have accused him of making her up entirely, in 2013 journalist Josh Levin reminded the nation what many older Chicago residents still remembered: Reagan's welfare queen was based on a real person, Linda Taylor. She lived her adult life mostly in that city and was a larger-than-life figure with more than eighty aliases with which she collected all sorts of benefits— food stamps, Medicaid, Social Security, and Aid to Families with Dependent Children. She was also likely white, as her birth certificate and death certificate recorded (although she did sometimes pass herself off as Black, Filipina, or Latina). As Levin argued, when Chicago authorities made her a symbol of welfare fraud, they also tacitly agreed to ignore much larger crimes— including child kidnapping, bigamy, and quite possibly murder as well—in order to keep the narrative simple and clear. He wrote, "A murder in Chicago is mundane. A sumptuously attired woman stealing from John Q. Taxpayer is a menace." She proved equally convenient for what ultimately became a national, bipartisan political project of using "Blackness" and "laziness" to end a slight but nevertheless crucial lifeline for mothers and their children.[15]

Initially, two different policy arguments drove the campaign for welfare reform. The first, favored by Reagan and some other conservatives, was that every adult should work as a matter of principle and character. They called their program "workfare." It was a fairly transparent pro-business argument designed to keep wages low—why do we care if our neighbors are "lazy," after all, if we don't need something from them? This actually generated a fair amount of opposition, mostly but not exclusively among Democrats, who thought the problems of poverty had more to do with the lack of well-paying jobs and health insurance and called policies forcing AFDC mothers into unpaid or sub-minimum-wage jobs "slave-fare" or "mass peonage."[16] (Others insisted that something had to be done about health care—Senator Daniel Patrick Moynihan argued, "It's a pretty rare mother who would rather take her chances with a $4-an-hour job and if one of her kids gets really sick just hope that there's a charity hospital around."[17]) Experiments in the eighties with workfare at state levels found that such policies had only a slight effect on employment rates: in any given year, the usual number of recipients who would stop receiving AFDC because they got a job was 55 percent; workfare programs that required work or job training nudged that number upward very modestly, to about 61 percent.[18] Improving wages and reliable access to health care across the population overall had a much bigger effect on reducing the welfare rolls (AFDC was indirectly but crucially a health care program, guaranteeing recipients and their children enrollment in Medicaid). However, workfare was a terrific government employment program for the middle class; it kept lots of middle-class welfare workers employed as they shuttled welfare recipients to their required 30-day jobs. Workfare was, everyone agreed, much more expensive than just giving benefits to recipients, but it offered a kind of "behavior modification" program for AFDC recipients, whom they infantilized, which seemed to be very satisfying to some people who weren't poor, providing the pleasure of white condescension to people imagined as Black (even if they weren't). Despite opposition and the expense, some form of workfare was enacted in forty states even before the Reagan administration's push in this direction, Many, though, believed workfare was half-hearted, as there were generally wide exemptions for mothers of young children and people with disabilities—the lion's share of people on AFDC.

What really energized the bipartisan effort to reform welfare was the idea of children being harmed by a "culture of poverty," an old idea given new energy from renewed concerns about teen pregnancy. From E. Franklin Frazier to the Moynihan Report, from Oscar Lewis's *La Vida* to Michael Harrington's *The Other America*, the belief that there is something about the lives and choices of Black and Latina poor women that leads them to perpetuate poverty across generations, particularly through the ways they raise their children, has a long genealogy in liberal social science and policy. Sociologist Charles Murray gave the idea new life in 1984, with his *Losing Ground*, which argued that receiving AFDC benefits was a kind of pathology, "dependency," that was both a cause and a consequence of teenage pregnancy (among young people implicitly understood to be Black or Latinx). Despite the immense diversity of people who received benefits from AFDC—including women who were widowed or divorced, those leaving abusive relationships, and people with disabilities—in the nineties public discourse become fixated on one particular story: teenage girls who got pregnant and didn't marry because AFDC made single motherhood a viable option. They, in turn, passed the habit of welfare dependency down to their children. Brilliantly but disturbingly, Murray argued that AFDC itself was *causing* poverty by rewarding female-headed households and should be eliminated. Poverty could be alleviated only if the government stopped giving money to poor people.[19]

It was Murray who offered the most brutal policy proposals. He wrote in the *Wall Street Journal* that "the first and central policy prescription [is] to end all economic support for single mothers. The AFDC (Aid to Families With Dependent Children) payment goes to zero. Single mothers are not eligible for subsidized housing or for food stamps. An assortment of other subsidies and in-kind benefits disappear." Why? Because "illegitimacy is the single most important social problem of our time—more important than crime, drugs, poverty, illiteracy, welfare, or homelessness because it drives everything else." Most effectively, Murray urged lawmakers to put these policy proposals into action by describing a specific racial threat. While teen pregnancy was a Black problem, AFDC was making it spread, in small but growing numbers, to white girls. The pathology of Black communities might be contagious (a danger to morally superior white reproduction that recalled the argument from the fifties and sixties that school desegregation would lead white girls to marry Black boys, or at least have sex with them).[20] "Workfare" had seemed mean-spirited and suggested a harsh solution to a problem that a lot of working mothers understood they were only one really bad fight with their husband away from: raising their children alone. But by the 1990s, teen pregnancy was becoming increasingly rare. Many felt insulated from being *that* kind of mother, but also eager to defend the compensatory privileges of whiteness even if it meant losing the only real safety net for mothers who might need to or want to leave their partners. And so Charles Murray's version of the world, in which all social ills were caused by teen mothers and their offspring, got legs. Vice president Dan Quayle argued that the unwed pregnancy of Murphy Brown, a fictional character on TV, caused the Los Angeles riots (he linked criticism of welfare, feminism, and gay parents under the banner of "family values)."[21] The welfare reform bill that ultimately passed in 1996 contained a long preamble that read like Charles Murray meets the Christian Right: marriage is the foundation of a successful society, teen pregnancy is terrible for children, the welfare rolls are growing, and the goal of cutting AFDC is to combat unmarried motherhood.

It needs to be said that the research does not actually bear out the common sense that teen pregnancy is bad for children.[22] While children born to teen mothers may, on average, get less schooling and be more likely to experience poverty as adults, it's not clear that the cause is being born to a teen mother. It may be that as teen pregnancy became rare (after being the condition of nearly half of all first births in the sixties), having a teen mother after 1980 was virtually a guarantee of having been born to a poor mother (and thus, most likely, into a community with underfunded schools). As class mobility in the United States continues to decline, that is a pretty good predictor of being poor oneself. It turns out that if you match the children of teen mothers with their real peers—not to all children born in the United States, but to these children's actual relatives, the children of the sisters who waited until they were older to have their babies—the results are not at all what Charles Murray predicted. The children born to teen mothers' siblings in their twenties do not do better than the children of teen mothers, and neither do their mothers. In fact, for African Americans in particular, they may actually do worse, an effect of the declining health status of their impoverished mothers—the "weathering" of bodies in a society that distributes risk differentially according to race, including stress, inadequate nutrition, chronic illness, or exposure to violence or environmental toxins. Indeed, because teen mothers have their children young, often while still living with their own parents, they have more of their lifespan in which to receive education and work without day care costs or dependents, ultimately earning more and contributing more in taxes than their sisters who had their babies later.[23] Teen pregnancy is not in itself a problem, although it is a marker of a problem in a society where good jobs are distributed almost exclusively to people who go through a long period of higher education. When girls believe, correctly, that neither they nor their children would be better off if they waited until their twenties to have their children, it means their opportunities are slim indeed. And that—rather than worries about sexually active girls—should trouble us a great deal.

The case for welfare reform, then, was an argument that receiving government benefits was so deviant that it warped and deformed the children. (Apparently this applied only to those who received AFDC but not to those who received *other* government benefits, like federal student loans, unemployment, workers comp, and the homeowner's tax deduction, or—wait for it—to those who accepted good roads, public schools, firefighting and policing.) These poor, stunted children had no choice but to eventually go on welfare themselves, completing a cycle of multigenerational dependency, often as teen mothers themselves. Charles Murray effectively made the race of these children explicit—they were Black, but if we weren't careful, they might be white in the future.

The reality of who was using AFDC was in fact both more heterogeneous and more ordinary. The majority used the benefits briefly, for two years or less. About 3 percent were teen mothers. They were mostly white mothers and their children who had left an abusive relationship or gotten divorced. They might not be getting child support, might have no work history, or need more education or job training. AFDC was primarily a stopgap that allowed women to leave a relationship or survive when their partner had left. A minority of welfare recipients used it for longer; these were generally people with disabilities (including mental illness) or other liabilities in the workforce, or they were mothers of children with disabilities. Stereotypes about hyperfertility and substance abuse notwithstanding, AFDC recipients were actually less likely than the general population to have two or more children or to use drugs.[24]

Newspapers (in this era before social media and other Internet media sources) played a major role in producing the New Right's story about exotic, pathological welfare queens, disturbed and disturbing, whose families looked nothing like everyone else's and who were seriously screwing up their children. After 1990, being a mother without a job—the statistical norm just over a decade earlier—suddenly became the most shameful of moral failings. Ellen Goodman at the *Boston Globe* pointed to the change:

> The photograph in the Maine newspaper showed a young, attractive mother and her two small children. "I'm a natural at motherhood," the woman had happily told the reporter. "It's my job."
>
> Nothing about these words or this job description would have stuck in my mind over the months since I read them except for one decidedly nontraditional fact of her life. The 20-year-old and her children were living on welfare.[25]

Goodman went on to express her disapproval of the attitude that it was okay to be a mother who considered that to be her job—and get benefits while her children were little.

Other journalists told the hard stories of families with mental illness, including parents and children struggling with sexual abuse, drug abuse, chronic illness, depression, and delusions—some problems grounded in poverty itself and the kinds of

low-wage jobs and hustles people used to get by, and others in
less apparent sources—and turned these folks into "typical"
welfare recipients enacting cycles of poverty. For example, Leon
Dash wrote an eight-part series for the *Washington Post* in September 1994 that chronicled the saga of Rosa Lee Cunningham,
a Black woman who had come to a segregated Washington, DC,
in the 1930s, a child refugee from the agrarian South, and gotten
hooked on heroin while working in nightclubs for fifteen years
to support her children. She only occasionally succeeded in
holding a job for long after that. AFDC made up the difference
with the younger of her eight children. Like a large number of
working-class women in this period, Rosa Lee had still been in
high school when her first baby was born, just as her mother, a
sharecropper, had been. Although her siblings and some of her
children were Great Migration success stories, getting respectable jobs and doing well, one of her daughters and a grandson
followed her into addiction, despair, and HIV/AIDS, using
AFDC and food stamps to get by. Theirs was a sad story, well
told by Dash, and was taken to be a tale of how welfare causes
teen pregnancy and multigenerational dependency. Never mind
that Dash could have picked different individuals in that same
family and told the opposite story. Never mind that the question
of why welfare—rather than heroin and HIV—turned out to be
the villain of the story seems ideological at best.[26]

Other newspapers in major cities followed suit, finding people
of color with mental illness and tragic stories and turning them
into "typical" welfare recipients, which they weren't. The stories
also made it seem like AFDC *caused* mental illness. In Boston,
Claribel Rivera Ventura, a Puerto Rican migrant with a sexual
abuse history, mental illness, a scary boyfriend, and a four-year-
old son whom she physically abused, became the symbol of how

welfare damaged families.[27] In Chicago, police looking for non-existent drugs ripped apart the apartment where families were doubling up after a fire; those families became, in the confused aftermath of the raid (in which the police blamed the mess on the families), a symbol of too many children, welfare, and children endangered by poor housing, cockroaches, and unfit mothers.[28] This story might have suggested that the Chicago police needed to stop tearing up poor children's homes for no reason. It might also have been an argument for the urgent need for better housing options, or even for churches or the Red Cross or (imagine!) the local public housing authority to provide temporary housing in emergencies. It didn't. It provided another cautionary tale about Black teens who got pregnant and got welfare.[29]

Columnist Howie Carr at the *Boston Herald* told the welfare queen story bluntly, crudely, and with an emphasis on white women's resentment of women of color and its compensatory function as white women were ground down by their jobs. He quoted a letter he said he had received from a working mother who loathed welfare recipients: she was "fed up with their junk-food bloated butts shoved into shiny spandex pants, watching the boob tube in their Section 8 apt., while scarfing down a bag of Cheetos." The writer complained about riding the bus home from work when two "welfare queens . . . got on with their strollers and their overflowing Filene's bags." One "whined loudly" about whether someone would give them a seat, and the writer "responded with a laugh, saying, 'Sorry, but I think the majority of the people on the bus worked hard all day so you'll just have to wait till you get home to work hard at your job, which I'm sure involves nothing more than lying on your back.'"[30] How the letter-writer knew that this tired stranger with a small child got a government check remains unstated—but it almost certainly was just because she was Black or Puerto Rican (spandex and big butts being racially coded).

While Carr's account is ugly, it shows how the fight over welfare provided a particularly racialized airing of the new demographic reality: that the majority of mothers (of whatever race) were in the workforce. The family-stress storm of the second shift was no longer confined to working-class and poor women, most often women of color; it had become a white middle-class reality as well. To women dealing with the grinding labor of full-time jobs and care labor—whom sociologist Arlie Hochschild described as "women [who] talked about sleep the way a hungry person talks about food"—the idea that government had a responsibility to help impoverished mothers who were out of the labor force seemed like a cruel joke. One social worker in a "welfare-to-work" program said welfare mothers were "not in the habit of getting up at seven in the morning, getting the kids ready and out the door, and then being ready to go to work."[31] No wonder the charge that welfare mothers were "lazy" resonated. Another social worker noted that these women were used to sleeping until they woke up. How crazy was that! Middle- and working-class mothers were performing heroics just to get through the week. That the situation of households carrying huge care burdens, having to put every adult into the labor force, and facing chronic sleep deprivation was unfair or unacceptable never crossed our collective political mind. The family wage was a thing of the past, and families, not government or business, were going to have to step into the breach in the new neoliberal order of things. But working mothers' anger, exhaustion, and frustration were real enough and leached out in public as an appetite for ever more vicious characterizations of welfare mothers.

Daniel Patrick Moynihan, who had been involved with poverty policy for decades, agreed that the flavor of the conversation was changed by the fact that most mothers were working:

> When the original welfare program began, the family was seen as an arrangement where the husband went out to work and the woman stayed home and kept house and raised the children. It was before washing machines and refrigerators and vacuum cleaners. So long as that assumption lasted, if you suggested that welfare recipients should work, you were suggesting that they be treated differently—and in some sense punitively—because you were saying, "All right, you are going to have to do what no self-respecting woman has to do." But then you looked up one day and women were working. Once it became a self-respecting thing to be in the work force, that changed the possibilities of discussing child support in a mode that would include the income from the mother as well as the father.[32]

Moynihan was probably better positioned than anyone in the country to know how the debate had been changed by the fact that the economy had pushed so many mothers into the workforce; he had been the public face and chief flack-catcher for welfare reform efforts in Republican and Democratic presidential administrations from Johnson in the 1960s to Reagan in the 1980s (the Department of Labor report he helped author has forever been called just the "Moynihan Report"). It may be, of course, that Moynihan the New Yorker never really understood that Southern politicians were so fiercely opposed to Black women receiving welfare because they had *never* seen Black women as respectable and had expected since slavery times that Black mothers worked, in agriculture and in other people's homes. But if previously there had been a struggle over whether unmarried mothers of whatever race could stay out of the workforce, by the 1980s, the argument for AFDC's (truly lousy) "wages for housework" and child care collapsed. From newspapers to policy makers, all agreed that the changing demographics of (white and middle-class) women working a second shift was driving the attacks on welfare—although they stopped short of asking what had happened to wages that was forcing so many into the workforce.

There was even an effort to make this punitive attitude toward nonworking mothers receiving benefits sound vaguely feminist, as Barbara Ehrenreich and Frances Fox Piven noted:

> A number of arguments are being advanced to give workfare a liberal, and even feminist, aura. First, it is said that workfare would help the poor by delivering them from the demoralizing "dependency syndrome" thought to be associated with welfare. Then there is the argument that most American women now work outside the home anyway. Workfare, according to this line of reasoning, is simply a way of updating the welfare state to take into account women's expanded role.[33]

Ehrenreich and Piven suggested increasing spending on welfare to make it possible for women to actually feed their children with their benefits. (Ironically, though spending increased for welfare at both the federal and state levels in Reagan's America, the benefits were never raised as high as the poverty level— welfare reform was mostly a giant jobs program for middle-class welfare officials, steadily expanding so they could police "fraud," essentially paying them to grind down poor women).

To quote welfare activist Johnnie Tillmon again, there was, in fact, nothing feminist about demonizing welfare mothers:

> People still believe that old lie that AFDC mothers keep on having kids just to get a bigger welfare check. On the average, another baby means $35 a month—barely enough for food and clothing. Having babies for profit is a lie that only men could make up and

only men could believe.... There are a lot of other lies that male society tells about welfare mothers: that AFDC mothers are immoral, that AFDC mothers are lazy, misuse their welfare checks, spend it all on booze, and are stupid and incompetent. If people are willing to believe these lies, its partly because they're just special versions of the lies that society tells about all women.[34]

Not feminism but misogyny and contempt for all mothers made it possible to mobilize fear and loathing of welfare mothers, she argued—and the unspoken but unmistakable fact of racism. That and the effort to make the double day mandatory for everyone. While only a handful of mothers were obviously in the cross-hairs (welfare was only 1 percent of the federal budget, and the actual numbers of recipients was quite small[35]), the scorn for welfare mothers provided an important cautionary note for all mothers, whether they were married, divorced, queer, or single: don't expect any respite from the hamster wheel of work for wages and work at home; give in to the pressure to get married or stay married at all costs, or you will be called a "welfare queen."

WHAT WELFARE WAS

AFDC had many shortcomings, including racial bias in who got discretionary benefits (such as back-to-school cash grants for children in September or new coats in the winter to replace the ones they always grew out of too fast) and a certain number of caseworkers who thought humiliating recipients was part of the job description.[36] Welfare offices were hard places: you had to arrive early in the morning to stake out your place in a long line, bring the paperwork you think they will want (which was never enough, necessitating repeating the whole procedure), and drag in the kids for all-day waits for frequent reauthorization. Still,

AFDC did at least provide a safety net for all sorts for mothers, especially those who were trying to leave abusive relationships. With benefits at around $132 a month per recipient as late as 1995,[37] it was certainly nothing approaching a decent standard of living, but it did keep body and soul together at critical times. According to a Massachusetts study, more than 70 percent of welfare recipients were victims of domestic violence, which is consistent with other studies that tell us that domestic violence is a primary cause of women's poverty.[38] Welfare was key to ending that violence; leaving an abusive husband or partner was not enough if one needed financial support from him—child support (which generally also meant visitation or shared custody) provided ongoing sites of violent conflict.[39] In fact, we could say that the federal approach to domestic violence shifted in the nineties from welfare support for victims to policing; the Violence Against Women Act of 1994 provided billions to local police departments, consistent with policies leading to mass incarceration and the hyped-up, militarized policing of the last decade.[40]

Welfare, a New Deal program enacted by feminists and expanded in the 1960s through the efforts of the Black freedom and anti-poverty movements, was by many measures an extraordinarily successful program.[41] Women on welfare received benefits, including health insurance, sometimes while going to school (including getting a BA), receiving job training, raising their small children to be old enough to go to school, or getting back on their feet. Others, including the 10–25 percent of recipients who had children with emotional or physical disabilities or chronic illnesses, the 12 percent who cared for an adult with disabilities, and another 20 percent who had a disability themselves,[42] cycled on and off AFDC. (This may explain why, beginning in 1990 when workfare's work requirements began to be enforced, the rate of people receiving Social Security disability insurance—SSI and SSDI—increased exponentially, growing by 93 percent in 11 years, as AFDC recipients shifted to being federal disability recipients.[43]) The expansion of AFDC in the 1960s eliminated the pervasive hunger that devastated children in many communities, especially Black communities in the South: the bowed legs of rickets, the bad teeth, the bloated bellies of kwashiorkor that led physicians to write prescriptions that simply said "food," the listlessness that the Black Panthers tried to address with breakfast programs because learning was all but impossible for chronically hungry children.[44] The overwhelming majority of mothers who received payments through AFDC (90 percent) received benefits for a short, transitional period of less than five years.[45] The average length of time that recipients got welfare payments was two years.[46]

REFORMING WELFARE: SUBSTANDARD DAY CARE AND NO HEALTH CARE

The case for welfare reform was originally based on experiments in Wisconsin and other states that seemed to show that less funding for welfare benefits meant higher incomes for former recipients. That state (among others) had moved aggressively to kick recipients off benefits in the 1980s. But the argument was a sleight of hand (as you might expect; only racism really allowed policy makers to believe that people would prefer the poverty of AFDC benefits to working for decent wages): Wisconsin was experiencing rapid economic growth, so when the state provided subsidized child care, health care, and transportation, many former welfare recipients were able to leverage these programs to get decent-paying jobs, and household incomes actually did go up.[47] But the Temporary Assistance for Needy Families (TANF) program that Congress finally enacted did not require that states provide day care subsidies (although it allowed them, producing an uneven patchwork of day care benefits), and Medicaid was often not available once people got off, or were kicked off, TANF.[48] When the recession finished the work that welfare reform had begun, subsidized day care was unavailable to most TANF recipients, health care availability (including for children) was uneven, and transportation assistance was virtually nonexistent.[49] Those who were working were concentrated in low-wage McJobs without health benefits, and the majority had lower incomes than when they had been covered by AFDC, some catastrophically so. Among those left with no income, the *New York Times* found single mothers scavenging trash bins, selling blood, returning to violent partners, moving in with friends, and turning to illegal means to survive.[50]

Even the day care subsidies that welfare reform *did* create were a far cry from feminists' 1971 call for affordable, high-quality day care. In 1996, speaker of the house Newt Gingrich famously said that he'd like to "take the children of welfare mothers and put them in orphanages." As I've written elsewhere, the post-AFDC welfare reform era indeed saw quite a lot of that—taking impoverished children and putting them in foster care.[51] Furthermore, TANF rules allow states to divert benefits for assistance to single mothers to foster care. But even for mothers who didn't lose their children, TANF was still quite Dickensian: it pushed kids into substandard day care,[52] sending recipients to unlicensed, untrained, and dramatically underpaid providers, generally in family day cares.[53]

Family day care is an often lightly regulated industry that allows people to care for children in their homes for a fee, usually much more cheaply than an accredited day care center with trained and licensed teachers. Though family day care centers are often staffed by good people who care about children, as a group they lack the resources to provide comprehensive early childhood education—developmental, progressive, and an essential base for later educational success—which is what middle-class and wealthy people get for their kids at accredited preschools and day care centers. Advocates of early childhood education argued that placing children with untrained providers institutionalized a next generation in poverty.[54] In two large-scale studies of family child care in the early 1990s involving hundreds of facilities across multiple states, researchers rated fewer than 5 percent as "excellent." Basically, these centers ran the gamut from poor to mediocre. Studies in 2007 and 2011 found the same thing, although the number providing high-quality care had risen slightly, to 10 percent—a still utterly depressing number.[55] The handful of really excellent family day cares hardly justified the massive investment in them by federal and state governments, which had suddenly become unwilling to let mothers care for their own children at home but were happy to let another mother care for them in her home, provided everyone got up early and got dressed.

Family day care was also a cheaper alternative to fully funding Head Start, the only actual early childhood education program for impoverished children (besides those for kids with disabilities). While Head Start's benefits have been well-documented—including large differences in mortality of children ages 5–9[56]—its resources are often unavailable to those who need them the most. Because of inadequate funding, it largely operates as a part-year, part-day program, which is not all that much help to working parents. As a result, fewer than 6 percent of children who were cared for by anyone other than their mother were in a Head Start program—a figure that includes those enrolled in Head Start grade schools.[57]

Early childhood education is incredibly important in establishing the basic wiring of the brain. Vocabulary and other skills learned before the age of five that are a fearsomely powerful predictor of school success and life chances, according to a recent Institute of Medicine study.[58] As a pair of education scholars explained:

> The quality of child care is important because it is closely linked with children's social, cognitive, and language development. Children in high-quality early childhood programs are more likely to be emotionally secure and self-confident, proficient in language use, able to regulate impulsive and aggressive inclinations, and advanced in cognitive development. Over time, these children may experience enhanced school achievement, higher earnings, and decreased involvement with the criminal justice system. In contrast, children who experience poor-quality child care are at risk for poor long-term developmental outcomes, including apathy, poor school skills, and heightened aggression.[59]

Research has been conducted among children of various socioeconomic classes and repeated over and over for decades, so there is not much mystery to what kids need. High-quality early childhood education leads to success in school and work—and even makes divorce less likely when these children are grown. Kids in poor or mediocre day care have an increased likelihood of aggression, school failure, dropping out without a degree, and even prison.

Parents and providers agree about the qualities that make a center excellent: child safety, the provider's and parents' communication about the child, and a warm, attentive relationship between the provider and child. This was difficult to sustain in the context of the extraordinary pressures of the state and federal child care voucher system, which provided day care to about 15 percent of the children who were eligible, kept wages for day care workers just above the poverty level, and was, by design, a cash-strapped system. Researcher Marcy Whitebook noted that while "voucher payments limited by market rate reimbursement policies increased as a proportion of public funding, the lion's share of the public resources flowed to the least-trained and worst-paid sectors of the industry."[60]

Despite some exciting organizing campaigns for better wages and broader subsidies, including one in California, where a ballot initiative for higher wages was defeated by a well-funded campaign by business, and the national Fight for $15 (an hour) campaign for day care and fast-food workers, for the most part, family day care workers are still little better off, politically and often financially, than the former welfare recipients they served.[61] It's striking, too, in the context of another federal government program started about the same time as "workfare" and TANF's day care vouchers: in 1989, the U.S. military began providing subsidized day care to soldiers and their families, and it did not use underfunded family day care. It opened hundreds of accredited early childhood education centers.[62]

Welfare reform also reduced the availability of Medicaid and other health benefits (which Obama's Affordable Care Act tried to restore.) It meant mothers and children died who wouldn't have under the old program. Comparing states with short TANF time limits with long ones in 2001 (before many states' time limits kicked in—and before the recession meant many people who were laid off after 2007 were ineligible for benefits), a research team found an excess of mortality of 16 infants in their first year per 100,000 babies that could be independently attributed to welfare reform.[63] Likewise, another study found an excess of adult deaths of 54 percent among recipients with more than two children (and hence were less likely to be able to work).[64] There was also a considerable increase in food insecurity. Consider the words of this mother in 2012, two decades and a recession later, after the dust had settled and the opponents of AFDC had won, talking about a jobless and penniless winter in Detroit, and what hunger feels like:

> Your fingers get slow, you know, your whole body slows down. You can't really do much, you try to put a good face on for the kids, but when they leave you just keep still, keep the covers around you. Almost like you kind of fold into the floor. Like you're just waiting it out. You don't really think about too much … November your stomach is crying at you but by December you know, you start to just shut down…. Around 3 you get up for the kids. Put on the space heaters, so they come home and it's warm in here.[65]

While early experiments with TANF-like restructuring of benefits initially meant that some recipients found better-paying employment, for those who were worst off (with no college or many children or dealing with their own or a child's disability), welfare reform also ensured that there were fewer poor people because they died.[66]

WHY POLITICIANS NEEDED WELFARE QUEENS

All of the arguments for welfare reform seem specious in retrospect. Workfare cost a lot of money for very slight gains in employment rates. Most people who used AFDC stopped within two years anyway. The babies of teen mothers are not worse off than those born to women in their early twenties. If it was really "all about the children," as conservative commentators and policy makers seemed to be saying, why were they sending children to low-cost day cares that we know offer children a tough start in life? Or pushing households into food and housing insecurity and higher mortality rates for children and adults alike? If not any of this, what?

Welfare reform provided an excellent cover story for policy makers who were eliminating popular programs that provided for poor people. Wahneema Lubiano defined cover stories as narratives that "cover or mask what they make invisible with an alternative presence; a presence that redirects our attention, that covers or makes absent what has to remain unseen if the *seen* is to function as the *scene* for a different drama. One story provides a cover that allows another story (or stories) to slink out of sight."[67] Whipping up racial resentment of mothers who were staying home with their kids—especially mothers who weren't married—and rendering them shameful, crazy, and pathological did a great deal to scare others into not acting like *that*, not applying for benefits for fear of being called ugly names or worse: for fear of losing their kids. It also provided an illusory "white privilege": in exchange for getting to believe their families were superior to families of color, white women agreed to be pushed into the labor force, to submit to having no time or resources to care for dependents, and to lose the one program that might help them if they had to leave an abusive partner (or even one who was just unloving).

While people were looking at all these supposed "welfare queens," exploring stories about Black teen mothers and multigenerational mental illness, Reagan's administration eliminated many popular programs that provided public benefits to support households and communities. It reduced housing subsidies and put people out of their homes; it cut aid to cities, including for transportation, elder day-care programs, and job training; it presided over pervasive redlining and racial discrimination by banks, real estate agents, and landlords monitored by the federal government; and top officials at the Department of Housing and Urban Development (HUD) shifted funds for housing subsidies to wealthy developers. They slashed low-income housing assistance (Section 8) and then blamed the people who were put out of doors: "people who are sleeping on the grates ... the homeless ... are homeless, you might say, by choice."[68] Or, even better, it blamed welfare. Commenting on the sudden appearance of homeless old ladies in Reagan's America, Lawrence Townsend, the much-lauded director of the welfare program in Riverside, California, said, "Every time I see a bag lady on the street, I wonder, 'Was that an A.F.D.C. mother who hit the menopause wall and can no longer reproduce and get money to support herself?'"[69] Meanwhile, deinstitutionalization of people with mental illness continued apace (begun by John F. Kennedy and the Community Mental Health Act of 1963, then accelerated by reductions in federal funding under Reagan), while the promised community-based infrastructure to support them never really materialized. Hundreds of thousands of people came to live in the street. People who would otherwise have left stayed with abusive partners for a modicum of economic security. Former welfare recipients wore all these faces.

The 1980s saw the beginning of a massive upward redistribution of wealth that has reconstructed class relations in the United States, reduced mobility from the working class to the middle class. Welfare was a convenient alibi at the moment U.S. corporations were taking well-paying manufacturing jobs offshore, driving wages down, and millions of people were being forced into a low-wage service sector—flipping burgers, selling the clothes Walmart was manufacturing in Guatemala and Vietnam, and cleaning homes and buildings—that was often part-time. Even at 40 hours a week, McJobs offered neither livable wages nor health insurance. As an added bonus, as the Fight for $15 campaign reminds us, they often came with a substantial amount of sexual harassment.[70]

In the United States, households with dependents, including conspicuously mothers—impoverished and otherwise—lost the most in this fight. The long feminist struggle against the double day that spanned the years from the 1930s to the 1970s was over after welfare reform, and this was clear to many at the time—every major national feminist organization opposed welfare reform.[71] Care work was privatized, so finding the time to do it and financial resources to support your household (little things like housing, food, and electricity) were your problem. While in many ways the sixties and seventies had been no better in reality, there had been optimism and momentum to build public support for care. But by the end of nineties, civic virtue and responsible motherhood had been redefined. Unless mothers had a trust fund, they had to have a job. For working-class and even a lot of middle-class families, children had to be warehoused in substandard day care with caregivers with little or no training and few resources. For the upper middle class, there were nannies and early childhood education. For others, though, public policy deliberately committed them to the stress storms of not enough money and not enough time, to the detriment of caregiving.

The New Right led with reproductive politics as a way to direct public attention to teen mothers while fundamentally reshaping government. The welfare reform discussion that began under Reagan provided the cultural cover to initiate this massive economic restructuring, and it involved a deliberate, policy-driven shift in political power away from unions, people of color, and women, and to corporations and the wealthy. It was mobilized in ways that particularly affected women and people of color and traded on negative stereotypes of those groups to effect its changes while not seeming callous. The poor, it told us, were responsible for their own poverty through their bad choices, involving that frequent object of horror in U.S. society: rampant teenage sex. If all those slutty girls would just keep their legs shut, it insisted (however implausibly), there wouldn't be poverty in America.

CHAPTER THREE

Offshoring Reproduction

In 1993, we got a snapshot of how neoliberal shifts in the relationship between households, wages, and public benefits were being lived by families of different classes in the United States through the political crisis that was called "Nannygate." In the weeks before Bill Clinton's inauguration in 1993, he announced an intention to put together a cabinet that "looked like America," by including women and people of color. His female nominees did not fare well because of a new spotlight on a practice that had become quite common among families of the CEO class—hiring undocumented nannies and housekeepers—which was taken to be a problem for mothers in particular (although an uncounted number of fathers were appointed to prominent positions without any inquiry into their families' child care arrangements).[1] The nomination of Zoë Baird, Clinton's pick for attorney general, turned into ground zero for the new anti-immigrant forces. Baird had readily admitted in the vetting process that she had two household employees, a nanny and chauffeur, who were undocumented. Because she was sponsoring them for green cards and it was not against the law to employ workers who were undocumented at the time she hired them, it never occurred to her or Clinton's team that she had committed more than a technical violation of the law—it was compared to a parking ticket. She paid a fine and some Social Security taxes, and that, they thought, was that.[2]

It wasn't. As the Clinton administration was about to find out, immigration was landing as a "crisis" of white nativism in US politics; the bipartisan agreement on immigration reform of a few years earlier that had legalized undocumented immigrants was giving way to ever more punitive calls to deport people and militarize the borders. It arrived, unsurprisingly, as an explosion over reproductive politics. The fundamental change in the relationship of government, business, and households in the United States—in which business took more and more time away from households, and government withdrew support (no welfare, elder day programs, and the like)—meant that households like Baird's were hiring undocumented immigrants to do their reproductive labor, immigration enforcement was keeping migrants trapped in these jobs, and immigrants themselves were supposed to either have no households or keep their children, elders, and other dependents in home countries.

This assumption that Zoë Baird had done nothing really wrong in hiring undocumented immigrants as household workers revealed a significant fault line in US culture. The nomination blew up; there was a huge backlash against Baird and another presumptive nominee, Kimba Wood, who had also hired an undocumented housekeeper and nanny. Middle-class folk (mostly women), overwhelmingly struggling with inadequate day care arrangements, didn't just resent impoverished "welfare mothers," but they were also brimming with anger at the relatively small number of the very wealthy who could afford nannies (the Census Bureau estimated less than 6 percent in 1987[3]). Baird was the perfect target for that anger, too; her close ties with big business and Washington insiders didn't help her case.[4]

The complex dance of white, class-based resentment worked a little differently in the anti-immigrant fervor mobilized by the Baird case than it had in relationship to welfare. It was the abject exploitability of immigrants that was infuriating here, as it had been throughout the 1970s and '80s, as unions raged helplessly against the offshoring of manufacturing and the shift to sites with ever-lower wages. While household laborers were certainly not taking union jobs away from anyone (except insofar as they made well-educated, usually white women available to the labor force), their position as the lowest-paid laborers was perceived, rightly or wrongly, to be depressing wages across the board. A follow-up *New York Times* article in January 1992 explored the rank exploitation that often characterized these relationships. It found that nanny-placing agencies in that city were quite open about offering mostly undocumented women as employees and that "legal" was a commodity that people could buy. "The reason that people hire immigrants without papers is that they're looking to save. If they want legal, they can get it, but it costs," Nedra Kleinman, who ran the All Home Services Agency on the Upper West Side of Manhattan, told the *Times*. While an occasional employer would actually help a worker go to school, find an apartment, and get situated as legal, it was mostly a utilitarian arrangement: employers sponsored workers for green cards and in exchange got women who were trapped in a live-in arrangement with low wages. One woman in Floral Park, Queens, told the *Times* quite bluntly that she was looking for an illegal immigrant who had not been in the country long to care for her newborn triplets.

"I want someone who cannot leave the country, who doesn't know anyone in New York, who basically does not have a life," the woman said. "I want someone who is completely dependent on me and loyal to my family."[5] One wonders what kind of "loyalty" she was likely to buy from someone whom she was clearly seeking in order to take advantage of. This kind of arrogance did not play well in white middle America. Despite the presumption of this well-off and frequently exploitative class, Baird's nomination and Wood's near-nomination went down in flames. Baird and Wood never did work in government. And no male nominee was ever asked about his household or child care arrangements.[6]

Immigrants' exploitation did not inspire a call for better wages and working conditions, however—much less solidarity. In the old, ugly bargain that the white working and middle classes has gotten since the end of slavery, they were invited to loathe people taken to be not-white in exchange for the illusory privileges of whiteness that got them little more than symbolic superiority,[7] while the CEO class ran the table in the absence of an organized working class and continued its successful campaign to freeze real wages for everyone. But the mobilization of white nativism in response to the Baird appointment led to expanded calls for deportations. A security apparatus rained down on the immigrants at the center of the controversy. The Immigration and Naturalization Service (INS) initiated deportation proceedings against the Peruvian couple, Lillian and Victor Cordero, whom Baird was sponsoring for green cards. They ultimately fled to Peru, insisting that they had been singled out and were the victims of unfair targeting by INS.[8]

These events turned out to be the opening salvo in a wave of new anti-immigrant measures. Nannygate occurred just a few years after the passage of the Immigration Reform and Control Act

(IRCA) of 1986. IRCA had allowed almost 3 million undocumented immigrants to regularize their status. At the same time, however, IRCA had made it a crime to hire people without proper documents and offered vague pledges about stepping up "enforcement"—which is to say, detention and deportation. The high profile example of the Corderos signaled the anti-immigrant terror that was to come. Within a few years, Clinton's administration inaugurated a new regime of deaths and deportation. Operation Gatekeeper put Border Patrol agents all along the highways and easy border crossings, while leaving open a dangerous pathway through Arizona's desert, which became the new migrant trail along which hundreds died every year.[9] Two additional measures—the Antiterrorism and Effective Death Penalty Act (1996) and the Illegal Immigration Reform and Immigrant Responsibility Act (IIRIRA, 1996) began to fast-track deportations, and, according to Human Rights Watch, "eliminated key defenses against deportation and subjected many more immigrants, including legal permanent residents, to detention and deportation."[10] This was the beginning of the criminalization of the quotidian existence of people who were undocumented and the making their routes into the United States hazardous and deadly—but, importantly, not impossible.

People without papers, a slight majority of them female, were coming into the United States (and a great many other places) largely to do reproductive labor: nanny work, housekeeping, and the like.[11] While women migrants come from every socioeconomic class and do all sorts of jobs, including a great number in professional positions, close to one million are household workers, and many of these are undocumented.[12] In short, immigration is significantly a question about how household and child care work are getting done in the aftermath of the neoliberal push to get all mothers and other caregivers into the workforce for 40 and more hours a week.

Like welfare reform, "immigration reform" was part of the political work by conservatives and business that allowed the state to shift more work to families—but this time not in the name of austerity or even eliminating "dependency." This time, the keyword was "security"—securing borders and producing "safety" for communities. (Ironically, Bill Clinton "tightened the borders" with his 1996 antiterrorism act in response to the bombing of the Oklahoma federal building—by a white US antigovernment figure, Timothy McVeigh.) It rolled back the security of all families by targeting the most vulnerable: communities of color and poor folks in particular.

Ironically, the "care crisis" faced by US households was mirrored by one that was at least as bad for impoverished and working-class Latin Americans. In their current configurations, as sociologist Rhacel Parreñas has argued, both are born out of a "cost of reproductive labor" question. After the Baird and Corderos fiasco, from the mid-nineties to the first decade after 2010, a rapidly growing number of middle-class households in the United States began adding domestic workers, most of Latin American origin or ancestry. They were relying on labor from elsewhere—"offshoring" reproductive labor—because they could pay women from Latin America lower wages to work in their homes than the women in the US household were earning outside the home. At the same time, migrant women who leave their children or other dependent household members in home countries are in a sense doing the same thing (though the consequences are not equivalent): relying on the lower cost of reproductive labor outside the United States.[13] If globalization is a story of manufacturing moving outside the United States to lower its cost, it is equally a story of relying on the offshoring of reproduction to lower the cost of *reproductive* labor.

Together with structural adjustment policies by the International Monetary Fund (IMF) and World Bank that used the fact of governmental debt to dictate harsh policies in the formerly colonized world, eliminating government support for food subsidies, schools, and health care, immigration "reform" in the United States (and parallel versions elsewhere) created a migratory workforce that was highly vulnerable to deportation and detention, and as a result, often separated parents from children. For employers, this was something of an ideal situation—women (in particular) who would work for almost any wage, no matter how low, to support family and household members back home, without the entanglements that come with dependents who are physically present, such as being late to work after a child's doctor's appointment, say, or the sick days that children or elders have so many of. That is, Arlie Hochschild's crisis of reproductive labor was shifted economically downward—to bring the who's-watching-the-kids (and elders and other dependents) crisis to a greater number of working-class households in the United States, or across national boundaries, as caregivers left children and loved ones in their home countries to support them by doing domestic work elsewhere. (Not that this was new in the Americas—during the three hundred years of slavery and the century after, a great many African and African-descended mothers were forced to leave their small children with inadequate or no care while they worked in the fields or in others' homes.[14])

STRATIFIED REPRODUCTION

In 1995, anthropologist Shellee Colen coined the term "stratified reproduction" to account for this process. She described the relationship between West Indian nannies and their New York City employers, arguing that when the IMF inaugurated structural adjustment policies designed to promote free markets and foreign direct investment, it created an economic crisis in the West Indies that pushed many women (among others) out of their home countries. As a condition of further loans—which many countries desperately needed just to make interest payments after the inflation of the late 1970s rendered their earlier loans extremely expensive—the IMF and the World Bank required governments to reduce spending on things like health care, schools, and food subsidies. In addition to making life very hard for poor people, many charged that these measures trashed domestic economies in order to make nations friendlier to the global economy. As Colen documented, most of the West Indian nannies in New York had been middle class at home. The women who employed them—usually but not always white, upper-middle class or wealthy—were increasingly in the labor force full-time in professional jobs. Gendered expectations meant that these working mothers were still largely responsible for child care and housework, although with few options to fulfill those expectations, as 50-, 60-, and even 80-hour workweeks made caring for their children and households impossible. Increasingly, they turned to the large West Indian female labor force in the city, because day care options were few and fragile and had too-short hours, and the conventional belief that children should be cared for in the home left many feeling more comfortable with nannies. Formerly middle-class West Indian women, whose own children were largely being fostered by family and friends in home countries, found nanny work attractive, as they needed sponsors for green cards (a role household employers might serve), and working with children sometimes assuaged their loneliness for their own children. Besides, gendered expectations about women's work in New York gave them few other options.[15]

Colen's term "stratified reproduction" took off among social scientists, because while Colen was documenting life for women in high-end jobs in a global city where day care options were particularly few and expensive and women from a part of the Caribbean that was particularly acutely hit by the early effects of structural adjustment, the economic and social relations she described were rapidly becoming a norm across the world and the United States. It seemed like a phrase that could be used to describe so much of the racial and class dynamics of reproductive politics in the post–Cold War era. Following a civil rights generation in which it had become decidedly uncommon outside the South to have a Black nanny and/or housekeeper, a new globalized reproductive order began to emerge in the late eighties and nineties. At the same time that impoverished, unmarried mothers and those leaving violent relationships were demonized as "welfare queens" in the public policy debate over mothers without jobs and forced into low-wage jobs, first wealthy and then middle-class women were solving the problem of the double day through the globalization of motherhood, as were women in the neoliberalizing global south.

But if immigrant women and their employers were engaged in parallel processes, they were not in it together. A 2012 study of two thousand domestic workers in fourteen cities found that paychecks and working conditions were abysmal for most of them. Live-in jobs were the worst: 67 percent of workers earned less than the minimum wage, and about the same number lacked health insurance; 82 percent had no paid sick days. Ninety-five percent were women; it is depressing but not surprising that women doing women's work earn tiny paychecks. But in addition, wages turned out to be intensively sensitive to race and immigration status. Nannies were better paid than housekeepers or elders' caregivers, but even at the top of the domestic labor pyramid, wages were not high enough to support a family. Latina nannies made $8.57 an hour, compared with $11.11 for Asian nannies. Black nannies earned still more: $12.71. But cutting the data differently suggests that migration status mattered even more: citizen nannies earned an average of $12.50 an hour, while those who were out of status earned an average of $9.86. Behind the closed doors of family homes, domestic workers reported routine sexual harassment, abuse, and assault. Many also said that they lacked even their own bed if they lived in; they were expected to sleep with the children in their care. Twenty-five percent of caregivers reported never being able to get more than five hours of sleep; 30 percent reported chronic health problems.[16]

In July 2010, New York became the first state in the nation to guarantee certain rights to nannies and domestic workers as a matter of law (joined by Hawaii, Massachusetts, and California within a few years): time and a half for overtime, one guaranteed day off a week, and, after a year of employment, three paid vacation days—that and a written contract. As slender as these benefits were, they were also more often ignored than observed; one legal clinic lawyer in New York said, "I have yet to see a live-in worker who's being paid overtime at the correct rate."[17] But anecdotally at least, it also widened the chasm between those who tried to treat domestic workers with respect and those who sought to hire illegal immigrants because, in a high-deportation climate, immigrant women have almost no recourse if their rights are violated.

THE WAGES OF IMMIGRATION

How are "illegal" immigrants made into cheap employees? By making them vulnerable to deportation, by making entry into the United States dangerous and deadly, meaning people will do almost anything to avoid having to leave once they get to the United States. The long view of immigration deportation and labor in the past century and a half suggests that the United States has pursued a policy that clamps down on immigrants—but not too much. It has needed immigrant labor and, in some periods, has needed their labor to be particularly cheap. It has not wanted their children nor their settlement. Although there are many crosscurrents and diverse agendas in policy conversations on immigration, the long view suggests that the effect of U.S. policy is not actually to deter immigration (although the 2008 recession did do that) but to make it sufficiently difficult to ensure that immigrant labor remains cheap. As immigrants became, in their majority, female, the effect was particularly to make domestic labor cheap.[18]

The United States has not always been so hostile to immigrants, but neither has it always welcomed them. The periodic paroxysms of anti-immigrant fervor have been interlaced with periods of relative peace. However, the narratives about why immigrants ought to be unwelcome have always been run through fairly predictable images of racial difference and gendered immorality. Contrary to popular myths of the United States as historically welcoming, racial immigration restriction is nearly as old as the nation; it was founded in a 1790 law that offered unrestricted immigration to *white* people. But the rights of immigrants to enter the United States actually remained untrammeled for almost a century after that, until the 1875 Page Act, which barred immigration for Chinese women, although not men, at a time when Chinese men were a crucial labor force in mining and building the railroad. The concern was ostensibly prostitution but might be more precisely described as wanting (men's) labor but not wanting them stay, reproduce, and have families. Chinese migrants were supposed to be "sojourners": to come, work, and leave. The period of restricting Chinese women was followed by a full-scale assault on the "yellow peril"—mob violence against Chinese communities and workers. An 1882 immigration restriction law barred the entry of most new Chinese and "Oriental" migrants—a somewhat paradoxical policy action, since Chinese labor continued to be economically crucial.[19]

Ironically, in terms of the center of much of the current panic about immigrants, the effort to regulate the comings and goings of Mexican and Central American migrants is relatively new in U.S. history. The harsh immigrant restriction acts of 1921, 1924, and 1929 never regulated immigration from Latin America. The vast area that is currently the U.S. Southwest—north to California and Colorado—was Mexico until 1848, when, after the Mexican-American war, the border divided families and communities, and disrupted historical work-migration patterns. Until the 1930s, though, the new international border was more an inconvenient formality than an actual bar to movement (although the new Mexican-Americans lost vast acreage of their land under the nineteenth-century inauguration of Anglo administration, and indigenous people lost land and water rights, both matters of life and death). That's not to say the border wasn't militarized; it was. The Texas Rangers, born as an Anglo vigilante group, harassed and sometimes killed Mexicans and Mexican Americans who were out of place or who engendered white anxieties about economic rivalry, and the Border Patrol, established in 1924, piled on. Public health officials believed Mexicans and Mexican Americans spread disease, and they sought to delouse, vaccinate, and otherwise make Mexicans more (supposedly) sanitary, resulting also in making it harder to cross the border and solidifying the belief that Mexicans represented a different (and dirtier) "race." Still, it bears remembering that the period in which visas were not required to enter the United States from Mexico was not so long ago—there are still residents of the United States, born in Mexico, who crossed legally in the 1920s, lived their whole lives on the US side of the border, and were made illegal by subsequent regimes of immigration. Mostly elderly, impoverished women, they never crossed the threshold of a court house or immigration office in their lives, and it never occurred to them to regularize their status when opportunities arose—first in 1929, then in 1986—when what the current debate is calling "amnesty" opened the doors to those who for all sorts of reasons were out of status. Despite the Depression-era push to drive Mexicans, particularly farmworkers, across the border into Mexico whatever their status (many were U.S. citizens), U.S. agriculture needed them, and some stayed.[20]

The 1940s, 1950s, and 1960s were the origin of the image of the Latino migrant as a man; the Bracero program recruited Mexicans to the West as temporary workers, requiring them to return to Mexico as a condition of their visas. But growers recruited many, many workers illegally, including women, children, and families— and some stayed, settled, and did great varieties of work. Growers then as now liked illegal workers for their exploitability; they could be paid less, and they were in no position to object to substandard conditions, even housed in shacks in fields with no running water or electricity.[21] Meanwhile, on the East Coast, crops were picked by people disenfranchised by race, not status, but no less outside the decent-paying labor market for all of that; first African Americans and then, as a civil rights movement enfranchised Black people to some degree, by Puerto Ricans. I grew up in a community that by the 1970s relied on Puerto Rican families—having cycled through Italians and Poles at the turn of the century and then African Americans from the South—to pick tobacco in the fields that were the majority of the acreage in our town, but I never saw a Puerto Rican kid in school. They were picking crops.

Although there were sporadic efforts to police people crossing the U.S.-Mexican border without papers in earlier decades—the fifties saw Operation Wetback, named for a racial slur—the current era in border era enforcement began in 1994. Called "Operation Gatekeeper," it was timed to begin with NAFTA—the free trade agreement that gutted Mexican agriculture by compelling Mexican farmers to compete with heavily subsidized produce of U.S. agribusiness. Cheap labor and hard work couldn't get them crops that were priced as low as the corn and other products that were subsidized by farm aid from the U.S. government, forcing farmers from Mexico (and then Central America after CAFTA) to migrate and work picking crops in U.S. fields. But while agricultural work in Mexico was becoming unprofitable, and growers in California and elsewhere had established a long work/migration pattern by recruiting Mexican laborers, this time, the federal government did not look the other way. By aggressively militarizing the border, first in San Diego and then along the Rio Grande, it stopped the easy and safe migration routes. It left open the long desert border with Arizona. Some say the Clinton administration deliberately made the crossing dangerous and difficult, rendering "illegal" labor available but leaving people ever less able to negotiate for decent wages and working conditions. Operation Gatekeeper also, perversely, halted circular and seasonal migration, ensuring a new wave of permanent settlement by Mexicans in the United States and, some argue, increasing the number of undocumented folks and mixed-status families in the United States.[22]

In the Contract-with-America climate of hostility to welfare mothers of the late 1990s, the press also began running significant numbers of stories about women coming across the border to have their babies, then using their U.S.-citizen children as an excuse to stay. Elena Gutiérrez argues that a discourse of immigrants "breeding like rabbits" and mothers who were hyperfertile "breeding machines" emerged sharply the late 1990s, not for the first time but at an amplified volume.[23] It was a period of recession in California. In an effort to criminalize immigration violations (which are civil offenses, like a parking ticket), voters passed Proposition 187, which sought to deny health care and education to migrants and their children, although it was later rolled back by a judge as unconstitutional. Still more draconian legislation, never passed, sought to deny birthright citizenship to migrants' children who were born in the United States.[24] The irony is ripe but bitter: The Fourteenth Amendment, designed to ensure the citizenship of former slaves in the aftermath of the Civil War, has long guaranteed citizenship to all who are born in the United States. It is painfully symmetrical that legislation that ignored the Fourteenth Amendment sought to create a new racialized underclass of "illegals" who could be exploited and underpaid—even, sometimes, unpaid, like slaves.

ARAB AMERICANS, IMMIGRANTS, AND TERRORISM

After the planes, the twin towers, and the Pentagon, after 9/11/2001, another wave of anti-immigrant and nativist racism

engulfed the United States, this one extending far beyond the
more local conflicts of California and the Southwest. The first
victims were Arab Americans and other Asian immigrants. In
the days after 9/11, in Phoenix, Arizona, a Sikh (non-Arab, non-
Muslim) gas station owner, Balbir Singh Sodhi, was murdered by
a nativist seeking to kill "towel heads," who felt that Sodhi's tur-
ban implicated him in the criminal actions of the 9/11 hijackers.
Thousands of Arabs and Arab Americans were rounded up by
the INS, many were deported, and the names of those detained
were kept secret. In New York, this meant some families spent
weeks wondering if loved ones had died in the Twin Towers or
been arrested on real or imagined immigration offenses.[25] Overnight, Arab Americans, who had often been characterized as
white in the dyadic black-white racial order of the United States,
became a racial threat. Registries of immigrants from certain
countries, deportation, "extraordinary rendition" (extrajudicial
kidnapping and deportation), and torture both reflected and
solidified this new racial order of things: the logic seemed to be
that if the United States is a democracy, then people who are
imprisoned in places like Guantánamo apparently without due
process must be an exceptional threat. Conservative activists like
David Horowitz and Robert Spencer (of the website Front Page
and the blog *Jihad Watch,* respectively) provided the neoconservative brain trust for the U.S. military and policy makers that
made Islam itself the problem; they, and scholars like Bernard
Lewis (*What Went Wrong?*), focused a domesticated war against
Islam that centrally targeted religious women's modest dress,
like the *hijab,* as the root of Arab-Islamic "backwardness" and
danger. Although traditions of religious diversity in the United
States made it impossible to ban head scarves (as happened in
French schools), observant Muslim women with covered heads

have been the victims of street harassment in the United States, including strangers attempting to rip off their clothes.[26]

One of the odder consequences of 9/11, though, has been a growing association of Mexican and Central American immigrants with "terrorism," although no evidence of links between the hijackers and Latin American migrants has ever even been suggested. Furthermore, not one of the 9/11 hijackers crossed a border without papers; they had simply overstayed ordinary visas. Nevertheless, calls to "protect our borders" were redoubled as a question of keeping "us" safe from violence. The years since have seen an intense militarization of the area around the U.S.-Mexico border, from a patchwork of walls to sensor arrays in the centers of small towns to the routine harassment and even jailing by the Border Patrol of all sorts of people who live in the area (including Anglos as well as Mexicans).[27]

Some of the harassment has specifically targeted mothers and children. Michelle Dallacroce founded Mothers Against Illegal Aliens, a white nativist group out of Phoenix, Arizona, which is not on the border, but two hundred miles north; still, it hosts significant Mexican and Mexican American populations. A *Los Angeles Times* reporter explained her motivations: "She heard only Spanish in some neighborhoods. Day laborers swarmed near her house, and a rash of burglaries plagued her upper-middle-class neighborhood. She ... concluded that Mexican immigrants were invading the country and weren't interested in assimilating. She formed Mothers Against Illegal Aliens ... because she feared for the future of her two young children, who could be ignored in a United States dominated by Mexican-born people."[28] On her website, Dallacroce claimed that Mexican immigrant women were "crossing our border to 'steal' the American Dream by giving birth."[29] Although like another group in Arizona, the Minutemen, Dallacroce was more of a media presence than an actual political organizer, nevertheless, the publicity itself was enough to make immigrants fearful and their lives more precarious.

Initially, the insistence that the Southwest is full of "criminal aliens" led to a defensive claim by Immigration and Customs Enforcement (ICE) that it was doing all it could to deport Latin Americans who had committed crimes, and people with DUI convictions decades old and people who were using a false ID were being sent to the country of their birth in record numbers (although under the Trump administration, ICE apparently embraced these claims about criminality in order to turn loose a deportation machine). The conflation of immigrants with criminals produced steadily rising deportation rates. The Obama administration deported more people in its first term than any other president in any four-year period.[30] The deceptively named Federation for American Immigration Reform (FAIR) stirred up anxiety by claiming that "Criminal aliens—noncitizens who commit crimes—are a growing threat to public safety and national security, as well as a drain on our scarce criminal justice resources," a belief amplified by Donald Trump when he stoked the white nativist id with his famous declaration that Mexico "is sending people that have lots of problems. They're bringing drugs. They're bringing crime. They're rapists."[31] In addition to the claim about criminality that was soon shown to be false by every reputable newspaper—immigrants are much less likely than others to commit crimes—was the other, less commented on absurdity: most Mexican immigrants are women. However, this proved to be a harbinger of things to come; his administration brought together Steve Bannon, Stephen Miller, and Jeff Sessions, who had all embraced this previously marginal position about criminality and actively promoted it through sites like Breitbart News.[32]

One case where an immigrant mother lost her child gives some insight into the making of the "criminal alien": the ways ordinary forms of survival were criminalized. María Luis, an indigenous Guatemalan woman in Grand Island, Nebraska, had her parental rights terminated following her arrest for lying to the police and subsequent deportation. María had taken her one-year-old daughter, Angelica, to the doctor for a respiratory infection. Although she was a Kiché speaker and, like many indigenous Guatemalans, did not speak Spanish, the doctors instructed her in Spanish about how to care for the child. When she failed to arrive for a follow-up appointment, social services went to her house with the police. When asked if she was her children's mother, María, frightened that she would be in trouble because of her immigration status, said she was the babysitter. The police arrested her on a criminal charge for falsely identifying herself to a police officer. While she was in prison, her two children were taken into foster care. Based on that charge, she was deported as a "criminal alien."[33] Her children were placed for adoption. Subsequent publicity and activism enabled her to get them back to her in Guatemala years later, but that made her case an exception, not the rule. Most women deported without their children lose them for good.[34]

Even before the Trump administration threatened to separate mothers and children intercepted at the border,[35] there was the Obama-era immigrant terror. While the Obama administration came to power claiming that it would end the abuses of an immigration system that had grown large in the years of the Bush administration, including in particular raising questions about the treatment of immigrants' children. Three years after the election, however, an investigation found more than five thousand children of deported immigrant parents in foster care. Most of the cases it reported were initiated after 2008. In 2013–16, when thousands of Central American children entered the United States seeking refugee status after the U.S.-supported Honduran coup and the exacerbation of state, police, and criminal violence—types of violence often indistinguishable from one another—throughout the Northern Triangle countries of Honduras, Guatemala, and El Salvador, the Obama administration responded with promises of more funding for Central American military and police and detention for the children and mothers with small children.[36]

NANNIES AND LONG-DISTANCE MOTHERHOOD

The climate of repression in the United States, including the mistreatment, detention, and separation of children from immigrant parents, motivates many parents to leave children at home when they move to the United States—that and financial insecurity, the difficulty of getting them here, and the desire to get established first. But one of the most significant obstacles is that the most common work immigrant women find is nanny, domestic, and home care work (for elders and people with disabilities). Especially for nannies and domestic workers, the expectation is often that women will live in—without their children.

Thus, as with nineteenth-century racial slavery in the United States, in the current regime of immigration and labor, disrupted families are not at all unusual. Sociologists Patricia Landolt and Wei Da call our attention to the fact that transnational business elites are also living much of their lives separated from children and spouses:

Workers—both men and women—are pressured to migrate across borders and into new labour markets in their search for a livelihood. Transnational business elites also navigate quite comfortably through the spaces of flows, profiting from their new-found border-crossing mobility and multinational experiences of inclusion. In turn, narrowing eligibility criteria in the immigration policies of receiving countries delay or disable plans for family reunification. These transformations suggest that the spatially unilocal family may become an increasingly rare form of family life.[37]

Women at both ends of the economic spectrum—the wealthiest business elites and the humblest rural, indigenous women displaced from agricultural work—are equally engaged in disrupted, spatially separated family life, where children and those who care for them are often in a different country from the working parents who send money home. (It's interesting to think of Anne-Marie Slaughter in this regard, who wrote a viral *Atlantic* article about working in the Obama administration in DC while her children stayed in Princeton, New Jersey. Long-distance motherhood was her problem, too, even though she was at the very pinnacle of professional success for a professor of international relations: participating in the policy-making process in the State Department.[38])

Although the growing global disruption of families may cut across class lines, the way children live these separations is not equal. Children in poor communities are much more likely to be without a caregiver than their wealthy counterparts. The unidirectional flows of care work—from South to North, from poor to wealthy—by definition signal an extractive economy of caring labor. Rhacel Parreñas writes of a "care deficit" in the Philippines, as children struggle to raise themselves and younger siblings when mothers migrate to do nanny and maid work in places like Hong Kong and the United States. (Fathers migrate, too, and in greater numbers, but conservative gender ideologies mean that migrating mothers are spoken of more harshly in the popular press, and this trickles down to children's sense of loss). One girl Parreñas interviewed spoke of how much she resented the children her mother cared for in New York. She said, "There was even a time when she told the children she was caring for that they are very lucky that she was taking care of them, while her children back in the Philippines don't even have a mom to take care of them. It's pathetic, but it's true. We were left alone by ourselves and we had to be responsible at a very young age without a mother. Can you imagine?"[39] Economists often speak of the extraction of raw materials and labor from the Global South; fewer notice that the dramatic rise of middle-class mothers working outside the home from the United States to Scandinavia has taken a toll on caring labor elsewhere.

While the care deficit is real, it is also important to recognize that some of the most alarmist language about children being "abandoned" and suffering irreparable emotional harm is essentially a reiteration of conservative gender stereotypes about who should care for children and what the (lifelong! devastating!) consequences are if they don't do it in the most conventional ways. Children and families adapt, and some develop quite functional strategies for dealing with a less than ideal situation—acknowledging that the absence of work in home countries and the real consequences of not migrating—which can include malnutrition, poor access to health care, and exclusion from schooling for children—are also not outcomes they would wish for. Another girl Parreñas interviewed, whom she called "Ellen," described some of these strategies:

I realize that my mother loves us very much. Even if she is far away, she would send us her love. She would make us feel like she really loved us. She would do this by always being there. She would just assure us that whenever we have problems to just call her and tell her. [Pauses.] And so I know that it has been more difficult for her than other mothers. She has had to do extra work because she is so far away from us.[40]

Ellen went on to say that she felt much closer to her mother than to her father, who had not migrated, in a telling assessment of what proximity can and cannot do. Furthermore, many of these children were able to complete schooling, even college; they lived in homes their families were able to buy; and they had access to a nest egg with which to start a business or a life. Despite the abysmal wages paid to domestic workers in global cities like New York or San Francisco, these workers can often send enough home to ensure a (very relative) middle-class existence for their children, a way of life that would have been completely unavailable had they not migrated, and the children obviously appreciated these advantages. Still, every child Parreñas spoke with gave the same answer when she asked if they would consider migrating and leaving their children behind: never.

CONCLUSION

The sea change in the relationship of government, business, and citizens in the United States that accelerated under Reagan, Bush, and then Clinton shifted the cost of reproductive labor from government to the "private" household at the same time that business was taking more and more labor time away from the household (by drawing mothers into the workforce without providing child care, for example). By the 1990s, this shift in state, household, and business relations was producing a broad crisis of reproductive labor that families and households solved in different ways depending on income and their place in the global economy. The solution for a considerable number was to "offshore" household and care work. That is, they hired nannies, housecleaners, and home care workers from Mexico, Central America, and elsewhere in the global South. Often, these migrant care workers felt compelled to globalize their own reproduction, leaving their children or other dependents in their home country, where their very low U.S. wages could offer financial support to caregivers, build a house, and send their children to school, even college. Immigration "reform" in the 1990s made this caregiving workforce precarious (by making people "illegal" and even, sometimes, stigmatizing their employers) and thus kept wages low, making household help affordable for a strapped middle class. The increasing alarm about "security" and foreign nationals in the United States—which spread for no clear reason to the Latin Americans who were doing the lion's share of paid household labor—hardened the labor process that was already well under way: namely, to make it more difficult for migrants to keep their children with them and to minimize their labor protections.

It is important to say that the explosion of immigrant nanny and household work was not an inevitable or even direct consequence of feminism in the United States. On the contrary, it was the endpoint of a long series of refusals on the part of government and business to meet the demands of the women's movement. As we have seen, in the 1950s and '60s, labor union women campaigned for an 8-hour day, which would let mothers care for their own children; in the 1970s the women's liberation movement called for high-quality, affordable day care (and was beaten back by the antifeminist wing of the Republican Party, which demanded that women return to the home). Feminists have never called for nannies for the rich. In the 1980s, it was declining real wages, not feminism, that forced women into the workforce in ever-expanding numbers. Feminist groups like the National Organization for Women and the labor group 9to5 campaigned to loosen immigration restrictions, and more than a hundred feminists were arrested in September 2013 in acts of civil disobedience on behalf of immigrant rights.[41] The expansion of a particularly vulnerable "illegal" nanny workforce in the 1990s and early 2000s by the invention of new crimes punishable with prison time— such as hiring someone who is out of status or misidentifying yourself to a police officer or having a false ID (that is, making human beings "illegal")—was also not a feminist initiative. Indeed, feminists fought for protections for women immigrants in the Violence Against Women Act (VAWA), which allowed special pathways to visas for women who were out of status and victims of domestic violence (often the two are causally linked, because of either partner or household employer violence).

The growing importance of immigrant household workers has often been spoken of as an inevitable flow of labor to fill a care gap in places like the United States, where middle-class mothers are in the workforce in unprecedented numbers. Yet there was nothing inevitable about it; it was a consequence of a political movement to shrink government, expand the gendered work of families, and ensure that business never picked up the tab. The women's movement's demand for 24-hour, high-quality, affordable day care could have been met, alongside other kinds of support for people with disabilities and dependents. Workplaces could have done a great deal more to accommodate the demands of parenting—flexible schedules, paid sick days,

paid maternity leaves, 40-hour workweeks, comp time—
acknowledging that we have a collective investment in the
reproduction of our species. School schedules for K-12 need no
longer be on an agricultural schedule, designed to free children
in summer and afternoons to pick crops for an economy built
around family farms. Relying on immigrant nannies (and others) may have been a predictable choice—in the sense that
immigrant labor is filling in sectors of the economy where workers must be "cheap," which is to say exploitable—but business
and government also chose not to step in to care for children.

While we rarely think of immigration to the United States as
a reproductive politics issue, that's exactly what it is. It was a
strategy, or a set of strategies, to make reproductive labor
cheaper by offshoring it. A discourse of danger, security, and
criminal aliens taken up with great vigor by the Trump administration not only masks the more ordinary realities of immigrant households and the paid work usually available to their
members—child care, elder care, housework, and cleaning
buildings—but it is a cover story that keeps immigrant workers
underpaid. The idea that there are a lot of "criminal aliens" out
there raping and murdering people—rather than frightened
mothers telling the police that they are their children's
babysitter—justified a new wave of repression that echoed previous ones. And that crackdown, not incidentally, arrived as a
reproductive politics issue: Nannygate.

CHAPTER FOUR

The Politics and Economy of Reproductive Technology and Black Infant Mortality

In 2008, the *New York Times* gave us another snapshot of how the wealthy were dealing with the problem of reproductive labor. Alex Kuczynski wrote a first-person story about hiring a gestational surrogate to carry a baby for her.[1] Featured on the cover of the Sunday magazine, the piece got noticed. Kuczynski, 39, wrote that she had been trying to get pregnant since she got married at 34. She suffered four miscarriages and underwent nearly a dozen cycles of in vitro fertilization (where her egg and her husband's sperm met in a petri dish and the resulting embryos were implanted in her uterus). Nearly the full cost ($8,000 per cycle) was borne by her and her husband, since their insurance didn't cover it—but she continued to have miscarriage after miscarriage. In the piece, she wrote about pain and hope—each cycle, each pregnancy marking new excitement about the possibility of a baby, and then, over the long, drawn-out process, that addictive hope being crushed. Ultimately, she paid another woman, Cathy Hilling, to become pregnant with one of her embryos. The questions her article asked about exploitation and Hilling's desire to be a surrogate traversed the usual moral territory, neither particularly thoughtful nor over-whelmingly obtuse. Kuczynski wrote that the $25,000 she paid Hilling would make a significant difference in Hilling's life, paying college tuition for one of her children, though she was not in real poverty. It mattered to Kuczynski that Hilling was middle-class, owned her own home, had a college degree, voted for Obama, had been a foster parent for more than forty children, and had worked as a gestational surrogate before. Kuczynski flayed herself in predictable ways: was she really the child's mother if she didn't go through the pregnancy? What would other people think? What story could she tell her child? Was this the dystopic future of Margaret Atwood's feminist novel *The Handmaid's Tale,* in which impoverished fertile women bore children serially—and without the freedom to say no—for the wealthy? Kuczynski failed to ask some big and important questions: What had become of the middle class if this was how you paid for college? What did it mean in this supposedly postfeminist age that she comforted herself with ideas about "renting a womb" and making Hilling the "vessel" for "their" embryo? Why had it become common for smart, ambitious women like Kuczynski to get married at 34, when on average their fertility is declining? Or, as we might put it, how, in the aftermath of welfare reform, immigration reform, and other neoliberal attacks on working-class households and their ability to keep body and soul together, were white and wealthy people living the new normal of the privatization of wealth and care?

The comments on Kuczynski's article—both at the *New York Times* site and in the wider blogosphere—were unsympathetic at best, often downright vicious, in ways only a public discussion of women's reproductive decision making could be, whether of "welfare queens," Nadya Suleman (aka "Octo-mom"), or Zoë Baird. We may be particularly unkind to really impoverished mothers, but we're not, collectively, all that generous to anyone who follows any but the most conventional route to getting pregnant and raising their kids. Kuczynski's narrative of pain about the difficulty of getting pregnant in her mid-thirties might have invited sympathy or even reflection about how we got to the point where her story of infertility was far more common than in previous generations (when trying to have a first child in one's mid-thirties was quite rare).[2] Kuczynski was clear that she would never have chosen surrogacy but for the four emotionally exhausting miscarriages, and she quoted her lawyer saying that she didn't believe anyone ever "chose" surrogacy as a way to avoid pregnancy. Yet people's contempt for Kuczynski's decision to hire a surrogate was angry and bottomless, picking up on a wider cultural narrative about the "designer babies" of the very rich—despite little evidence that there actually are any, unless you want to include medical decisions to screen out embryos carrying genes for serious illness in families with a history of things like hemophilia or cystic fibrosis. But those who wrote in to the comments section loathed Kuczynski for confessing relief that she was not pregnant and that she went skiing and white-water rafting in the ninth month of Hilling's pregnancy (because apparently no real mother in the history of the world ever wished to evade the physical discomfort of late pregnancy, and no men were ever celebrated for hiring someone else to do labor for them while they went skiing, either). The photographer and editor who created the layout for the piece produced an explicit subtext for the article about wealth, privilege, and exploitation, contrasting Kuczynski and baby on her estate-like property with Hilling, nine months pregnant, on her porch with couch and dog. The photographer, Gillian Laub, went out of her way to include the damaged foundation of Hilling's house in the photo. Furthermore, the photo of Kuczynski, with her house's stately pillars and her Black baby nurse, Dudley Stevenson, recalled nothing so much as the classic image of a Southern plantation during slavery times. It looked like Tara. As one commentator wrote, the biggest thing wrong with the article was the photographs.[3] Or, as a reprotech clinic's blog reported, reading the article on a text-only computer was a completely different experience than seeing it the next day with photos, which must have been more or less how Kuczynski felt as a writer.[4]

The feminist blog *Jezebel* was ever-so-slightly more sympathetic but suggested another narrative about how messed up Kuczynski was: "Kuczynski is self-aware enough to know that paying a ton of money (about $25,000) for a baby-carrier when so many foster children need a good home will be considered by some to be immensely selfish." That fostering is "considered by some" the most morally appropriate response to infertility represents common sense in this sentence, a generous choice contrasted with the privileged position of hiring a gestational surrogate. Yet would providing a "good home" for a foster child really offer a different set of exploitative race and class dynamics than those Kuczynski is being criticized for? After all, the surrogacy contract was at least in some sense a choice for Hilling, and for Stevenson the nanny job paid, even if these choices were terribly constrained in this world of stratified reproduction and however queasy we might feel about these "reproductive bits" of child care and generation being split off and paid for.[5] Losing your children to foster care, on the other hand, is pretty much the epitome of a lack of choice: nearly all children in the system have been taken involuntarily from their impoverished, often nonwhite mothers (or fathers) who are being punished for something—most commonly poor housing or some other kind of neglect that may or may not be essentially just the bad luck of being poor.[6] Foster care is the very definition of reproductive coercion, and, as many have argued, works together with adoption to transfer children from poor, usually racially minoritized mothers to whiter and wealthier ones. Dorothy Roberts predicts:

> One hundred years from now, today's child welfare system will surely be condemned as a racist institution—one that compounded the effects of discrimination on Black families by taking children from their parents, allowing them to languish in a damaging foster care system or to be adopted by more privileged people. School children will marvel that so many scholars and politicians defended this devastation of Black families in the name of protecting Black children.[7]

Compared to surrogacy, foster care seems like taking somebody's generative and child care labor without even the niceties of contracts or payment.[8]

It's no surprise that IVF, infertility, and what is often its close companion, infant mortality, are issues of reproductive politics, but in this chapter I want to argue that they are also political and economic in the sense I've been exploring. That is, they are the new normal of reproduction and its disruptions after the withdrawal of government support and declining real wages that mark the neoliberal era. When each individual household has a privatized responsibility for reproduction, care, wages, and survival, women who seek the education necessary for admission to the middle class may delay reproduction. Infant mortality rates are a marker of intense racial disparities in health, and the difference between white and Black infant mortality rates widened significantly during the neoliberal era. In recent years, public health researchers have suggested racism as a primary cause of inflated infant mortality rates, sharply raising the questions of whether the ways racism was lived and embodied was intensified after 1980. IVF, surrogacy, infant mortality, and infertility are profoundly about the structure of the economy and race, and not just in the predictable ways. While Kuczynski and those who've recently been positioned as akin to her—Anne-Marie Slaughter and Sheryl Sandberg—have come in for a fair amount of jeering as overprivileged women who are not an appropriate face for a feminism committed to ameliorating the conditions of those who are most oppressed, I find them more interesting than that. I want to suggest that they and the difficulties they encounter are actually diagnostic of deep and real problems of structural infertility and the ways that changes in the economy are affecting care and reproductive labor across class and race.

The comments about Kuczynski were hardly the only or most important things that can be said about the racial and class politics of surrogacy and reproductive technology. Certainly, they are the most common—it is a white, wealthy thing, indulged in by women who don't want to be pregnant or who want a perfect child. It is, we say, a selfish move by those who overvalue genetic relatedness. IVF is about the desire to have a designer baby: you can get prescreened embryos (with or without the intended parents' gametes) that result in babies and pregnancies without the usual risks of disability, disease, or miscarriage, and even choose the sex![9] These are the powerful cultural narratives about assisted reproductive technologies (ARTs): rich folks, almost always white, are avoiding most of the pain and hassle of pregnancy by using them; feminists have argued that they are also intensifying the stigma of and lack of public support for disability by making it, increasingly, something only poor children struggle with, as preimplantation genetic diagnosis and other screening procedures make having eugenic, healthy, gender-selected children easy enough that rich folks can avoid having to face old-fashioned, random pregnancy.

There is good reason for the sense that ARTs are haunted by eugenics. They are. ARTs primarily serve to enable the reproduction of a largely (though not exclusively) white professional class—the very group that eugenicists in the early twentieth century worried were not having enough offspring. ARTs' users and practitioners are preoccupied with questions of health and disability, as signaled by the development of preimplantation genetic testing of embryos. It relies on the bodily labor and, arguably, exploitation of young women and men who are less powerful or wealthy than those whose fertility they are enhancing or enabling—whether it is the monk-like abstinence demanded of sperm donors or the hormone regimens that women undergo to donate ova. These drugs are far from risk-free, and they lead to a small but real danger of ovarian hyperstimulation syndrome (which can cause serious illness and even death). Egg "donation" also decreases the ovarian reserve of the women who are having their eggs surgically removed in these procedures, making it more likely that they will themselves face impaired fertility in the future.[10] The reproductive cells of gamete donors (who are not really donors, of course, but are paid—albeit a fraction of what reproductive "consumers" pay) are advertised in catalogues in terms of their original possessor's race and intelligence, as measured by SAT scores.

Banking sperm has a deeply eugenic history, rooted in the ambition of Hermann Müller, one of the giants of twentieth-century eugenic biology, to save the sperm of great men. Müller, who saw eugenics as a means broadly of improving the inheritance of the next generation, longed to offer the sperm of great scientists, political leaders, and humanitarians to everyone. (For him, it was a democratic longing of sorts, born of the desire to give all children opportunity, talent, and brilliance and to create a society of people like Lenin, Pasteur, Beethoven, Omar Khayyam, Sun Yat-Sen, and Marx.[11]) Such a sperm bank was in fact attempted in the 1980s and '90s, when Robert Graham tried to stock one with the gametes of Nobel laureates. The only Nobel-winning volunteer was William Shockley, famous for his work in physics but infamous for his eugenic arguments that African Americans had congenitally low IQs and his efforts to pay some to get sterilized.[12] Gestational surrogacy is governed by a particularly harsh logic of the market: those who "rent" their wombs in India, Cambodia, or parts of the United States are almost all of a class that could never hire a surrogate themselves, marking this as a kind of "biocapitalism," like selling kidneys, where the wealthy rely insatiably on the bodily labor of the poor—not unlike the cultural logic of manual labor, which is available to sell only as long as the worker is possessed of a strong and healthy body.[13]

Indeed, the logic of public benefits and state-mandated private benefits is precisely eugenic: as a matter of law and regulation, insurers pay for the poor to get birth control and for the rich to get IVF. Private health insurers in more than ten states are required to provide infertility treatment to their employees, but none of those states provides it as a Medicaid benefit. Although the U.S. Supreme Court has concluded that private employers need not cover employees' birth control, Medicaid mandates it—without a co-pay—and also covers sterilization.[14] So those who have private insurance can get ARTs but not necessarily birth control, and those on Medicaid can get birth control or sterilization but not ARTs. As anthropologist Dána-ain

Davis notes in her incisive article on Nadya Suleman, this is the cultural (and policy) logic whereby "women of color, or women marked as being of color, poor or low income women, and single women do not have fertility problems that should be addressed."[15] They do, however, apparently need birth control.

Still, looking at ARTs exclusively through the lens of modern-day eugenics too often turns to a framework that is still about individual choice—like Kuczynski's—and fails to account for how much the reproduction of middle-class and even wealthy women is constrained by economics and career options and does little to account for the ways well-to-do women's reproductive choices elicit almost as much over-the-top anger and loathing as impoverished women's. It may also lead us to misunderstand some significant things. For example, absent from most of this public discourse is the important fact that ARTs don't work very well: if you use IVF to get a designer baby, you are more likely to get *no* baby than a beautiful genius or an exceptional athlete. The success rate of IVF hovers around 30–40 percent,[16] and the rate is even lower for gestational surrogacy that doesn't use the "surrogate's" eggs. Some evidence also suggests that children born via ARTs have higher, not lower, rates of disability.[17] In addition, it's easy to overstate how important genetic relatedness is to intended parents, because gametes—eggs and sperm—are often bought and sold in these procedures, meaning any resulting offspring may have no genetic relationship to one or both parents.

Furthermore, it's not just the rich who use ARTs—not by any stretch. Because many states and insurance plans in the United States cover ARTs only partially or not at all, the ability to find $20,000 to $30,000 is often a decisive factor in using IVF; consequently, reprotech clinics and banks are increasingly offering fertility financing.[18] That assistance, together with credit cards and some insurance coverage, means that a surprising number of people can access even $50,000 for gestational surrogacy. There is also a significant market for ARTs among queer folks, whether it is lesbians and trans men using frozen sperm at the doctor's office (frozen so the donor can be tested for HIV after the donation—it takes a while after infection for the test to turn positive) or gay men seeking surrogacy. And it's not just a white-people thing: there is sufficient demand for gametes by "African Americans"—however diverse, complex, and poorly defined that category may be—that "Black" women's eggs may be priced higher than "white" women's (because Black "donors" are hard to recruit, the relatively steady demand by Black buyers makes them more expensive.)[19] Further, military health plans offer good infertility coverage, and at least one clinic offers a subsidized Soldiercryo[TM] program, designed to allow those being deployed the opportunity to bank sperm or eggs; one of the most common injuries in the wars in Iraq and Afghanistan is damage to testes from improvised explosive devices (IEDs).[20]

Internationally, IVF and other reproductive technologies have spread rapidly among not just the wealthiest classes of Europe, Egypt, and Latin America but also among Turks in Germany, the middle classes of Egypt and Iran, indigenous people in the Andes, and people from all over Africa and Asia who can make it to the United Arab Emirates.[21] Even transnational gestation surrogacy, which seems to many like the height of "First World" exploitation of impoverished "Third World" women, doesn't exactly work like that. India's thriving surrogacy market, priced to undercut California's, has diasporic and resident Indians as the majority of its clients.[22] With ARTs costing about the same as a mid-sized car, growing insurance coverage and a thriving neoliberal debt market happy to exploit people's urgent desire for children have made ART use almost as ubiquitous as automobiles.

I want to suggest a different way of thinking about ARTs. As with the migration of domestic workers, interracial and transnational adoption, and welfare reform, ARTs are intensely about economics and racial politics. More precisely, they are a response to two or three forces. For a still expanding swath of the middle class, nationally and internationally, ARTs are how people are coping with the structural infertility of the long period of education and economic insecurity that is the price of the ticket these days to the middle class but that virtually requires delayed childbearing. Not only can you go into debt for an education and a house, but the high cost of ARTs means you can send repayment checks to the bank for decades for a child—or the failed attempt to have a child. Impoverished people, in contrast, may be more likely to try to get pregnant earlier but are also at higher risk of exposure to toxic substances that impair fertility, inadequate health care, poor diet, and stress. Black women are twice as likely as white women to experience infertility and its close cousin, infant mortality, and this disparity is not explained by class, prenatal care, or nutrition—something we will take up in detail in the latter half of this chapter. Women outside (and inside) the United States and Western Europe are also contending with the reproductive health effects of inadequate access to safe, legal abortion, including infertility as a result of infection and scarring.

ARTs (not unlike adoption) represent a huge, $4 billion industry that has grown massively, largely in response to the failure of the workplace to accommodate reproduction and the reality that humans, and households, care for children and other kinds of dependents. Reprotech is hugely expensive, and it doesn't work very well. The race and class concerns we ought to have about IVF, surrogacy, and other ARTs certainly include the question of the exploitation of the women whose "body bits" fuel the industry, but perhaps that is not the *only* worry we ought to have. Maybe we should also be concerned about how the normative childlessness of both students and workers are feeding an intensely privatized ART industry, just as it is fueling women's immigration to do the reproductive labor of caring for children, homes, and dependents. Racist concerns about the changing racial and ethnic demographics of the United States put pressure on white women to have children because some people think that, in the words of Iowa congressman Steve King, "We can't restore our civilization with somebody else's babies."[23] Welfare reform's blaming of poverty on teen pregnancy is part of a larger discourse about the horrors of young childbearing that puts pressure on everyone to delay it. The infertility of young women and men in their twenties, whether caused by illness, poor nutrition, or unsafe environments, is less often treated than the structural infertility of women in their thirties because they are more likely to be poor and their treatment is unlikely to be covered by insurance, but it is nevertheless a real part of the *need* for ARTs, if not their use. This is not my mother's generation's infertility. This infertility is induced by the labor market—and the toxic health by-products of racial and other inequalities—and it is driving a highly profitable but not very effective ART industry.

FREEZING EGGS

All these years after the 1970s fight over whether middle-class and white women needed to stay home with the children, pronatalism still drives the conversation about women and work—but now it's full of maddening double binds. Women should have children, but not too early and not too late and not at the expense of work or career. In the fall of 2014, for example, the blogosphere and social and traditional media lit up with discussions of the perfect exemplar of this kind of craziness: enhanced insurance packages at Facebook and Apple that would allow women to freeze their eggs so that they could have babies later in life. "Not since the birth control pill has a medical technology had such potential to change family and career planning," trumpeted a front-page story in *Businessweek*. "Company-Paid Egg Freezing Will Be the Great Equalizer," read a *Time* magazine headline.[24] And NBC News explained that it was really just another effort by tech giants to get a "leg up" in the race to attract "female talent." In notoriously male-dominated Silicon Valley, egg freezing was a way to attract young women who wanted to spend their twenties and early thirties focusing on their education and careers without sacrificing the possibility of later motherhood.[25]

Some objected to the cheerful "feminism-lite" argument on the grounds that Facebook, Apple, and others seemed to be setting a new standard in the expectation of normative childlessness at work (J. P. Morgan and Citibank apparently also offer the perk, although they didn't send out press releases[26]). Previously it had been a clear but unspoken expectation that you would work all the time. Really, what else can you say about a Silicon Valley tech sector that seems to expect that you aren't going to find time away from work to do the most minimal reproductive labor, even for yourself—Google offers rides to work on its own bus, makes your meals in their cafeteria, and has on-site haircut, laundry, and nap facilities. Egg freezing seemed to be just another explicit message that workers should not expect to get home in time to make dinner for children or arrive late enough to drop them at school, much less take time off when they get sick. Chirped one commentator in *Business Insider:* "Practically, this isn't about changing the system. It's about making it easier for ambitious women to exist in the world we have. And we should applaud the companies that give women this choice." Some choice. The same editorial acknowledged the normative effects of what it called "the system" when it assured readers that this perk was not going to change things all that much. "There are plenty of women (most of them, I'll bet you) who are going to want to have children before age 35. The time off, the career setbacks, the pay inequity—all trade-offs that high-achieving women knowingly accept when they decide to have a kid. To most women, it's worth it, and will continue to be worth it."[27] The writer claimed she really did want to change the "culture" of overwork and its sexist effects (although "policy" might be a better word than "culture," because unwritten rules often have more force than written ones when it comes to retention, promotion, and advancement). Still, her cheerful comments about giving women the "choice" to freeze their eggs—even though it's an ART that is unlikely to produce a pregnancy—seemed to belie the seriousness of her desire for better working conditions.

The proximate cause of all this discussion of egg freezing was that in 2012, the American Society for Reproductive Medicine (ASRM) had dropped the "experimental" label from egg freezing—until that time it had mostly been used by women facing chemotherapy-related infertility. Changes in the freezing procedure had made it slightly less of a complete failure (with some claiming as high as a 20 percent pregnancy rate with a woman's own previously frozen eggs[28]), although it is hard to think of many other kinds of medical procedures regarded as effective with rates that low (would you get an appendectomy if someone told you that it helped in 20 percent of cases?). While the cost might seem prohibitive without insurance, the business press cheerfully advised fertility financing—which, not incidentally, aligns fertility clinics with one of the most lucrative parts of the neoliberal financial services industry: credit and debt. "For most 30-year-olds, $8,000 is a big nut" to pay for egg freezing, Gina Bartasi told *Businessweek*. So she formed Fertility Authority to offer financing, arranging credit for women who couldn't afford the procedure. For example, they can pay a gamete-freezing company called Eggbanxx $1,500 down, and then roughly $250 a month for the next 24 months, essentially putting their eggs on layaway. "There's very little health-care coverage for fertility treatments, and I saw a hole in the market for a business to get in on that."[29] Spending two years putting a big chunk of your paycheck into something that has an 80 percent chance of failure—to say nothing of an additional $20,000–$50,000 price tag for IVF to try to achieve a pregnancy—seems like a very big nut indeed.

A whole slew of advice books had been debating this very issue for a decade. In 2002, Sylvia Ann Hewlett's *Creating a Life: Professional Women and the Quest for Children* advised women to make career sacrifices in order to have children earlier. It was written deliberately to alarm young women, arguing that 40 percent of women earning $50,000 or more were childless at age 45 (echoing public service announcements by the ASRM in 2001 that warned women of the decline in their fertility by age 30).[30] Lori Gottlieb followed up with *Marry Him: The Case for Settling for Mr. Good Enough*,[31] arguing that women should refuse that cool assignment for a year in a faraway place and give up on ambitious, challenging jobs that require a large time commitment, long apprenticeship, or extended education. Elizabeth Gregory's 2007 *Ready: Why Women Are Embracing the New Later*

Motherhood took issue with this view, arguing that for middle-class women, being older at their first birth (30 for women with a master's degree) is a good thing: older mothers have a larger income, more stable relationships, and a greater ability to provide high-quality, reliable child care that enables them to stay in the workforce (which, in turn, provides huge dividends in lifetime earnings), and their children have "better outcomes," gauged by standardized test scores and behavioral measures. Sarah Ann Richards offered a related, cheerful message that was apparently received by Silicon Valley executives, with her *Motherhood, Rescheduled: The New Frontier in Egg Freezing and the Women Who Tried It.*[32] Despite the fact that only one of the ten women she interviewed actually had had a baby from the eggs she had frozen (probably a not-bad measure of the effectiveness of the procedure), Richards argued that it was still better advice than that offered by Hewlett and others. Although this was a conversation dominated by heterosexuality, there were also nods to the idea that queer women might also be better off starting early, with younger eggs, although having two sets of eggs seemed to take off a lot of the pressure. (And while egg banking or sperm banking and its timing in the life course are certainly relevant questions for trans folk who wish to preserve reproductive potential before transition or while taking a pause from hormones, they don't seem to appear in this cisgender-focused advice literature.[33])

CHANGING THE WORKPLACE?

It's interesting to contrast these prescriptions for how women should change their private lives with two other accounts that suggested that the workplace might have to change. In June 2012, Anne-Marie Slaughter wrote a piece for *The Atlantic* that quickly went viral.[34] In it, she complained that for her, even at the very pinnacle of women's success, where everything was going right—State Department job, supportive feminist boss, terrific husband with flexible work hours who was happy to do more than half the child care—the act of "balancing" work and children wasn't working. A few months later, Sheryl Sandberg, chief operating officer of Facebook, published *Lean In*, suggesting, similarly, that women shouldn't have to choose between a successful career and having children.[35]

As everyone who was reading a newspaper or social media that wasn't about cute kittens in February or March 2013 knows, the response to Sandberg's book was swift and punitive. Anna Holmes noted in a *New Yorker* blog that the firestorm generated by *Lean In* included many high-profile commentaries by people who hadn't read the book.[36] The essence of the critique—which was similar to the critique of Anne-Marie Slaughter—was that Sandberg was too successful to complain about much of anything, never mind the difficulties women face with child care or careers. The redoubtable Maureen Dowd reported, "Sandberg describes taking her kids to a business conference last year and realizing en route that her daughter had head lice. But the good news was that she was on the private eBay jet."[37] Because ... head lice aren't awful? Because most mothers don't instantly feel like it's a huge, embarrassing comment on what a terrible parent they are that their kids got head lice at day care—even if they didn't? Because it doesn't call attention to all the ways that she was violating business norms by bringing her kids to work? No, wait ... it's that it's unfairly easy to cope with such a problem on a private jet, when the rest of us would be on the bus. Really? The *New York Times* dealt with the question in its characteristic way, by turning the divergences between Slaughter's and Sandberg's accounts into fodder for its long-standing "mommy wars" machine, publishing two separate pieces in two weeks highlighting the differences between them.[38] Where Sandberg highlighted the self-esteem crisis that comes from figuring out how to maneuver in a system rigged against you, Slaughter highlighted the unfairness of that system. These are hardly two people who could never get on the same page. But the mommy wars—the alleged catfight between stay-at-home mothers who sacrifice their careers and work lives for their kids and mothers who park their kids at day care without a care for the damage done to them in order to climb the corporate ladder—have been selling for decades, so why should the fact that these descriptors don't fit either of them (or very many other mothers) stop anyone now?

Sandberg and Slaughter weren't actually guilty of what they were busted for. They were in fact acutely aware of how privileged and anomalous their situations were. This is precisely why each said she was writing—because if what corporations call "work-life balance" and sociologists call the "crisis of care work" was unsolvable for them, it certainly wasn't solvable for women with less power and fewer resources. Even if money could buy them out of housework and routine child care, it couldn't resolve the fundamental contradiction between the new-normal 65-hour workweek and the responsibility to care for little humans who need time and thoughtful engagement 24/7. Further, Sandberg and Slaughter claimed, refreshingly, a solidarity with those who are less privileged: they thought they had an obligation to speak up, because their voices might actually get heard, unlike others, and they should use their power and authority to make things better for those with less power and money. Not a terrible thought, that. Imagine if that had been the norm at Enron when the company was causing rolling blackouts across California in 2000–2001 and its officials were caught on tape laughing about "stealing" $1 million a day from California and fleecing "Grandma Millie" while bringing Enron record profits?[39] Or if that had been the norm in banks like Wells Fargo that systematically sold subprime mortgages to those who were apparently eligible for better loans and "robo-signed" foreclosure documents, kicking people into the streets who had restructured their loans or otherwise should not have been foreclosed on?[40] In an era of unembarrassed predatory practices by the wealthy in the name of making money, we might have appreciated those who even nominally tried to use their power to make things better for the poor and powerless as well as the middle class. But, being women talking about reproductive labor, Sandberg and Slaughter were mocked instead.

Still, the solutions they offered were inadequate to the problem they identified, and, frankly, rather unimaginative stuff. Slaughter argued for things like making it easier to Skype into meetings and finishing the revolution that e-mail had begun of treating home and work as a continuous, Möbius-strip-like space, while Sandberg suggested that men should do more child care so that women need not blunt their ambitions in the service of someone else's career, that women need to know that they will be the victims of unconscious bias, that it helps to know that lots of highly qualified women feel like imposters, and that women need mentors and should be encouraged to speak up in meetings and not be afraid to assume leadership roles. This is actually rather standard advice; a group as staid as the National Science Foundation offers a similar list as the basic set of obstacles faced by women in careers in science, technology, engineering, and mathematics (STEM) fields. There's nothing wrong with all this, except that these are individual solutions to what even Slaughter and Sandberg know are structural problems that implicate wages for care workers, the question of who pays for care (or doesn't), the sharp decline of the 40-hour workweek, the gendered denigration of care work (and of the young, the old, and others who need care), the relative lack of power of women in heterosexual couples and the households they form, and the ferocious rise in business's power to define how we live.[41] Further, the alternative view, that, as Rosa Brooks put it in the *Foreign Policy,* middle-class women might "recline" rather than "lean in"—have friends, have time off, enjoy children, drink wine, and read novels—is nowhere in evidence.[42]

What's interesting, though, are two things. First, Slaughter and Sandberg hit a nerve, bringing to mind the poet Muriel Rukeyser's question: "What would happen if one woman told the truth about her life? The world would split open." Slaughter's piece in *The Atlantic* generated more hits in a day than the total hits for any other article in the history of the magazine's digital existence Someone who wasn't a celebrity—a Princeton professor of international affairs and a development policy analyst for the state department (that is, a total wonk)—was merely describing, in detail, why it was hard to hold a high-level job and be a mother. Something about the impossibility of her dilemma resonated. Sandberg's firestorm played out differently, but the basic plot line was the same. In Sandberg's case, it was a TED talk video that went viral,[43] and the press ripped apart the book before it even came out. Still, it was a best seller, and Amazon. com's customer reviews were full of testimonials by those who described themselves as middle-class or single mothers and had found comfort in the book, especially Sandberg's self-deprecating stories about everything she had done wrong as an employee and as a parent.[44] Something about the misery and double-binds their work described clicked.

Second, even their mild prescriptions for changing the workplace generated ferocious backlash. It seemed to evidence a deep-seated resistance to having a broad, thoughtful, and sympathetic public conversation about the topic that everyone who's ever stood on a playground with parents of young children knows occupies a tremendous amount of their attention: how to care for children and work. That the workplace might have to change, as both Slaughter and Sandberg suggested to varying degrees, is apparently not an answer that mainstream policy discourse wanted to entertain.

WAGES OF INFERTILITY

The liberal, kind-of-feminist-sounding pronatalism that warned middle-class and upper-class women to begin families early, select a partner when they were in their twenties, and freeze eggs worked alongside a much more coercive *Handmaid's Tale*–style pronatalism, which metastasized in public policy after about 2000 as efforts to deny women access to contraception—as "conscience clauses" that allowed pharmacists to refuse to fill a prescription for the pill and as the full-court press to gut the Affordable Care Act's guarantees of prescription coverage for birth control and enact state regulations prohibiting insurance coverage of abortion. These worked together with increasing burdens on abortion clinics and their patients that resulted in fewer providers and hard-to-get procedures. It's what the Democrats were calling the Republican "war on women" in the national elections of 2012. Although "soft" pronatalism wanted to pressure women to "choose" pregnancy and "hard" (conservative) pronatalism seemed happy to force it as part of a prescribed gender role—even endorsing efforts to eliminate abortions for pregnancies due to rape and incest (through claims that women don't get pregnant from "real rape")—the effect was similar: women becoming pregnant earlier and more often than they might have wanted.[45]

As the response to Slaughter and Sandberg suggests, it was apparently impossible in 2012 and 2013 to sustain a vigorous mainstream conversation about why we don't organize work and care in ways that are compatible with the reproduction of the species and gentle and generous care of elders and other adults who cannot care for themselves, whether that is with attendant care, a family caregiver, or well-funded professional facilities. Nor can we have a discussion of a 40-hour workweek or the fact that the vicious cast of our racial politics has a relationship to reproduction and labor—and what that has to do with the transformation of work, government, reproduction, and wages for everyone. While Elizabeth Gregory's *Ready* celebrated the fact that older mothers can hire a caregiver for their children and not have to miss work, that kind of choice is also driving appalling changes in the resources that impoverished women—the caregivers serving those "older mothers"—can bring to their own families or dependents, whether they have migrated without them or leave them to care for each other while they are working. It also perpetuates the normative expectation that women can tidily tuck reproductive labor into their "private" life while they work full-time, which drove the elimination of AFDC in an effort to force impoverished women to flip burgers and work at Walmart.

The business press and the feminism-lite crowd that advocated egg freezing frequently compared it to the pill in its ability to revolutionize the world of sex and pregnancy. I would agree, although on a less celebratory note. Egg freezing offers an expansion of the revolution that the pill began: it allows women to curtail any awkward reproduction on company time. Women who use the pill (and abortion when it fails) are the other side of the coin of this culture's stereotype of teen mothers and "welfare mothers": they are the good planners, the ones who delay parenthood until they are "ready," until they can afford to support their children. The pronatalism directed at white professional women is all about timing—and, in its own way, quite cruel. It fosters the desire for babies at a time when women are least likely to get pregnant.

In fact, some feminists have argued that the infertility industry is essentially a fraud, hiding its low success rates, causing untold pain and charging a fortune for the privilege.[46] It is a tremendously privatized medical specialty, operating mostly as free-standing clinics that until recently received very little oversight. For decades, the fertility industry avoided controversy in part because it rarely received public money—after a National Science Foundation (NSF) grant for research on human embryos in 1979 ran into tremendous antiabortion controversy, researchers (and the NSF) started to avoid federal funding for anything to do with embryos. In some ways, the de facto ban on NSF funding for IVF research also freed reproductive medicine from much federal oversight. Reproductive medicine groups also kept their heads down by essentially following the most conservative guidelines of the much more public adoption establishment—at first, serving only married clients and banning gays and lesbians and single women.[47]

At the same time, ART clinics have been immensely responsive to public pressure, steadily expanding access to their services. In recent years, they have shifted frameworks from an adoption-based "best interest of the [potential] child" standard to one having more to do with reproductive privacy—a framework borrowed from *Roe v. Wade* and the Supreme Court decisions related first to sodomy and then gay marriage. "Private" works in two senses for clinics and in US politics more generally: that which is decided at home, away from the moral oversight of a meddling "public," and that which is associated with the free market, not paid for by state money. Charis Thompson argues in an ethnography of IVF, *Making Parents,* that it is a peculiar fact about the United States that we think what is truly dangerous in reproductive politics is the involvement of the state (as in Nazi eugenics or Medicaid funding for abortion).[48] By largely keeping the state out of it, the ASRM has avoided the kind of robust debate about ARTs that resulted in commercial surrogacy being banned throughout much of the European Union (although many nations still allow "altruistic" surrogacy, as if only money and not, say, family pressure, could be a source of coercion). In Costa Rica, IVF is regulated like abortion. Access to buying eggs and sperm is severely curtailed in many places, conspicuously France, particularly if you are queer.[49] By contrast, the United States has an almost unregulated free market for medically assisted reproduction.

When there have been serious efforts to debate the ethics of the industry, the ASRM has adroitly maneuvered around it by offering to oversee itself, in the kind of "regulation" that both business and many politicians (mostly Republican of late) have preferred. While President Jimmy Carter convened a federal ethics panel to oversee reproductive technology, his successor Ronald Reagan allowed its mandate to lapse, and the ASRM convened its own ethics panel in 1985. When Congress moved to demand that the fertility industry reveal how many clients actually get a baby for their trouble and money, the ASRM sponsored the Fertility Clinic Success Rate and Certification Act and even funded the data collection. However, the data it chose to collect—now available on the Center for Disease Control's website—obscures as much as it reveals: pregnancy rates *per cycle* rather than "take home babies" per client.[50]

Although the most visible mainstream, kind-of-feminist debate about women and ARTs is between the pronatalism of Sylvia Ann Hewlett (get partnered and pregnant, preferably before 30) versus the wait-till-you're-ready position of Elizabeth Gregory and Peggy Orenstein, who suggest that pregnancy after 35 or even 40 is a totally viable option, even if you have to buy eggs or sperm, there is another, much more critical feminist position. The Feminist International Network of Resistance to Reproductive and Genetic Engineering (FINRRAGE) began asking questions decades ago about the consequences of this industry. Beginning in the mid-1980s—only a few years after the 1976 birth of "test-tube baby" Louise Brown—feminists like Rita Arditti and Gena Corea were arguing that IVF and similar procedures were essentially experiments carried out with the patients' own money.[51] Whether or not that was true in the 1980s, all that experimentation has not moved the needle much on success rates: from about 30 percent to about 40 percent.[52] Most clients still go home without a baby, often after years of ruinously expensive "treatment."

Pretending that we can all have children whenever we want (and multiples of them, celebrated in the most pronatalist of ways, provided the couple is white and married)—straight! gay! over 65! doesn't matter!—has deflected a different conversation: the one where we reckon with the impossibility of middle-class lives for a growing swath of people, including wage workers, people with student loan debt, those who cannot get together a down payment for a house that would reduce their tax rate and allow them to build wealth (at least in theory—the bursting of the housing bubble suggests that it's a market that can be dangerously manipulated by speculation and banks), or anyone who does not live in a family that can put two people in the professional work force for some significant period of time. The more that even people who are white with professional parents have to delay childbearing to be middle class, the higher the rates of involuntary childlessness or having fewer children than one wishes climb *as a matter of policy,* or at least as a predictable set of consequences associated with the absence of policies that would clip the wings of the business, state, academic, and military enterprises that benefit from the lower wages, benefits, and taxes that result from the success of a conservative movement for a neoliberal economy and politics. A real reproductive rights movement or workers' movement in the United States and elsewhere might demand an end to the highly predictable, not to say deliberate, result of these changes to the conditions of life, work, childbearing, and child rearing.

THE OTHER INFERTILITY: THOSE WHO ARE NOT SUPPOSED TO GET PREGNANT

If structural infertility related to education and the job market affects the majority of those who attend college for at least some period of time, different kinds of infertility—or highly stigmatized fertility—are associated with being impoverished. This is the other side of the eugenic coin. Let us begin with the growing group of people who may or may not be able to get pregnant but are not "supposed" to: teens, working-class people earning minimum wage, unmarried people, many people of color, and anyone relying on Medicaid. While beliefs about what level of material well-being is necessary to have children drive a great deal of the popular conversation about who "should" have children, there is of course no particular standard. That there is even a relationship between material well-being and childbearing is a twentieth-century, middle-class, and to some extent white belief.[53] Further, the evidence that teen pregnancy leads to bad outcomes—in terms of health, educational, or lifetime-earnings—is mixed at best and highly class dependent. Indeed, as we have seen, some research argues persuasively that for African American girls in high-poverty urban areas, having children in their mid to late teens is actually a good idea, producing healthier babies and better earnings, allowing them to stay in the work force longer (as their children get older) and evading some of the health consequences for newborns of having a mother whose body has been brutalized by being poor, because younger mothers have suffered less "weathering."[54] Needless to say, no one has proposed that impoverished Black teens who are trying to get pregnant but cannot should have access to fertility treatment through Medicaid. The difficulty of even imagining such a thing—despite some evident reasons for it— suggests something about how strongly we believe that only some people "ought" to get pregnant.

Indeed, only a minority of all people who can't achieve a pregnancy seek fertility treatment, but of those who do, there are sharp income differences. Of those experiencing impaired fertility or infertility, only 5 percent without a college degree were treated with ARTs compared to 20 percent of those with a college degree.[55] In addition to class, there are significant racial disparities that exceed those produced by the unequal racial distribution of poverty.[56]

Another cause of infertility in Black and impoverished communities in the United States is the use of long-acting, physician-controlled contraceptives like Norplant and Depo-Provera. Depo-Provera in particular has been associated with impaired fertility for more than a year after its expected or intended use. In a study of lifetime contraceptive use, Depo was used about three times more often by women without a high school diploma or GED. It is particularly pushed for teenagers, despite an FDA black box warning that suggests that its use may put them at high risk for disabling osteoporosis later in life.[57] The use of Depo and Norplant is much more common among US Black women (44 percent) and Latina women (38 percent) than among white women (31 percent).[58] Many have suggested that health practitioners prefer it for young, poorly educated, disabled, and/or racially minoritized women and girls because they are perceived as poor decision makers and poor contraceptive users. Depo-Provera and Norplant are injected or implanted by a nurse or physician, who effectively then has control over whether they get pregnant. Although less permanent than tubal ligation, and undoubtedly a method of choice for some, physician-controlled long-acting contraceptives are in a sense the technological inheritors of the social impulse embodied by eugenic sterilization in an earlier generation.

For all these reasons, together with baseline health, racially dispossessed and impoverished groups are much more likely than white and middle-class people to suffer from infertility.[59] According to the National Survey of Family Growth, married Black women are twice as likely as married white women to be dealing with involuntary infertility—but only half as likely to use infertility services. In populations with equal access to insurance coverage for infertility—notably those in the military—the racial disparities in accessing reproductive medicine disappear.[60] African Americans are also the most likely to lose pregnancies to miscarriage and stillbirth and to lose infants to early death. In one large study, the rate of miscarriage for Black women, after controlling for confounders (Black women in the study were less likely to smoke or drink during pregnancy) was 57 percent higher overall and 93 percent higher after week 10 of pregnancy.[61] The causes of these racial disparities cannot be accounted for in the medical literature without taking account of racism—significant disparities continue to exist even after controlling for known risks.[62]

From 1980 to 2008, racial disparities in infant mortality climbed to unprecedented rates. At first this rise was misattributed to drugs, specifically crack cocaine, but subsequent research found that crack had little effect on infant mortality rates—albeit after hundreds of women were sent to jail for using it during pregnancy, and thousands lost their children to foster care[63]— and as crack use declined, racial disparities in infant mortality continued to climb. An emerging body of medical and public health research is arguing that the root causes of racial disparities in infant mortality are stress and racism. Public health researchers such as those involved in the Harlem BirthRight Project make an argument that is deeply congruent with the issues I am raising: that the increasing time people are expected to spend at their formal job and the resulting stress on households and communities, together with a decline in public supports, are having eugenic effects. People of color in general and Black women in particular experience an intensified form of this generalized problem, and it is showing up, among other places, in high rates of infant mortality.

Beyond the grief that the death of an infant leaves in the lives of the people who cared about that baby, in the aggregate, disproportionate rates of infant mortality tell us that something is wrong. Internationally, we use the infant mortality rate (IMR) as an index of people's health, a measure that reflects not just the safety of childbirth or the quality of infant care but lifelong diet, health care, exposure to toxic substances, and stress. High infant mortality indicates that in the aggregate people are not doing very well. We think of countries like Afghanistan, plagued by war with the United States and by rural poverty, which has one of the highest IMRs in the world at more than 112 deaths per 1,000 live births. Or countries like Guatemala, where communities struggle with malnutrition, at nearly 22 infant deaths per 1,000 born. The United States is much lower, at only 5.8 deaths per 1,000. Still, that's not a very low rate. It's higher than all of Western Europe, Canada, Australia, and much of Eastern Europe. Out of 225 countries and territories where infant mortality is measured, Monaco is lowest, with fewer than 1.8 infant deaths per 1,000 babies.[64] For 2014, the United States ranked between the Slovak Republic and Russia.[65] Within the United States, infant deaths are highly variable, but the rates are also predictable by zip code. The primary reason that U.S. infant mortality is so high compared to other countries is that African Americans suffer a staggering rate. If Black America were its own country, it would be ranked between China and Turkey.[66] Alongside trouble getting pregnant and a greater likelihood of miscarriage, disproportionate rates of infant mortality are a reason African American women are much more likely than white women not to have or raise the children they want. This phenomenon partly overlaps with—and is also different from—higher rates of infertility and miscarriage among impoverished people in the United States.

Highly disparate rates of infant mortality are the persistent and even deepening effect of what we might call a specifically neoliberal racism. That is, it's the flip side of a Manichean system of stratified reproduction that benefits no one except the business sector, which relies on a work force whose reproductive labor it continues to imagine is not its problem, enabling it to evade taxes that might help pay for day care, elder care and other costs of maintaining the species. It is a cultural system where Black women are seen as caregivers to white infants on the one hand and as illegitimate, less qualified, and, hence, underpaid employees on the other. If the neoliberal moment is characterized by a business sector and government that don't care about anyone's reproduction or reproductive labor, as I have been arguing, they *really* don't care about Black women's. Black women are disproportionately concentrated in low-wage, high-stress employment sectors without health insurance or even sick days.[67] Even when Black women have good jobs, they often experience disproportionate stress, being expected to do more than a similarly situated white worker and facing assumptions that they are unqualified, as has been documented repeatedly, for example, for Black women university professors.[68] On the government support side, as we have seen, the neoliberal efforts to reduce public benefits for reproductive labor began by targeting "welfare"—inaccurately but persistently understood as a program most likely to be used by Black mothers. The crumbling of other state supports—for housing, day care, education, disaster relief, public health, and elder care, for example—together with an exacerbation of policing, imprisonment, and the militarization and surveillance of communities of color produce a climate in the United States and the material conditions that would seem to virtually guarantee to increase the stress of Black mothers.

After decades of avoiding saying so, a growing number of medical and public health researchers are concluding that the racial disparities in infant mortality are caused by stress and racism. These include the dirty looks and habitual discounting that social scientists have started calling "microaggressions," such as the story that made the rounds on social media in 2016 of a Black woman being told to sit down when a flight attendant asked for a physician to help someone who had become ill, because the flight attendant refused to believe that a Black woman was a doctor.[69] Furthermore, substandard schools, challenges in finding a healthy diet and good housing, working long hours to combat employment discrimination, fears about what the police might do to their children, and physician racism are increasingly being identified as contributors to Black mothers' stress.[70] In addition, if generations of activists have insisted that women face a double day—work for wages and work for the household—some have suggested that this effect is exacerbated for women of color, who face a "triple day" of labor in the workplace, household, and community.[71]

Racial disparities in infant mortality have increased in the era of neoliberalism, the forty years since Reagan (see table 1). While the overall rate of infant death continued to decline, the difference between deaths of white and Black infants increased. The contradictions and violence of neoliberalism is lived with particular intensity by African Americans, whether the increasing stress of maternal and child poverty in the era after workfare and the end of AFDC—the era when impoverished mothers scrounge in dumpsters or stay with violent partners[72]—or try to juggle long work hours and do care work for families and communities in an era of declining funding for schools and militarization of the police. Racial wage disparities have also intensified in this same period.[73] The infant mortality rate for Black mothers is more than twice that of infants with white mothers. (There

TABLE I

Black and White Infant Mortality Rates Per 1,000 Births
in the United States, 1980–2013

Year	Black	White	Ratio	Year	Black	White	Ratio
1980	22.2	10.9	2.0	1997	14.2	6.0	2.4
1981	20.8	10.3	2.0	1998	14.3	6.0	2.4
1982	20.5	9.9	2.1	1999	14.6	5.8	2.5
1983	20.0	9.6	2.1	2000	13.6	5.7	2.4
1984	19.2	9.3	2.1	2001	13.3	5.7	2.3
1985	19.0	9.2	2.1	2002	13.8	5.8	2.4
1986	18.9	8.8	2.1	2003	13.5	5.7	2.4
1987	18.8	8.5	2.2	2004	13.2	5.7	2.3
1988	18.5	8.4	2.2	2005	13.6	5.7	2.4
1989	18.6	8.1	2.3	2006	13.3	5.6	2.4
1990	18.0	7.6	2.4	2007	13.3	5.6	2.4
1991	17.6	7.3	2.4	2008	12.7	5.5	2.3
1992	16.8	6.9	2.4	2009	12.4	5.3	2.3
1993	16.5	6.8	2.4	2010	11.5	5.2	2.2
1994	15.8	6.6	2.4	2011	11.5	5.1	2.3
1995	15.1	6.3	2.4	2012	11.2	5.0	2.2
1996	14.7	6.1	2.4	2013	11.1	5.1	2.2

SOURCES: Centers for Disease Control, "Infant Mortality and Low Birth Weight among Black and White Infants—United States, 1980–2000," *Morbidity and Mortality Weekly Report* 51, no. 27 (July 12, 2002): 589–92; T.J. Mathews, Marian F. MacDorman, and Marie E. Thoma, "Infant Mortality Statistics from the 2013 Period Linked Birth/Infant Death Data Set," *National Vital Statistics Reports* 64, no. 9 (August 6, 2015), www.cdc.gov/nchs/data/nvsr/nvsr64/nvsr64_09.pdf; and T.J. Mathews and Marian MacDorman, "Infant Mortality Statistics from the 2005 Period Linked Birth/Infant Death Data Set," *National Vital Statistics Reports* 57, no. 2 (July 30, 2008), www.cdc.gov/nchs/data/nvsr/nvsr57/nvsr57_02.pdf.

are also somewhat elevated rates for Native Americans, Asian Americans, and Latinxs, particularly Puerto Ricans, but this data set has much greater variation, because "Native women," who come from different tribal nations, and "Latinxs," who come from different Latin American countries, have very different health experiences from one another, and have not been made into coherent groups the way African Americans have. Some Latinxs and Native people have even higher infant mortality than Black people, while others have much lower rates).[74]

While some medical researchers have suggested that this unexplained higher rate might be due to some as-yet unidentified genetic component, it makes little sense to try to ascribe differences by "race" to genetics. "Race" defines a social and political group, not a biological one ("race" in all these studies, after all, is how the mother self-identifies, without any effort to standardize or even describe what mothers mean when they characterize their race).[75] No one has ever tried to separate out different African national ancestries in these studies or to compare the health of African Americans to that of Afro-Cubans or Afro-Brazilians, which is to say, to compare populations where race has different social effects, even though these are the kinds of studies that would be necessary to even suggest a genetic component. Another piece of evidence that a very specific form of ill health characterizes racialized U.S. minorities is the fact that among African diasporic populations in the United States, those born outside the country have lower infant mortality than those born within its borders.[76]

Despite the problems with that research, it's at least an improvement over what commentators and the medical literature were saying during the Reagan years, when disparities in infant mortality were being attributed to drugs, especially crack cocaine. Crack—the cheap form of cocaine—was believed to be driving the rising rates of infant mortality and disability, despite little evidence. As we've seen, throughout the 1980s, Black women in particular were sent to prison and lost their children to foster care at astonishing rates. Poster campaigns, television news, and multipage spreads in major city newspapers gave us images of low-birth-weight babies fighting for life in neonatal intensive care units and criminally irresponsible mothers—who were overwhelmingly Black and Latina. By 2001, a special issue of the *Journal of the American Medical Association* was arguing that on the contrary, cocaine had much smaller effects on pregnancy than smoking did, and that the hysteria about "crack babies" was unwarranted, overblown, and had ugly racial undertones. While racial disparities in health, housing, experiences of violence, and infant mortality were real enough, crack was not the cause. This was, of course, little comfort to women who had lost their babies to death or foster care, much less to women who had gone to jail.[77]

More recently, scholars have argued that even when you "control for" poverty (as if that were possible, when the unequal distribution of poverty in the United States is hardly an incidental feature of racialization), Black rates of infant and maternal mortality remain at about twice the white rate. That is, when white and Black outcomes are measured across populations that have equal access to things like prenatal care, nutrition, and insurance, African American babies are much more likely to die. In other words, something about being Black in the United States—not necessarily poor, or uninsured, or unhealthy, or undereducated, but simply African American—contributes to the likelihood that a baby will die before its first birthday. Some argue that disparities in care and physician racism account for at least some of this difference,[78] while others point to "stress" as a catchall for the physiological effects of racism.[79] Those trying to understand elevated infant mortality plausibly look to the many ways race is materially constituted in overt as well as unintended ways—as a market segment, as groups characterized by certain neighborhoods or certain kinds of housing (for example, racial disparities in asthma might be attributed to exposure to the droppings and exoskeletons of cockroaches more commonly found in rental housing controlled by slumlords.)[80]

As we have seen, what we might call (without disparagement or disrespect) "white feelings" about infertility, delayed reproduction, and the like get wide play in the public sphere, but black grief about lost babies or even infertility has virtually no public voice. The popular "biological clock" books offer some kind of collectivity—a group of people who are moving in concert to figure out the conundrum of when to get married, when to have babies, whether to freeze their eggs. Even when the advice is bad or depressing, white middle-class people at least are part of some humanized collective with recognizable feelings. The infant mortality literature, in contrast, generally operates on two distinct but equally distancing registers: the broad statistical portrait and the individualized and pathological pregnant woman.[81] The big picture delivers a steady stream of bad news. In the United States, infant mortality has steadily declined over the hundred years that data has been collected—90 percent over the course of the twentieth century, as better nutrition, better access to health care, vaccinations, antibiotics, and clean municipal water systems have reduced the prevalence of contagious diseases.[82] However, just as access to these things has differed by population group and region, infant mortality has declined at different rates for different population groups, and it is this inequality that accounts for the difference between the United

States and other wealthy nations. While some populations within the United States—notably whites, especially in the Northeast—have infant mortality rates equivalent to the top-ranked nations, African American rates are much larger, and even aggregating them misses some of the differences: for example, in Washington, DC, infants born in the poorest neighborhoods are ten times more likely to die before their first birthday than those in the wealthiest parts of the same city. Further, despite high levels of spending on health care per capita, the United States has steadily and rapidly lost ground in comparative terms. In 1980, the United States and Germany had comparable infant mortality rates, but thirty-five years later, babies were twice as likely to die in the United States. Compared to other nations, inequality in the United States is drastic—and not improving at any significant rate.[83]

Overwhelmingly, the effort to explain high rates of Black infant mortality immediately slips to the register of the pathological, attributing it to mothers' smoking, co-sleeping, failure to get prenatal care, or illegal drug use. On the one hand, this view leads to policing solutions (because only criminals would do such a thing to their helpless newborn baby, the logic seems to go). Black pregnant women are disproportionately screened for the presence of illegal drugs in their bodies and then jailed for crimes that have been essentially made up for the purpose of criminalizing "bad" pregnancy and parenthood, like fetal child abuse, and the rates at which Black parents lose children to foster care for "neglect" is also entirely disproportionate.[84] On the positive side, there are the cheerful posters from the CDC Office of Minority Health "A Healthy Baby Begins with You," which emphasize things like eating well and managing your stress (as if stress were just an individual bad decision). Political theorist Annie Menzel notes that local campaigns also emphasize individual pathologies—even as the research indicates that systemic racism may have a much bigger role to play.[85] Monica Casper and Lisa Jean Moore argue that the focus on big demographic narratives rather than the fine-grained, textured stories of families and communities that lose babies—and the material lives of infants—means that scholars and policy makers fail to do justice to the complexity of people's lives or produce solutions that work.[86]

Despite the growing body of medical research that suggests structural, not individual causes for Black infant mortality, the responses to it are also instructive, suggesting the need of some researchers to return to individualizing pathology. For example, in 1992 Kenneth Schoendorf and Carol Hogue published an article in the *New England Journal of Medicine* with two significant findings: (1) college-educated African Americans still experienced twice the white rate of infant mortality, and (2) the cause seemed to be low birth weight. This suggested a host of things. First, the "bad" behavioral traits usually attributed to Black families with dead or frail infants—poverty, unemployment, substandard housing, lack of insurance or prenatal care, youth, single parenthood—seemed not to apply to this college-educated cohort, and there could be no attribution of poor infant care (such as smoking) because the only thing that differed between the Black and white families in this group was birth weight, not behavior. Further, the low birth weight of these predominantly full-term infants might suggest something about lifetime ill health or stress. Nevertheless, a series of letters to the *Journal* tried to find individual causes, suggesting how committed physicians can be to Black pathology arguments. The mothers probably smoked during their pregnancies, argued one; African Americans smoke more than whites. Another suggested that the mothers in Schoendorf's study had failed to gain enough weight to grow a healthy baby (in an interesting counterpoint to the usual arguments about maternal obesity); nutrition in pregnancy was no doubt the cause. Yet Schoendorf and Hogue had pointed out that Black mothers are *less,* not more, likely to smoke during pregnancy.[87] Furthermore, a subsequent study noted that even Black women with really fabulous nutrition during pregnancy had higher rates of infant mortality.[88] That is to say, the infant health disparities they documented could not be reduced to "bad" maternal behavior.

Despite a century-long preference for pathologizing African Americans to account for disproportionate Black infant mortality—from an explanation that insisted on the health *benefits* of slavery to various kinds of accounts of absolute differences between Black and white bodies and babies—more recently, a growing body of scholarship seems to point to something it calls "stress" to account for racial disparities in infant mortality. "Stress" is a bit of a black-box term without any clear meaning, but it at least begins to get at the ways the whole condition of people's lives, from housing to lifelong health and nutrition to how jobs and relationships affect pregnancy and the resulting health of infants. Indeed, it suggests some of the ways the daily toxic effects of racism in all its historical specificity might impact pregnancy outcomes, including the specific contexts of the shrinking of government programs, housing crises, and deindustrialization and unemployment in the latter third of the twentieth century.

Black infant mortality has been about twice as high as white infant mortality for as long as we've measured it—since the period just after slavery—except for a brief time from the War on Poverty until the election of Ronald Reagan, during which time it dropped to only one and a half times as high.[89] We use infant mortality internationally as a portable abacus that can compare the overall health of populations.[90] In that vein, I want to argue that we might also use the changing ratios of white and Black rates as a kind of historical index of the differences in how the political category of "race" impacts people's health—even, perhaps, as a sensitive measure of racism itself. Attending to differential rates separates broad changes in health and well-being (resulting in healthier babies overall) from the specific effects of what Ruth Gilmore calls the very definition of racism: "group-differentiated vulnerability to premature death."[91] The years when it was lowest—the decades of the 1960s and '70s were not only the decades of President Lyndon B. Johnson's legislative efforts to improve health, health care, nutrition, and housing, his War on Poverty, but, as we have seen, also the decades of activism that expanded access to AFDC, built community health centers, offered the hopefulness and commonality of purpose that can characterize times of political mobilization, and sought to reduce racism, unemployment, poverty, and income inequality.

The election of Ronald Reagan marked the end of that era, and from 1980 to 2005, the differences in Black and white IMRs grew and stayed high, reaching two and a half times higher for African Americans in 1999, and declining only slowly thereafter.[92] The availability of social services, health insurance, health care and income supports declined drastically in this period, while rates of incarceration increased sharply (by 790 percent between 1980 and 2012[93]). While it is hard to know how long the lag time might be (since IMRs measure pregnant women's well-being not only during the nine months of pregnancy but across their lifetime) or how to measure all the factors that might contribute to infant mortality, it's clear that these were years in which health indicators for white and Black well-being have diverged.

Although the decades after 1980 saw extraordinary changes in neonatal medicine and the quality of care in neonatal intensive care units (NICUs), the disparity between the number of Black and white babies born alive who died before their first birthday steadily increased. We can think of this as an index of inequality, one that measures everything from maternal stress to the quality of care to social inequality. While "white feelings" about structural infertility, delayed childbearing, and changes in the workplace—things that certainly affected Black (and Latinx, Asian, and Native) communities as well—could be measured by the number of books about the right time to have babies, we could read this disparity as an index of disproportionate Black grief about babies who never came home from the hospital or only for a short time.

Leith Mullings and Alaka Wali offer a compelling account of where we might look for the causes of what the public health and medical literature have begun to call Black women's "stress" that ends in more babies who do not make it through their first year. The results of their remarkable multidisciplinary Harlem BirthRight Project were published as a book, *Stress and Resil-* *ience*.[94] They narrate a story about a Black community where one shopkeeper remarked that "every day, somebody comes in to buy a card for some baby's funeral" and where women were coping with chronic stress related to employment and income, which in turn put pressure on housing, nutrition, child care, and the safety of their environment. The rise in female-headed households also added considerable stress for women, even as the study found that men, often under considerable strain themselves in the context of difficult economic and social conditions, contributed a great deal more to the support of these households than is generally acknowledged. The study also found that social

Social support

support from family, friends, and coworkers eased these stressors, from coworkers who throw baby showers to help purchase key items to family and friends who listen.[95]

Individuals and communities devoted significant time, care, and resources to helping babies survive. The Harlem BirthRight Project found a lot more informal support for pregnant and parenting women than the most apocalyptic accounts suggest (Single mothers! Raising children alone! Declining marriage rates!). Middle-class women relied on friends and coworkers, and working-class and impoverished women found practical support from extended family members, from a place to stay to meals. Fathers, meanwhile, were meaningfully involved in their children's lives to a much greater extent than rates of marriage or living together would suggest, bringing everything from diapers to dinner to babysitting and other kinds of time with their kids.

So how can we describe why Black babies die? Mullings and Wali offer the framework of the "Sojourner syndrome" as a way to account for how increasing social and racial inequality can attach itself to bodies as infant mortality. The Sojourner syndrome is comparable to Sherman James's notion of "John Henryism," a term he used to characterize Black men's stress in a 1994 paper to account for the racial disparity in rates of high blood pressure. John Henry, the legendary "steel-driving man," is said to have worked side by side with the industrial steam hammer to prove he could work as fast and as hard as it could. John Henry won, only to lie down and die when the contest was over. John Henryism, in James's account, is the bodily experience of hardworking, hard-driving Black men perennially at risk of being replaced—in the 1860s and '70s by the steam hammer on the railroads and in the 1980s by the export of US manufacturing jobs.[96] Similarly, Mullings and Wali suggest that Black women's stress can be measured in relation to Sojourner Truth's "Ain't I a Woman" speech for women's rights from 1851. They argue that even now, it does an excellent job of describing the differential conditions of Black women's lives—the disparate responsibilities, hardships, and griefs of Black women. One version that survives of that speech, with Truth's characteristic preacher's rhythms, is this:

> That man over there says that women need to be helped into carriages, and lifted over ditches, and to have the best place everywhere. Nobody ever helps me into carriages, or over mud-puddles, or gives me any best place, and ain't I a woman? Look at me! Look at my arm. I have ploughed, and planted and gathered into barns, and no man could head me! And ain't I a woman? I could work as hard and eat as much as a man—when I could get it—and bear the lash as well! And ain't I a woman? I have borne thirteen children, and seen most all sold off to slavery, and when I cried out with my mother's grief, none but Jesus heard me. And ain't I a woman?[97]

Mullings and Wali write of how this shadows the contemporary situation of pregnant African Americans. Decades of redlining have ensured that Black communities are disproportionately concentrated in substandard housing; educational and employment discrimination have resulted in chronic economic stress; good nutrition is a struggle in the so-called food deserts of central cities. Community activism is essential in keeping everyone afloat—even as it demands scarce resources of time and money. They write that Black women's stress comes from

> the assumption of economic, household, and community responsibilities, which express themselves in family headship, working outside the home (like a man), and the constant need to address community empowerment—often carried out in conditions made difficult by discrimination and scarce resources. In addition,

Sojourner Truth speaks to the contradiction between ideal models of gender and the lives of black women: exclusions from the protections of private patriarchy offered to white women by concepts of womanhood, motherhood, and femininity; the experience of being silenced; and, not least, the loss of children.[98]

While Mullins and Wali's voices—as anthropologists working in the community—are still a ways away from the engaging, opinionated, and rich public discourse about (implicitly white) structural infertility, they at least begin to map a more nuanced set of narratives about the conditions of Black infant death and the material circumstances that give rise to it in Black women's (and trans men's) lives. Intensifying economic pressure, declining time and support for households and care labor, and perhaps (although it's hard to measure) intensifying racism are contributing to higher rates of infant mortality.

Another anthropologist, Sandra Lane, studied a slightly wider phenomenon: racial disparities in miscarriage as well as infant mortality. Working with a Healthy Start program in Syracuse, New York, Lane marked the ways the construction of African Americans as a market segment may have contributed to pregnancy and infant loss: the disproportionate use of douches and menthol cigarettes. She noted that using a protein marker in infants' urine to measure how much nicotine they had been exposed to, even when mothers did not smoke, showed that Black infants had significantly more nicotine exposure than white ones, suggesting that ambient exposure to secondhand smoke might be a factor. But why particularly for Black infants, when secondhand smoke is everywhere? Menthol, argues Lane. Beginning in the 1960s and '70s, tobacco companies began marketing menthol cigarettes aggressively to Black communities (using location-specific billboards and Black models). Menthol cools the cigarette smoke, causing those who inhale it to hold it in their lungs longer—including, apparently, babies. An R.J. Reynolds executive admitted that they understood its dangers: "We don't smoke this shit, we just sell it. We reserve that right for the young, the poor, the black, and the stupid."[99] Although this doesn't comport entirely with other studies showing less exposure to cigarette smoke for African American infants, this may be a piece of the puzzle for infants who do come home and are subsequently lost.

The cause of higher rates of miscarriage in Lane's group, she argued compellingly, was bacterial vaginosis. Untreated, bacteria can travel up from the vagina into the uterus and inflame the amniotic sac, causing miscarriage. Her project at Syracuse Healthy Start was able, for a time, to significantly reduce pregnancy loss rates by treating bacterial vaginosis, though the infection seems to readily recur, causing little harm to women between pregnancies, but requiring treatment with each new pregnancy. The differential rates of bacterial vaginosis in Black women, Lane argues, seemed to be caused by douching—a procedure that confers no health benefits and is entirely unnecessary, but preys on women's shame about bodies and their smells. At one point, Lane confessed, she dreamed of doing civil disobedience in the drugstores of Syracuse, removing the douche products that disproportionately cluttered the shelves in Black neighborhoods.

Most important for the argument I am making here, though, is that (following Mullings) the increasing burden of both work and care fall disproportionately on people of color.[100] Across the economic spectrum, people of color are disproportionately seen as either imposters and "affirmative action hires" at the high end or paid less and working more at the low end (whether as a result of pushing mothers into the workforce through welfare reform or just the growing disparity between rich and poor). They are more likely to experience, or to have family members for whom they have duties of care experience, time-consuming, stressful crises: cars that break down; housing crises; educational failure and disproportionate K-12 suspensions and expulsions, especially of kids with disabilities; chronic disease and addiction; and hyperpolicing and incarceration, to name a few. The more the workplace demands of everyone, the more it specifically demands of African Americans to prove that they are not imposters, not slackers, not thugs or entitled incompetents. The more we privatize wealth, dependency, and care work, the more those who disproportionately bear care burdens or struggle with the unequal distribution of poverty and illness in the United States suffer. The name of all of this is stress, and stress has adverse health effects across the life span, including on infertility, miscarriage, and infant mortality.

The major racial disparities in fertility and the availability of fertility treatment—particularly between Black women and white women—suggest another face of racism and racial justice activism: demands for healthier housing, neighborhoods, and food, which would improve Black women's overall health, which in turn would increase the likelihood of getting pregnant and improve pregnancy outcomes. When public health researcher Arlene Geronimus notes that the early to mid-teens is the "best" time for inner city young Black women and girls to get pregnant because their infants are less likely to be born with low or very low birth weight, she is telling us a distressing story about the effect of stress and other suffering on Black girls' bodies that is parallel to this broad question of racial disparities in infant mortality at the extreme low end of the income scale.[101] Girls start showing effects of unhealthy environments or diet by the age of 20. Because these are geographical health effects—predictable by zip code or neighborhood—it is hard to say they are the outcome of "bad choices" as our public policy debates so often do (indeed, our public policy conversation sees these pregnancies themselves as the outcomes of bad choices)—rather than aggregate disadvantage. Better environments, an end to racism-induced stress, better access to health care in general and reproductive health care in particular, better treatment for Black women in health care settings, together perhaps with an end to certain marketing practices, ought also to be part of any kind of real conversation about infertility—not just egg freezing for employees of J. P. Morgan Chase.

[margin annotation: bad choice vs. structural causes]

Throughout the whole public conversation about Sheryl Sandberg's *Lean In* and the aftermath of Anne-Marie Slaughter's *Atlantic* piece, commentators complained that this was pretty much a white and middle-class problem. Well, yes—but only up to a point. Black infant mortality rates tell a different story: of care burdens and work pressures that put differential stress on African American women before, during, and after pregnancies. Whether impoverished, middle-class, or wealthy, Black women, men, and households live that class position with greater vulnerability to stress because of racism. We know that because babies die.

Infertility, ARTs, later childbearing, pregnancy loss, and infant mortality are more than "just" reproductive issues; they are how we are living racially differentiated transformations in the economy, public benefits, and the wider culture. In the United States, we have in recent decades seen the exacerbation of at least two kinds of structural, predictable reproductive disruption: that caused by workforce demands to delay childbearing and that caused by racialized dispossession and resulting ill health. Although these appear to be at odds with each other—

one group is expected to have children, albeit later in life, and the other group's children are the subject of fairly unremitting hostility in public discourse or lack of concern about differential death rates—certainly neither group could be said to be able to have the children they want under the conditions of their choosing. We have been debating abortion, birth control, and the means of preventing unwanted pregnancies vigorously and at length for two generations, but while we were looking there, many people lost the ability to have the children they wanted, not only through the involuntary sterilization of people of color and those of any race with disabilities, as activists have been protesting for generations now, but also through involuntary, structural infertility as a result of economic changes and unsafe jobs.

CHAPTER FIVE

Gay Married, with Children

If structural infertility and a high degree of racial disparity in infant mortality rates are faces of the "new normal" of the reduced support for reproductive labor and the privatization of dependency, so too are the gay married. Throughout the 1970s, a new antigay right-wing movement defined homosexuals as those who had a lot of sex but did not do reproductive labor. In Florida, Anita Bryant's Save Our Children campaign imagined queer people who had no children of their own (and so threatened straight people's). In California, the Briggs Initiative tried to keep "the gays" away from positions of responsibility with respect to youth—to fire them as teachers, guidance counselors, and child psychologists. These campaigns—and even liberal books like *Everything You Always Wanted to Know about Sex but Were Afraid to Ask*—imagined queer folks as antisocial, mentally ill members of a dark subculture founded in furtive sexual encounters or deviant, even violent relationships. The everyday social reproductive work of gay liberation groups and people who knew each other from bars and built political, social, and erotic

149

communities was invisible to those outside, for the most part. With the AIDS crisis—and its fights over whether lovers could care for their sick and bury their dead without losing control to the sick men's parents—the infrastructure of queer caring labor was rendered abruptly visible, full of devastating grief. An army of volunteers kept many gay men from passing through illness and death alone, even when hospitals were leaving food trays at the end of the hallway out of fear of contagion. And then in the 1990s, seemingly without warning, there was a gayby boom, queer kids were on the street and in foster care, and the long fight for gay marriage began. Gayness became genetic, not contagious, and suddenly queers were all about the reproductive labor (and not so much about the sex). This, at least, was the outline of the story as told by the mainstream press.[1]

While the narrative I want to offer is definitely more complicated (queer folks have obviously had children and done reproductive labor for a lot longer than it was visible to those outside the gay community), I am particularly interested in the ways gay political demands for marriage, for protection for reproductive labor—from caring for children and sick or disabled partners to marriage—tracked the larger story I have been telling in this book about how reproductive labor has changed by becoming much more privatized. Gay marriage was in many ways a deeply conservative political project—as we have seen, a racist account of the moral failings of (implicitly Black) unmarried mothers was the cornerstone of the policy move to "reform" welfare. A similarly racist account of properly gendered marriage also informed settler colonialist efforts to remove Native Americans from their land in the name of morality and exclude Chinese, Muslim, and other polygamous immigrants.[2] Yet as the state did less and corporations did nothing to acknowledge or support the space to care for dependents, the outlaw status of gay households and communities became more and more unsupportable. If the only place that could care for dependents was "the (legally recognized) family," then gay people needed one too. Gay marriage, I am saying, is a reproductive politics issue.

For many, gay marriage was not a first choice, but a difficult pill to swallow that nevertheless prevented others from breaking up their households and separating them from chosen kin. For others, it conferred dignity and legitimacy on their relationships, providing a space for their love to be acknowledged in public. Even—or maybe especially—those gay folks most harmed by the white supremacist attacks on Black or immigrant households—which, as a result of the structure of racism in the United States, could never be thought to be gendered right—turned to the politics of marriage.[3] It wasn't, of course, what people needed: comprehensive family rights for all kinds of people—single moms, blended families, divorced people, elderly folks living together, older siblings raising younger ones or caring for a brother or sister with a disability—but a rather narrow set of legal rights for conjugal couples, opposite sex or same sex—a context in which only 69 percent of children under 17 reside.[4] Above all, it wasn't what the LGBT movement had demanded, but rather what it settled for.

GAY AND LESBIAN PARENTS

For the courts and queer folks alike, one of the most important questions animating the quest for gay marriage has been the protection of gay and lesbian parental rights. There have, of course, been gay parents as long as there have been gay people: People who stayed in heterosexual marriages so they could keep their kids. Lesbians who did heterosexual sex work for the money and inadvertently but not necessarily unhappily got pregnant. Beginning in the late 1960s, with the intensification of a gay liberation movement, lesbians and gay men came out to a small circle of friends or a larger, more public one, left heterosexual marriages, and fought to keep custody of their children or at least visitation rights even when their ex knew or suspected that they were gay. Others went underground, taking their children and running, hiding from ex-spouses. By the 1970s, some parents and lawyers were organizing groups like the Lesbian Mothers' Defense Fund, the Lesbian Mothers' Union, the Lesbian Rights Project, and Lambda Legal Defense to help provide expert witnesses, lawyers, and financial support. Still, until at least the mid-1980s, mostly these gay parents lost their children in custody hearings or agreed to settle without going to court, preserving visitation by not asking for custody, or agreeing to custody without child support (lest this sound like ancient history: as I write this in 2017 as a university professor, there is currently a cohort of children of queer parents the age of my students who are not able to go to college or are attending less expensive schools closer to home because of those nonsupport agreements).[5]

The activist organizations and literature of the gay movement of the 1960s and '70s are suffused with this melancholic legacy of lost children. Bruce Voeller founded the National Gay Task Force and was its executive director at a time when he was engaged in a very public battle to maintain visitation rights with his children. It was a fight he ultimately won, but with restrictions that left his children out of his life in any meaningful way: they could not go to his home, meet his lover, or go to any locations where other gay men were present. Abilly Jones-Hennin, founder of the National Coalition of Black Gays, was also a father and organized gay parents' groups in the Washington, DC, area. Among the five demands of the 1979 March on Washington for Lesbian and Gay Rights was this one: "End discrimination in lesbian mother and gay father custody cases."[6] Minnie Bruce Pratt's collection *Crime Against Nature,* which received a prestigious designation as a Lamont Poetry Selection from the Academy of American Poets, found its title in the sodomy laws that made it unthinkable that she would be able to keep her boys; she relinquished them to her ex-husband in order to preserve visitation. It contains these lines:

> Years back, at the beach, with piles of shells
> In our laps, with the first final separation on us,
> One asked: *How do we know you won't forget us?*
> I told them how they had moved in my womb: each
> Distinct, the impatient older, the steady younger.
> I said: *I can never forget you. You moved inside me.*
> I meant: *The sound of your blood crossed into mine.*[7]

Queer communities organized to demand that parents be allowed to keep their children, taking on names like the Mary Jo Risher Appeal Fund and the Jeanne Jullion Defense Committee that echoed other political trials of groups from the Popular Front to the Black Panthers. Nearly all gay and lesbian parents lost their custody cases in the 1970s and '80s. Still, there were unexpected moral victories, as when Risher's case became a made-for-TV movie, *A Question of Love,* that portrayed her sympathetically, as a grieving mother who had heartbreakingly lost her 7-year-old son. The terror of losing children—whose dependence inflected the love and affection of bonds with parents in a way that could make being unable to care for them seem like the worst kind of betrayal—queer families' relationships with their children even when they faced little danger that they would actually lose them. The risk, too, that a heterosexual ex-spouse could reopen the custody agreement if a parent's homosexuality became known slammed the closet door shut for many. Even gay folk who didn't have children and didn't want them knew about these issues if they were connected to the increasingly politically activist queer community, as these campaigns populated the pages of newspapers like San Francisco's *Bay Area Reporter,* Washington's *Gay Blade,* and Boston's *Gay Community News.* Even the resolutely apolitical bar crowd couldn't entirely miss the rallies and contingents in gay pride parades. It was a grief that permeated gay communities.

At the same time, there was an exuberant freedom in queer struggles to keep children: the refusals to stay in dead marriages, to believe that parenthood was incompatible with living out the wildness and unpredictability of love and desire, to accept that there were only very conservative definitions of family available, defined by shared blood or even who you were having sex with at the time. "Come to your life like a warrior," sang Cris Williamson in the "women's music" genre that, together with typed and stapled newsletters like *Lesbian Connection,* urban collective households, and rural land cooperatives knit lesbian communities together, demanding and celebrating risking everything to be free. Carl Wittman in "A Gay Manifesto" in 1977 argued that "traditional marriage is a rotten, oppressive institution," adding that "liberation for gay people is defining for ourselves how and with whom we live, instead of measuring our relationship[s] in comparison to straight ones, with straight values."[8] Gay and lesbian people laid claim to heterodox meanings of kin and family, even as they measured the likelihood that they would be kicked out of their families of origin ("Not in this family!").[9] People spoke of friends as family, of "families we choose."[10] One of the key nodes of urban gay politics was queer collective households, which, as Stephen Vider notes, were an effort to imagine a future without atomized nuclear families and all they entailed with respect to consumerism, sexist distribution of reproductive labor, and ways of teaching gender roles to children.[11] Emily Hobson writes that collective households "provided locations from which to challenge gendered domestic labor (including child care), to destabilize the centrality of couples to domestic life, and to create new intimate bonds that blurred the boundaries between sexual relationships and other bonds of family, including political brotherhood and sisterhood."[12] In the coded language of the underground community of gay and lesbian people in the 1980s, if you wanted to find out if someone was queer in mixed company, you asked, "Are they *family?*" One bumper sticker and political slogan named ex-lovers as family and comrades: "An Army of ex-lovers cannot fail." The demand by activist queer folk to keep their children drew on feminist and antiracist critiques of marriage as a relationship of property, of the fiction of a male head-of-household as the only person in a household in which slaves, wives, and children were property and in which slaves and others were presumed to have no other genealogies or kin.[13] The gay a capella group The Flirtations (often heard on the streets of Provincetown, and featuring Michael Callen, one of the most prominent AIDS activists of that generation, before his death at 38) sang songs like "Everything Possible," Fred Small's lullaby for free children ("I will sing you a song no one sang to me/May it keep you good company/You can be anybody that you want to be/You can love whomever you will/ ... /And know that I will love you still"), and "Your children/are not your children/They are the sons and the daughters of life's longing for itself," the words of Kahil Gibran set to music by the Black freedom, lesbian feminist musicians of Sweet Honey in the Rock. They were claiming the legitimacy of gay fathers and lesbian mothers raising children—with the promise, too, that they would do it differently, better, and in the service of a more just world. "Try to imagine," said Callen in the introduction to "Everything Possible," "how different you might be, and how different the world might be, if more parents would sing lullabies like this to their children."

These were not respectability politics. The movements for lesbian and gay custody did not operate in a vacuum, but were part of a broader coalition to transform what counted as a legitimate family. Historian Daniel Winunwe Rivers notes that these groups maintained strong intellectual and political links with welfare rights, the Black Panther Party, opposition to sterilization abuse against women of color, and a broader reproductive politics agenda. Dykes with Tykes, a New York lesbian mothers' group, wrote that their political work included fighting for "the right to have a family if we choose, for the custody of our children, and the resources to sustain them."[14] Lesbian mother activists also had roots in antiwar, civil rights, and Black power movements.

During this same period, the conservative antigay campaigns of the era were engaged in fierce gay shaming whose politics also centered around children—claiming that homosexuals, essentially by definition, molested children. Anita Bryant's 1977–78 crusade against an antidiscrimination ordinance in Miami that sought to protect gay and lesbian people in housing, employment, and public accommodations—things that had little or nothing to do with children—was organized around the slogan "Save Our Children." Her group claimed that "the recruitment of our children is absolutely necessary for the survival and growth of the homosexual movement." The Briggs Initiative in

California targeting gay teachers, child psychiatrists, and juvenile probation officers was essentially about defining anything gay folks did as like having sex, such that organizing a lesbian brunch group could be seen as on a spectrum with molesting children. The initiative targeted people who were engaged in "public homosexual activity" but defined it, as custody cases often did, to include any kind of political activity on behalf of gay, lesbian, or trans folks. Public homosexuality in this account was quite capacious, including sex at home, in public restrooms, or the speech act of saying "I am gay/lesbian"—and all implicated you in child molestation. Gay rebellion and its reaction could also lie quite close together. In 1987, *Gay Community News* published an essay entitled "Tremble, Hetero Swine," that began by describing itself as "an outré, madness, a tragic, cruel fantasy, an eruption of inner rage, on how the oppressed desperately dream of being the oppressor." It continued with the lines

> We shall sodomize your sons, emblems of your feeble masculinity, of your shallow dreams and vulgar lies. We shall seduce them in your schools, in your dormitories, in your gymnasiums, in your locker rooms, in your sports arenas, in your seminaries, in your youth groups, in your movie theater bathrooms, in your army bunkhouses, in your truck stops, in your all male clubs, in your houses of Congress, wherever men are with men together.... The family unit, which only dampens imagination and curbs free will, must be eliminated. Perfect boys will be conceived and grown in the genetic laboratory.

The emergent Christian right, never good at irony, dropped the first line and called the rest of it "The Homosexual Agenda," even reading it into the Congressional Record from the second sentence on.[15]

GAYBIES

In the 1980s, the arrival of significant numbers of "gaybies"—deliberately conceived offspring of gay and lesbian folks—deepened the political urgency for queer family rights. Ironically, as Daniel Rivers has brilliantly pointed out, it was the most nationalist corner of lesbian separatism that really began to expand the practices of queer parenthood by thinking through the ways lesbians could get pregnant without heterosexual sex. In workshops at the Michigan Womyn's Music Festival and conversations on women's land, lesbian feminists began to explore the possibilities of replication from an ova alone by parthenogenesis or gynogenesis—particularly hoping these could result in the conception of only girl children, thus eliminating the thorny problems associated with boy children, whom some argued carried too much "male energy" to be on womyn's land and could too easily be associated with rape and other kinds of patriarchal violence to be part of the radical political and spiritual experiment of building the lesbian amazon nation outside mainstream society. (Others argued for raising a tribe of nonsexist boys and men. Whatever their politics on this issue, though, in practice a great many lesbian feminists were deeply uncomfortable with excluding boy children and their mothers.) As it became increasingly clear that parthenogenesis was unlikely anytime soon for species that were not frogs, womyn's communities began to turn their focus to the possibilities of conception without heterosexual sex or medical intervention by soliciting donor sperm and conceiving with the help of turkey basters, pipettes, and glass jars—sometimes relying on a go-between to preserve anonymity and address worries about the courts inventing paternity rights even for gay sperm donors (which they did). In the late

1970s and early 1980s, lesbian feminists were organizing coffee-houses, bike repair and home repair collectives—and "artificial insemination" collectives. Groups formed in Boston, New York City, Burlington, VT, and Oakland, CA, that eventually gave rise to sperm banks primarily for lesbians.[16]

In the 1980s and '90s, lesbians and gay men in their families of choice started getting pregnant in real numbers. Barred from nearly all commercial sperm banks, they relied on turkey basters and each other to achieve pregnancy and parenthood. Gay and feminist health centers such as the Feminist Health Center of Oakland, the Vermont Women's Health Center, and the Feminist Women's Health Center in Los Angeles, and Fenway Community Health Center in Boston offered "alternative fertilization," or sperm banking for lesbian clients. Lesbians looking for a cheaper or more connected option and those far from a major gay urban center leaned on friends for sperm or had strategic reproductive intercourse with a male partner. They formed complex families, offering sperm donors varying degrees of participation. Some women, usually lesbians, even carried babies for gay male friends. Gay community children were raised with three, four, or even more parents with varying levels of responsibility and related-ness. (Lest this sound like an uncontrolled experiment with children's lives, it's worth remarking that since currently about 50 percent of marriages end in divorce, many of these involving children, complex queer family formation was no more chaotic and often much more thoughtful and loving than remarriage—giving children four parents—or other heterosexual postdivorce relationships.) In the 1980s, even the mainstream press was commenting on a "gayby boom."[17] These "lesbian nation" efforts eventually gave rise to pressure on traditional sperm banks to rethink their goal of serving only heterosexual married couples having trouble getting pregnant and, in turn, ultimately also led to gay men's turn to surrogacy. Ironically, anecdotally at least, lesbian feminists using artificial insemination disproportionately conceived boys (perhaps because the procedure favored the Y-carrying faster but weaker swimmers), also contributing to the eventual dissolution of most of the womyn-only spaces and land collectives.

The increasing number of lesbian and gay families with children did not come with an expansion of legal security for those families. All was well unless something brought them to court, but humans being humans, relationships failed, good intentions unraveled, former lovers and friends left with the kids, and those who had helped raise those children took their exes to court. Lesbian and gay parents in their intentional families faced the same issues previous generations of queer parents who had conceived in heterosexual families had: sperm donors who wanted to claim paternity rights were awarded them because courts found that artificial insemination outside a medical context (and without payment) did not terminate a donor's parental rights; when the parents' relationship ended, courts for decades consistently awarded custody to the bio-parent when there was a dispute, denying that even coparents with extensive and long relationships to children had a claim to custody, even if they were named on a birth certificate. In the mid-1990s in California and a few other states, lesbian rights lawyers persuaded some judges to issue orders for what they called "second-parent" adoptions, where a non-bio-parent was recognized as akin to a stepparent. With these, a handful of non-bio-parents began to be able to win visitation or even custody in disputed parental separations, but most lesbian and gay families remained legally naked and vulnerable.

Within a decade, as sociologist Laura Mamo has pointed out, lesbians and gay men came to rely in ever-expanding numbers on the infertility industry: commercial sperm banks and surrogacy. Expanding access came at tremendous financial expense, but it also made lesbian and gay reproduction much more routine, taking it beyond word-of-mouth communities and ghettoized gay institutions. Mamo asks what was lost and gained as conception became much more medicalized after infertility treatment was opened to queer folks.[18] Avoiding legal insecurity, of course, was as much a motivation as the opening of the fertility clinics' doors; with courts continuing through the 1980s to regularly take children from gay bio-parents (usually in the context of divorce), what rights could a nonbiological lesbian parent hope to have if something went terribly wrong and the sperm "donor" sought parental rights? Sperm banks offered protection from this eventuality; courts seemed to regard the exchange of money—the buying and selling of sperm—to decisively terminate a sperm donors' parental rights, when the exchange of commitments to that effect were not similarly understood. The legal innovation of second-parent adoption (and eventually, gay marriage) went even further than financial gamete transactions in protecting non-bio-parental rights and giving chosen family legal legitimacy, but it also enshrined the couple as the logical and legal parents. Other, more creative family forms did not disappear, but they certainly receded as the norm in queer family life.

BRING SHARON KOWALSKI HOME!

Of course, relationships with children were not the only ones that needed protecting. Two kinds of issues in the 1980s made it clear that love was *not* actually enough to make a family. Throughout that decade, two things—AIDS and a case involving Sharon Kowalski and her lover—haunted gay community efforts to remake reproductive politics, family, and community by reminding queer folk that when their family of origin was hostile to their homosexuality and chosen family, the courts could take them away from the people they loved.

In 1983, Karen Thompson and Sharon Kowalski were two gym teachers living together in St. Cloud, Minnesota (Karen had a job at the University of Minnesota). Though they had exchanged rings and bought a house, they told almost no one of their relationship. When a drunk driver hit Kowalski's car one day as she was driving a niece and nephew home, she suffered a serious traumatic brain injury (her 4-year-old niece was killed; the nephew survived and recovered). Thompson was the first to the hospital but was denied information or the opportunity to visit her seriously injured lover, a situation that proved predictive of how things were to be. Kowalski's parents grew suspicious that Thompson was spending so much time at the hospital, and when she confessed the nature of their relationship, the parents ultimately sought guardianship and prevented Thompson from visiting her lover. As the relationship between Thompson and Kowalski's parents deteriorated, in 1985 her parents moved Kowalski from a rehabilitation facility to a nursing home closer to their home and for three and a half years banned Thompson from visiting her, despite the fact that with Thompson's help, Kowalski had meaningfully improved in the rehab facility: learning how to spell and use a spelling board to communicate, standing, and leaving the facility for visits. In the nursing home, she lay in bed as her muscles tightened and she lost intellectual capacity. Still, Kowalski continued to affirm her desire to live with Thompson. As

Thompson lost petition after petition in court, she turned to the gay and lesbian community to publicize their story and raise money for legal expenses. In 1988, after the publication of Thompson's book *Why Can't Sharon Kowalski Come Home?*, August 7 was designated as a national day of action to "Free Sharon Kowalski," with events in twenty-one cities. Thompson spoke all over the country to feminist and gay groups, urging gay and lesbian people to sign durable powers of attorney for each other as a legal stopgap against this kind of nightmare. In 1991, Kowalski's father, Donald Kowalski, relinquished his guardianship, citing his own health problems and exhaustion about the endless legal battles. In the final twist of the knife, a Minnesota court then gave guardianship to a family friend, Karen Tomberlin, chastising Thompson for telling Kowalski's parents that she was a lesbian and making her sexuality public at rallies. Finally, eight years after the accident, in December 1991, a Minnesota appeals court gave custody to Thompson, saying that they were a "family of affinity," that Thompson's house was wheelchair accessible, and that Kowalski had continuously expressed a preference to live with Thompson. While the outcome was a relief, finally, for Thompson and the community that had supported her, nothing could undo the effects of the three and half years in which Kowalski had received no rehabilitation, or the fear that the protracted court battle had spread across especially lesbian communities about whether their families could be forcibly torn apart in the same way.[19]

HIV/AIDS

At the same time that the Kowalski case and organizing around custody cases were making their way through lesbian communities, AIDS was raising some of the same kinds of family issues for gay men and their lesbian friends and allies. As gay men sickened and died, their partners were finding that if bio-parents intervened, they had no right to care for their lover, attend his funeral, have a say in where he was buried, inherit his property, or even stay in the apartment they had shared if they were not on the lease. It can be hard for people who were not there to understand the extent of the epidemic's devastation of urban gay communities in the 1980s and early 1990s, but one statistic might give a sense of the concentrated devastation: historian Daniel Rivers estimates that 80–90 percent of the hundreds of people active in the San Francisco gay fathers' organization died in the 1980s.[20]

AIDS forced a great many people to come out who had previously not been visible nor involved in gay liberation politics—their gay community was found in rest-stop bathrooms, in the bushes at public parks, in bathhouses and porn theaters, or in semiclandestine communities of men who were married but knew about each other, on the down low in Black and Puerto Rican communities or cross-border encounters in the Southwest. The AIDS epidemic also saw an influx of more respectable men—with money, power, and conservative politics—into gay activism. The results were contradictory and uneven, but they ultimately signaled the decline of the centrality of left politics, or any coherent political orientation, in the queer community.

The Braschi case, for example, brought a different class of queer folks into the fold at the same time that it brought a new victory to the struggle for gay family rights, this time in the context of bereavement and AIDS. In 1976, Leslie Blanchard, a Manhattan hairdresser to stars (including Mary Tyler Moore, Meryl Streep, and Robert De Niro), exchanged Cartier bracelets with his twenty-years-younger Puerto Rican lover, Miguel

Braschi. Ten years later, Blanchard died of AIDS in Braschi's arms. Three months later, Braschi received a notice of eviction from the rent-controlled apartment in Manhattan they had shared, since only Blanchard's name was on the lease and only spouses or family members could assume a lease under New York's rent control laws. The real estate magnate who owned the apartment, Stanley Stahl, wanted to make the apartment more profitable and was part of the growing effort in New York to gut the rent stabilization laws and gentrify the city (memorialized in *Rent,* among other places). Braschi vowed to fight the eviction in court, telling a friend, "They don't understand who they are dealing with." The case ultimately wound up with attorney Bill Rubenstein and the Lesbian and Gay Rights Project of the ACLU.

Braschi was a great plaintiff; he and Blanchard had completely integrated their finances and their lives. Blanchard had made him the nearly exclusive beneficiary of his $5 million estate (although the will referred to him as a "friend," in the discreet language so many gay and lesbian people used for their families in the '80s). They had been together long-term, were on close terms with each other's families, and Braschi had been Blanchard's primary caretaker throughout his illness. Interestingly, Rubenstein decided not to pursue the strategy of claiming that Braschi was Blanchard's spouse, despite some pressure to do so, arguing both practical reasons—"spouse" had a clear legal definition that they could not meet—and political ones—if they succeeded in getting the court to redefine "family," it would make it easier not only for same-sex couples but also others, such as unmarried straight couples or elderly folks who called each other family without having any relationship of blood or marriage, to win other kinds of family rights, including hospital and jail visitation, health insurance, and bereavement leave. Braschi stayed in the apartment as the court case progressed. Three years later, he won a judgment from an appellate court that he was, indeed, family. Although the case had limited value as precedent, applying only to housing law in New York, it was quickly joined to the growing political momentum for some kind of family rights for gay and lesbian people. Immediately after the ruling, *Braschi* was an issue in the New York mayoral race. Republican candidate Rudolph Giuliani decried its effort to make "a gay couple a family unit." Democratic candidates Ed Koch and David Dinkins called for domestic partner benefits for city employees.[21]

These victories were double-edged. On the one hand, sometimes courts did the right thing. Sharon Kowalski went to live with Karen Thompson, who by this time was living with another lover, and together they were able to offer Kowalski more care and independence than they would have been able to otherwise, forming a three-person family with more legal recognition, perhaps, than marriage of one or the other of the conjugal couples might have allowed. Braschi won, although as scholar Carlos Ball has argued, the case may have succeeded in significant measure because so many others lost—and the partners of people with AIDS, many sick themselves, were swelling the ranks of New York's homeless population.[22] Most importantly, most gay people didn't live in New York. Some "second parents" won the legal right to have an ongoing relationship to their children, although most queer folks who lived outside gay enclaves like New York and San Francisco did not. I for example did not, in 2000, win a legal adoption of my oldest in Tucson, Arizona, meaning that the times when it mattered most, like in the emergency room or one awful night when she was held in juvenile detention, I was unable to get her care or visit her, and I wasn't allowed to register her for school.

After decades of legal struggle, by the late 1980s, most gay and lesbian folks still had little assurance that they had any rights in their families that courts were bound to respect, whether custody of their children, the right to care for sick or disabled lovers, or visitation in hospitals or jails. Queer folks had no expectation of pensions through their partners, the ability to inherit even the property that they had shared, or—except in New York City rent controlled apartments—the ability to keep their housing. Unless families of origin, landlords, or the random employees of banks, schools, hospitals, and prisons that gay folks met (as clients or visitors or denizens) chose to treat their love and kinship with respect, there was nothing they could do.

A POLITICAL MOVEMENT FOR SAME-SEX MARRIAGE?

Although same-sex marriage ultimately became a way to defend against these legal liabilities, at first, it seemed like an outlandish idea. While in a handful of early cases in Minnesota, Washington, and Kentucky gay folk had sought marriage licenses in the 1970s,[23] these failed quickly, although not without punitive effects. The University of Minnesota dismissed a librarian—James McConnell—who had filed suit for a marriage license. In *McConnell v. Anderson,* the court acknowledged that McConnell was qualified for the position but objected to the fact that he had refused to stay in the closet and was asking for "the right to pursue an activist role in *implementing* his unconventional ideas concerning the societal status to be accorded homosexuals and, thereby, to foist tacit approval of this socially repugnant concept upon his employer, who is, in this instance, an institution of higher learning." The court concluded, "We know of no constitutional fiat or binding principle of decisional law which requires an employer to accede to such extravagant demands."[24]

Together, these three kinds of legal assaults on gay families— losing children in custody cases, guardianship of partners with severe disabilities, and the inability to protect the right to care for partners or hold on to common property in the face of HIV/AIDS—brought some gay and lesbian people to the city clerk's office to ask for marriage licenses. Bill Rubenstein, speaking to the *New York Times* about the Sharon Kowalski case in 1991, said, "This case, and AIDS, have been the defining events of the 1980s in this area. It's underscored why we need legal protection, and created a terrific incentive to fight for these kinds of marital rights and recognition of domestic partnership."[25] The movement for domestic partnership benefits was gaining some political traction, as big cities and towns with considerable gay communities like Berkeley, Los Angeles, West Hollywood, Seattle, and Madison began to grant benefits to the same-sex partners of municipal employees.[26]

Choosing marriage, choosing a politics of respectability, seemed to some like a fundamental betrayal of what many gay and lesbian groups had been fighting for: rights for love and passion beyond the bounds of traditional domesticity and for custodial relations with children and other dependents marked by love and care rather than the kind of legal contract with the state that feminists had been criticizing robustly for decades. Why would lesbian and gay folk want to enter into an institution that had historically denied women legal personhood and the right to own property, hidden violent abuse of partners and children behind a veil of privacy, demanded sexual exclusivity, and produced norms about the division of reproductive labor that left some (female) people with all the work? Wasn't the point of being queer that you didn't have to deal with all that, and could create something different?

Marriage politics sharply divided gay communities and activists in the 1980s and '90s. In 1986 and 1987, the effects of the influx of more conservative gay and lesbian people as a result of the AIDS crisis were sharply felt. The organizing for the March on Washington for Lesbian and Gay Rights was the site of substantial conflict about the political orientation of queer communities—about feminism and antiracism broadly; whether opposition to wars in Central America and apartheid South Africa should be listed among the demands of the march (they were); whether people with AIDS or Cesar Chavez of the United Farm Workers, who had been an early and vocal opponent of the Briggs Initiative in California in the '70s to fire gay teachers, and Ellie Smeal of the National Organization of Women should lead the march. The march turned into a three-day series of events. These included the first national viewing of the AIDS memorial quilt; a protest at the Supreme Court against *Bowers v. Hardwick,* which had affirmed the right of a cop who had been accused of gay-bashing to enter someone's bedroom and arrest him for sodomy; the march itself (led, in fact, by Chavez and Smeal); and the Wedding.

Marriage emerged as possibly the most divisive issue of all. *Gay Community News* staged a debate in which the affinity group Positively Revolting denounced gay marriage as of a piece with gay gentrification and other kinds of (upper-) class warfare against single mothers and impoverished communities, objecting that it divided the lesbian and gay community into "respectable" and unrespectable queers, objecting to its demands for monogamy and consumer goods, its unequal forms of labor (the double day), and reminding readers that in many states, marriage still legalized rape because a man couldn't be prosecuted for raping his wife.[27] Against these objections, supporters of same-sex marriage named the myriad forms of economic and legal discrimination deriving from lesbian and gay couples' exclusion from marriage, including tax and insurance benefits and child custody.[28] The day before the march, on October 10, 1987, thousands of lesbian and gay couples exchanged vows in a mass wedding, with the slogan "Love makes a family." Karen Thompson told the crowd, "If I'd been a 'normal' spouse, I'd have been encouraged to help Sharon recover, instead of blocked at every turn." Comedian Robin Tyler asked, "How can we support a patriarchal institution? We are not here to parrot heterosexual marriage, an unequal bond between unequal partners—that's sick." Demands included the right to equal treatment in fostering, adoption, and child custody and full legal status in insurance and taxes.[29]

In subsequent years, this fight was restaged as an argument about the priorities of lesbian and gay movement lawyers and legal organizations. In 1989, San Francisco's *Outlook* magazine published a debate between Lambda Legal Defense's legal director, Paula Ettelbrick, and its executive director, Tom Stoddard. Lambda had worked on the Kowalski case, and although marriage seemed quite distant on the horizon, the Wedding at the march on Washington had raised the question of movement priorities sharply. In "Since When Is Marriage a Path to Liberation?," Ettelbrick, while acknowledging that marriage was a strategy for gaining family rights, argued that "marriage runs contrary to two of the primary goals of the lesbian and gay movement: the affirmation of gay identity and culture; and the validation of many forms of relationships."[30] Stoddard admitted to not being particularly enthusiastic about the sexist institution of marriage, but, citing the Supreme Court's description of marriage as "intimate to the degree of being sacred" and "noble" in

Griswold v. Connecticut (which gave married couples the right to use contraception in 1965), argued that the second-class status of gay relationships could end only when gay couples were allowed to enter in to this "sacred" and "noble" institution.[31] While both acknowledged the practical benefits of marriage—from tax breaks to health insurance—for both, it seems, the symbolic significance of marriage was actually more important. Ettelbrick and Stoddard subsequently took this debate on the road, staging the conversation in one urban gay center after another.

Another significant voice in the debate was Andrew Sullivan, who in 1989 penned "Here Comes the Groom: A (Conservative) Case for Gay Marriage" for the *New Republic* in response to the *Braschi* case.[32] He argued that having courts determine who was a family was a mess, and that domestic partner statutes provided a lesser and burdensome alternative to marriage—often requiring bank statements showing evidence that finances were comingled and a lease or other documents showing that the partners were living together. (Another objection to domestic partner registries—not voiced by Sullivan but circulating in gay communities—was that they were "roundup lists" if anyone wanted to come after the gays, akin to the data provided by the Census Bureau to aid in Japanese internment during World War II.[33]) But Sullivan mostly hated the fact that "activist" judges were going to determine who constituted a family, and he argued that marriage, in contrast, would bring gays into the conservative fold—or at least into lives that resembled mainstream America's. Marriage would reduce promiscuity, make gay folks more responsible and "foster social cohesion, emotional security, and economic prudence," not to mention "the healthy rearing of the next generation." (The other name for this, in queer scholar-activist Lisa Duggan's formulation, was "homonormativity": "a politics that does not contest dominant heteronormative assumptions and institutions, but upholds and sustains them, while promising the possibility of demobilized gay constituency and a privatized, depoliticized gay culture anchored in domesticity and consumption."[34]) Further, Sullivan reiterated the slanderous welfare-reform case against Black single mothers and what Moynihan in the sixties had called their "matriarchal" families, albeit in muted form: "In the context of the weakened family's effect upon the poor, it might also invite social disintegration" to not promote gay marriage. Sullivan's case for gay marriage basically tried to drop a bomb on the gay-liberation dream of freedom to choose alternative forms of kinship and the feminist vision of solidarity among single mothers, battered women, and queer folk as refugees from the patriarchal property relationship of marriage.

From the 1990s all the way through 2015, an organized queer left bemoaned the fundamental conservatism of gay marriage and the failure of imagination of a politics of organizing for rights and benefits according to who people were having sex with. Many scholars and queer-activist opponents of same-sex marriage complained, together with Leo Bersani, that it spelled an end to the freedom and the fun of "lawless homosexuality," in legal scholar Katherine Franke's phrase. She argued that what same-sex marriage gave us was gay people who put financial penalties for adultery into prenuptial agreements, and she asked whether that was really the goal of a gay liberation movement.[35] Many queer opponents blamed the turn toward marriage on Sullivan, his well-heeled cadre of gay Republicans, and the lawyers in the big gay legal organizations like Lambda who, despite their initial reluctance, ultimately did join gay marriage cases.

I want to suggest that this account gives Sullivan too much credit; the bigger "problem," if it was one, was that ordinary gay folk also sought to protect their family rights through marriage. It's important to remember that there were thousands of people at the Wedding in Washington in 1987 and to notice where gay marriage cases came from. The organized, activist gay community— whether lawyers or activists—wasn't very enthusiastic about marriage, and the households of those in the gay enclaves of New York and San Francisco, where many of the movement organizations found their homes, were relatively well-protected legally by the eighties and nineties. Furthermore, when new gay marriage cases cropped up, first one by one and then by the fistful, movement lawyers were initially very reluctant to participate. The first cases, in Hawaii, involved gay folks who just went down to the county clerk and asked for a marriage license, then cast around for someone to help them sue. (I was writing for *Gay Community News* at the time. The activist gay community was so small that I remember standing around and asking, "Do we know these people?" We didn't.) This was the problem for gay movement lawyers for mapping activist strategy for a community and a movement that people could join overnight.

LGBT movement lawyers couldn't act like the NAACP, the racial equality group that still stands as *the* model for legal civil rights activism. The legal efforts to overturn *Plessy v. Ferguson,* which instantiated "separate but equal"—the social practice of Jim Crow—all the way up to the success of *Brown v. Board of Education,* the school desegregation case that broke open the legal dam defending segregation in public accommodation, were defined by the NAACP. It enacted a careful, deliberate course. The NAACP was able to select respectable, middle-class plaintiffs and the cases that most sympathetically and effectively portrayed the harm of racial segregation—like sweet little Black third-grade girls who went to church on Sunday in white dresses, whose preference for white dolls over Black ones demonstrated to a whole generation of jurists and psychologists that school segregation was inimical to the mental health of Black children.[36] Gay folks had no such legal discipline. Anyone who was gay could apply for a marriage license, and they could probably, through informal networks, find some lawyer who was gay who would take their case to court, which would leave movement lawyers between the rock of a case they didn't see advancing movement goals and the hard place of possible losses in court that would set back the status of gay folk. So, for example, in 1990, Lambda Legal refused to participate in the first major gay marriage case, in Hawai'i. The organized gay legal community had recently lost *Bowers v. Hardwick,* the carefully chosen sodomy case that was supposed to move gay rights forward but instead resulted in the Supreme Court upholding laws criminalizing gay sex. So it came to the Hawai'i chapter of the ACLU, which took it up only reluctantly.[37] Nan Hunter of the ACLU's Lesbian and Gay Rights Project urged Hawaii's ACLU to take the temperature of gay groups in the islands before it joined the suit (which some pronounced insulting, arguing that "individual and civil rights should never be construed as a popular opinion issue"[38]). Even as late as 2009, movement lawyers were trying to stop the torrent of marriage cases, issuing an urgent missive to the gay community to stop suing states for the right to marry, "Make Change, Not Lawsuits."[39]

Up to and including the cases that were consolidated in *Obergefell v. Hodges* by 2015, the Supreme Court case that finally made same-sex marriage legal in the fifty states (and US territories and possessions, although that took a little longer to establish[40]), the plaintiffs were often the same folks at the center of the gayby boom: not necessarily white and often far from urban centers (indeed, the very demographic least likely to live in nuclear families). However, as the conservative "family-values" 1990s marched on, in the aftermath of welfare reform and other kinds of assaults on the well-being of "nontraditional" families, the persistent, growing, and widespread absence of a social safety net together with active hostility from institutions like hospitals and schools to recognizing gay kinship meant that, increasingly, family was the only obvious means for queer folks to care for dependents, and it needed to be a "legal" family. The constitutive exclusions of a gay marriage strategy—the vast numbers of gay or straight (or nonsexually tied) households and kin or family networks that were raising children outside of conjugal couples—were sometimes less important than the fact that gay marriage did get basic resources (like insurance and protection of family ties) for some.

As happened with HIV/AIDS, the politics of raising children in same-sex relationships had brought out a very different constituency than traditional gay politics had—but most weren't exchanging Cartier bracelets. By the 2000 census, it was clear that the urban white queer folks in New York and San Francisco who had long been the center of LGBT political movements were not also the center of the gayby boom. Gay parents were disproportionately likely to be Southern, rural, and people of color.[41] The census found 2 million children being raised by two same-sex parents. Their families were disproportionately poor, about twice as likely to live in poverty as the children of married, heterosexual couples. Forty-one percent of same-sex couples with children identified as people of color, compared to only 27 percent of different-sex parents. Same-sex couples lived in 96 percent of US counties, and same-sex couples in the South were more likely to be raising children than those in other regions. They also were particularly likely to be immigrants, with 6 percent of same-sex couples being of mixed status, one a U.S. citizen and the other not. Far removed geographically and socially from the urban centers in which it might have seemed imaginable to organize politically for inclusive solutions like universal health care and second (or third and fourth) parent adoption, Southern, rural gay people sought to solve the problem of their family's rights in the simplest and most obvious ways possible: through same-sex marriage.

In other contexts, the very limitations of marriage produced unlikely coalitions for domestic partnership in the hinterlands. Arizona, for example, produced the first failure of a statewide ballot measure for a "defense of marriage" act through a campaign that emphasized that it would take away domestic-partner benefits for heterosexual households where partners preserved resources (such as a pension from a previously deceased spouse) by remaining unmarried and likewise fought for domestic-partners' insurance when the legislation to ban its extension to state employees also took it away from adult dependents with disabilities, who had previously had it through parents or other household members.[42]

Legal scholar Katherine Franke has argued that the gay rights movement should have continued the strategy of fighting for rights through lawsuits like the *Braschi* case and special documents, like medical powers of attorney that carve out rights for specific individuals named as family. However, a marriage license typically costs less than $100, while the raft of documents (a will, power of attorney, durable power of attorney for medical care for the partner, and health care proxy and power of attorney for each of the children, plus in states that allow it, a home study and adoption for a second parent) that are needed to produce some family rights for queer folk requires a lawyer and thousands of dollars—and these documents don't in and of themselves have the power to compel the myriad people who are not judges or lawyers to do what you need them to do in an emergency. In 2007, for example, Lisa Pond slipped into unconsciousness alone in a Florida hospital after a brain aneurysm while her partner—who had a medical power of attorney, precisely as Karen Thompson had advocated decades earlier—and four adopted children fought to get in, or even get information about her condition, and failed. They were on vacation from Washington state when Pond collapsed suddenly and was taken by ambulance to a Miami hospital. When her partner, Janice Langbehn, arrived with the children at around 3:30 p.m., she was told by a social worker that she was in "an antigay city and state" and would need a health care proxy to get in to see her partner. Although she scrambled to get those documents faxed to the hospital at 4:15 p.m. and showed the staff the children's birth certificates with Pond's name on them, it wasn't until Pond's sister arrived near midnight that they learned from her that Pond had been moved to intensive care, got her room number, and saw their now-unconscious mother and partner, who was pronounced dead in the morning. Or similarly, Sharon Reed was denied overnight visitation with her partner, Jo Ann Richie, who was dying of liver cancer when a nurse from an employment agency barred her because she wasn't a "real" family member.[43] Although in both cases the hospital employee may have been wrong legally, that was little consolation to the families who weren't able to see their loved one when it mattered most. Everyone knows what a marriage certificate means (whether they like gay folks or not), but trying to hang onto the appropriate legal agreements or court orders and explain them to school officials, juvenile detention officers, nurses, border security guards, or TSA and airline officials (as one tries to travel with children and family members) creates myriad hassles for gay folk at best, and personal grief and tragedy at worst.

THE COURTS DO IT FOR THE CHILDREN

As lesbian and gay folks lurched, uneasily and divided, toward a politics of same-sex marriage, the courts jumped on the bandwagon of doing it "for the children." In the first successful gay marriage case, *Goodridge v. Department of Public Health* (2003), the majority decision turned on the question of children (and, to a lesser extent, other kinds of dependency, such as the plaintiffs' caring for elderly parents or each other in the event of illness or disability). Before it made it to the state supreme court, a superior court judge in Massachusetts ruled against same-sex marriage on "child" grounds, arguing that (all?) heterosexuals were "theoretically … capable of procreation," while gay folk had to rely on "inherently more cumbersome" nonsexual forms of reproduction.[44] Essentially, the judge found against gay marriage on aesthetic grounds—queer procreation wasn't sufficiently elegant.

In 2004, when the Massachusetts state supreme court's Margaret Marshall found that state policy was discriminatory and same-sex couples should be allowed to marry, her decision found that the *children* of gay folk were unfairly disadvantaged by its absence (citing issues like health insurance, taxes, and other material burdens on nonmarried couples), although she took pains to note that the state had for decades sought to eliminate any particular disadvantage to children stemming from who their parents were, such as the old legal status of "illegitimacy" or "bastardy." The opposing side had made three arguments about the purpose of restricting marriage to heterosexuals, all of which turned on children or dependency. The purpose of marriage, they suggested, was "(1) providing a 'favorable setting for procreation'; (2) ensuring the optimal setting for child rearing, which the department defines as 'a two-parent family with one parent of each sex'; and (3) preserving scarce State and private financial resources."[45] On the contrary, Marshall insisted, procreation was *not* the primary purpose of marriage, or at any rate, it was a private decision, and the state supported many forms of procreation and, since the 1980s and '90s, had done away with categorical bans on homosexuals as adoptive parents or preventing them from continuing to parent their children if they had come out in the context of divorce. Gay folks could be "excellent" parents.[46] As for the third argument, founded on the idea that gay people were less likely to comingle their finances and hence had weaker bonds not deserving of state benefits, Marshall pointed out that the plaintiffs had all joined their finances, especially for purposes of raising their children or caring for elderly parents.[47]

Although this was certainly a victory for lesbian and gay family rights, it is also worth noting what the decision did *not* say. Another justice, John Greaney, wrote a concurring opinion that argued that much of this analysis was unnecessary, that simple equality—equal protection—was sufficient to establish that lesbian and gay people ought to be granted the right to marry, as it had been in *Loving v. Virginia,* the Supreme Court decision that had overturned antimiscegenation laws as improperly racially discriminatory. The decision was also much more conservative than what lesbian and gay movement lawyers had asked for. The brief from Mary Bonauto and her cocounsels from Gay and Lesbian Advocates and Defenders (GLAD) was a ringing testament to a Massachusetts tradition of freedom and equality, reaching back to the Quock Walker case in 1781, in which a man born enslaved had successfully sued for his freedom, ending racial slavery in Massachusetts. The brief then turned to the rights of prisoners in the state and the rulings that ended eugenic sterilization, and explored the many kinds of interdependence that the state and private entities grant only to married couples, from emergency hospital visitation to health insurance and pensions to care for disabled or elderly relations.

But the court did not find for either freedom or equality. Instead, what the state supreme court granted was far more limited and couched in the neoliberal language of privatizing responsibility for dependency. The court argued that marriage, straight or gay, "provides for the orderly distribution of property, ensures that children and adults are cared for and supported whenever possible from private rather than public funds." Marriage serves to free the state from certain kinds of responsibilities (and costs), and so gay marriage could be understood to be a public good. It was about the privatization.

Whether judges found for or against same-sex marriage, they persisted in the argument that it was about the children. In *Goodridge,* the dissents were all about how having a father and mother was best for children.[48] In an Indiana case, *Morrison v. Sadler* (2005), and then again in 2006, in a New York case, *Hernandez v. Robles,* the courts found a novel reason to deny same-sex marriage—namely, the fragility of heterosexual parenting: "such relationships are all too often casual or temporary." They held that an important function of marriage was to create more stability and permanence in the relationships that cause children to be born. The state thus could choose to offer an inducement—in the form of marriage and its attendant benefits—to opposite-sex couples who make a solemn, long-term commitment to each other."[49]

Subsequent courts followed these conservatizing lines—gay marriage is about the children and privatizing responsibility for care. In fact, the 2008 California supreme court case, *In re Marriage Cases,* (subsequently upended by a ballot proposition, then affirmed by the US Supreme Court) argued:

> Society ... has an overriding interest in the welfare of children, and the role marriage plays in facilitating a stable family setting in which children may be raised by two loving parents unquestionably furthers the welfare of children and society. In addition, the role of the family in educating and socializing children serves society's interest by perpetuating the social and political culture and providing continuing support for society over generations.

It also elaborated the rhetoric of the way the state benefits from privatizing responsibilities for care:

> The legal obligations of support that are an integral part of marital and family relationships relieve society of the obligation of caring for individuals who may become incapacitated or who are otherwise unable to support themselves.[50] Society ... relies on families to play a crucial role in caring for the young, the aged, the sick, the severely disabled, and the needy. Even in advanced welfare states, families at all levels are a major resource for government, sharing the burdens of dependency with public agencies in various ways and to greater and lesser degrees.[51]

It couldn't be clearer than that: the purpose of gay marriage is to privatize dependency. A generation earlier, custody was being denied to lesbians and gay men because sodomy laws made them criminals; now, in a stunning reversal, gay folks were being made respectable because having children made them citizens.

That these were fundamentally conservative arguments was not lost on gay movement activists; this critique was the heart and soul of the "Beyond Same-Sex Marriage" statement of 2006, in which LGBT activists and intellectuals put forth a sustained argument for not making gay marriage the center and focus of queer activism. "Winning marriage equality in order to access our partners' benefits," they argued, "makes little sense if the benefits that we seek are being shredded." Marriage, they suggested, was a poor substitute for a social safety net.[52]

The case that opened the floodgates for successful same-sex marriage claims in court was the *United States v. Windsor* case, which overturned the federal Defense of Marriage Act (DOMA) in 2013. Ironically, it is the exception that really underscored the extent to which court decisions about gay marriage were all about the children and privatizing reproductive labor. The case was about estate taxes and a couple that had never had children. It, and the cases that followed from it, might reasonably have been expected to be about the right of gay and lesbian couples to be free from the tax burdens imposed on unmarried people who inherit property. On the contrary, though, Justice Anthony Kennedy, arguing for the majority, wrote about the harm inflicted on the children of queer folks, saying that DOMA "humiliates tens of thousands of children now being raised by same-sex couples. The law in question makes it even more difficult for the children to understand the integrity and closeness of their own family and its concord with other families in their community and in their daily lives."[53] This language of "humiliation" actually extended the argument about children much further; it reintroduced the concept of bastardy or illegitimacy (which previous cases had been at pains to avoid) in a Moynihanesque move that echoed neoconservative arguments about the psychological and moral harm to children of unmarried parents; it was an argument that carried distinctly racial undertones.[54] (It's also an imaginative leap; can you imagine the conversation on the elementary school playground that goes, "Nah, nah, your parents are gay!" "Yeah, but they are *married!*"? Neither can I.) While the lawyers in *Windsor* (again, not movement lawyers, it's worth noting) had solicited amicus briefs that said gay marriage would be good for children, these briefs made that claim based on the tax cost and reduced benefits to gay people, and actually specifically argued against bastardy or illegitimacy as reasonable legal concepts.[55]

Although *Windsor* was decided on federalist grounds—the federal DOMA should not be allowed to trump New York state's decision to recognize Edie Windsor's marriage to her deceased partner, Thea Spyer—it opened the door to circuit courts around the country finding a federally protected right of same-sex couples to marry under the Fourteenth Amendment's promise (originally to the freed slaves) of equal protection by US laws. In the next two years, at least forty court cases found a right to gay marriage in the Constitution. Further, following *Windsor*, courts discovered the children of queer folks—in part because a Williams Institute amicus brief in that case pointed to the 2000 census measure of how many children were being raised in lesbian and gay couples.[56] For example, the following year, in a Utah case, the Tenth Circuit found: "Like opposite-sex couples, same-sex couples may decide to marry partly or primarily for the benefits and support that marriage can provide to the children the couple is raising or plans to raise."[57] In a Virginia case, also in 2014, *Bostic v. Schaefer,* the Fourth Circuit reiterated Kennedy's language arguing for urgency about same-sex marriage, that waiting for legislation to permit gay marriage ignores the "the stigma, humiliation and prejudice that would be visited upon these citizens' children, as they continue to wait for this possibility to become realized."[58] Similarly, in *De León v.*

Perry (2015), the Fifth Circuit, combining cases from Texas, Mississippi, and Louisiana, argued, "There is no doubt that the welfare of children is a legitimate state interest; however, limiting marriage to opposite-sex couples fails to further this interest. Instead, it causes needless stigmatization and humiliation for children being raised by the loving same-sex couples being targeted."[59] Even where there were no children, the courts argued that same-sex marriage was crucial for the children.

In June 2015, the Supreme Court issued a sweeping ruling in *Obergefell* that legalized same-sex marriage. Again the majority opinion was written by Anthony Kennedy, and again he wrote solicitously about the harm to gay folks' children. Citing the Fourteenth Amendment, he found a right to "dignity" in the Constitution, embedded in the language that no state can deprive anyone of life, liberty, or property without due process of law. Writing in ringing terms, he argued that the right to same-sex marriage was animated by four principles: liberty, intimacy and privacy, the protection of children, and marriage's being fundamental to the social order. In addition to reiterating the humiliation language from *Windsor* ("The marriage laws at issue harm and humiliate the children of same-sex couples"), the decision enumerated the specific financial harms to children of denying same-sex marriage—taxing health insurance benefits of domestic partners, for example; the court also confounded the right to same-sex marriage with the right to second parent adoption, arguing that a Michigan case where a couple was forced to divide their children, each adopting some of them, visited specific harms on children who then had no legal relationship to their second parent, with all the attendant issues of being able to get medical care, register them for schools, be guaranteed an orderly custody procedure in the event of divorce or a parents' death, and so forth. While it might indeed be difficult to bar a parent's spouse from adopting, it is difficult to see exactly how this was an argument for same-sex marriage—many, many states had permitted second-parent adoption without same-sex marriage.[60] Again, the ideological force of binding marriage and children together seemed to render logical and inevitable that which was neither. Further, as Kennedy said, "without the recognition, stability, and predictability marriage offers, their children suffer the stigma of knowing their families are somehow lesser."[61]

Legal scholars would point out, correctly, that there is a difference between the legal principles espoused in *Windsor* and *Obergefell* (equal protection and due process), which have value as precedent, and the dicta, which are just basically things the justices said, which can be disregarded. But as Nan Hunter and Antonin Scalia both pointed out (for really different reasons), Kennedy's opinions in both cases relied on a notion of a constitutional affirmation of "dignity"—the dignity of gay relationships that can only be fully affirmed by marriage—that was seemingly original with him.[62]

When gay and lesbian people began fighting for the right to raise their children in the 1970s—usually but not always in the context of custody battles—and to inherit, to care for disabled or ill lovers in the context of HIV/AIDS and the Kowalski case, to stay in their housing, as in *Braschi,* they were certainly fighting for family rights. Whether they were fighting for marriage is much less clear—lesbians' fights to keep their children in custody battles while still being able to have lovers stay the night might be said to have more in common with welfare mothers' and single mothers' battles than any fight for the "dignity" of marriage. Indeed, for most of the past forty years, the "dignity" of marriage has been deployed more often and more thoroughly as weapon against the families of gay folks than for them. While *Obergefell* and other gay marriage rulings and legislative battles certainly conferred rights on some gay and lesbian families, they did nothing for others, especially where the parents are not a conjugal couple but may include three or more people, either as a nonmonogamous relationship or as an extended "chosen family." By upholding the special circle drawn around married couples and granting them family rights—even as it made that circle bigger by including same-sex couples—the courts affirmed the specialness of certain kinds of families even as it denied the importance of other kinds of families—of siblings raising each other or sharing homes as adults, of "Golden Girls"–style relationships between elderly folks, and above all, of single mothers.[63]

Gay marriage represented a turn to the new normal, in the aftermath of decades of destruction of security for various kinds of families: those headed by single mothers, working mothers, immigrant families. While the courts finding a constitutional right to gay marriage for the children might, superficially, seem like the opposite of the conservative pressure on reproductive labor represented by the failure of business or government to make it possible for people to take time off to care for children, elders, or other dependent family members (whether through longer work hours or declining real wages), in another sense they are close kin. The double day may be nearly impossible to pull off, but it's all there is. What queer folks learned in the 1980s is that there's no else to do care work than *legal* families joined by marriage; anyone else can be torn away by courts and homophobes. Furthermore, beginning in the late 1970s, the dream of a state (much less business or any other employment sector) that would support the reproductive labor of households died a long, slow, agonizing death. What was left in its place were the intensely privatized bonds of care in the family (some laced through with affection and love, others with violence and threats). Individuals outside of households could not be dependent on others for care; the mechanisms that might have existed to support chosen families and paid caregivers—state pensions for the elderly, AFDC for single (or battered) women and their kids, well-paid (and hence reliable) attendant care for people with disabilities—were all vanishing into thin air. Gay families were similarly essential for people's security (gaybies, elderly, sick, disabled queers—everyone at some point in their lives), and the more the legal assault on their well-being continued, the more essential gay marriage became. As a reproductive politics issue, same-sex marriage facilitated the privatization of dependency in both a queerly affirming and profoundly conservative way.

Epilogue

The Subprime

This chapter argues that reproductive labor, its relationship to what we formally consider politics and economics, and how we differently value people's lives by race are at the heart of most of the things we disagree about in the United States: feminism, welfare, immigration, infertility and infant mortality, gay marriage. The massive neoliberal shift that began in the late 1970s fundamentally realigned the relationships of households, government, and business such that social reproduction and reproductive labor stopped receiving much support from government (including for schools, housing, and public safety), and frozen real wages sent every available adult into the labor force and then to try their luck on debt markets, in an effort to keep their household afloat. This neoliberal privatization of care has been the core question at the back of nearly every other public policy issue, including the election of Donald Trump, who campaigned with the old racist promise to white people: white working people's pockets are empty because of people of color (immigrants and Black criminals); put your faith in the white ruling class (we'll keep your wages low but you'll get to feel superior to nonwhite people). Trump offered "globalization," a racialized boogeyman of immigrants and free trade agreements, as the name of the problem in place of "neoliberalism," the political movement among the 1 percent to shrink government, unions, and wages and redistribute wealth upwards. For decades, the neoliberal movement accomplished its political goals in particular through race-based shaming of supposedly irresponsible reproductive behavior—an account of Black "welfare queens" and Latina "breeding machines."

Trump's presidency has been portrayed by some as an historical earthquake, radically discontinuous with what came before. Who could have predicted that at a time of rising employment rates, US Americans would vote economic resentment of the Democratic Party? Wall Street would, of course, continue to back the Republican promise of low taxes and small government, but how would they pick up enough other votes to win power? How could one foresee a hostile takeover of the Republican Party by business interests that had long been slightly offstage, the recentering of racism in US public life in a way it hadn't been since Reconstruction (or at least the anti–civil rights backlash), and the upending of democratic traditions in favor of an authoritarian populism that may or may not resemble fascism? From one perspective, it was a radical shift. But the historical developments I've been pursuing in this book provide plenty of evidence of continuities. Welfare reform and anti-immigrant deportation and detention (in a labor sector dominated by household workers) over the past thirty years suggest something of the centrality of racism in our public policy, even if they happened under the more comforting pretexts of ending "dependency" or crime. The economic misery of the 99 percent has been periodically evident in uprisings like the

Occupy movement, but in quite a sustained way in our struggles over households and reproductive labor.

My argument in this book has been that the reproductive politics of households has been one of the key sites where the racist argument for neoliberalism has been advanced and where we have lived our immiseration—not just as less money but also as time famine, where there is never enough of it to allow for kind and generous care of dependents because the formal labor market has sucked up so much of it. The politics of households is also where anxiety about the state of the economy and a vigorous suppression of claims for public support for reproductive labor have been debated as public policy. Further, even as households have less time, they have more responsibilities as the space of public, shared labor and support for dependents disappears. For example, the anxiety around the public school Common Core curriculum might be crystallized in the web pages for parents about how to help their kindergartner (or tenth grader) with Common Core concepts.[1] When, exactly, did we start looking to parents rather than teachers to take responsibility for a community's children's learning? Presumably it was sometime around when neoliberal tax cutting producing scarcity and austerity hit communities and their school budgets—a slightly different moment depending on how impoverished the school systems (and communities) were to begin with, clearly, but certainly a problem that has been creeping up the economic ladder. Even parents who were not Christian Right homeschoolers (who avoided public school because of the teaching of evolution and climate change) became de facto teachers as communities disinvested in schools through tax reduction and budget cuts.

If this argument is correct, we can perform this analysis on nearly any issue—my contention is that reproductive politics govern a great deal of what we have said, and not said, in public discourse. Consider, for example, the work of creating the kinds of safe communities people need to raise their kids, free from police harassment and violence. Mass incarceration—the doubling of the percentage of the US population that goes to jail or prison since the 1970s—has a devastating effect on children: 10 million kids (including one in nine Black children) have experienced parental incarceration, and the increasing use of police officers in schools to handle routine discipline has given rise to what activists terms a "school to prison pipeline."[2] The charter school movement takes money out of the mainstream public schools even as charter schools cherry pick which kids they educate,[3] and some environmental movements blame environmental degradation on too many kids even as polluting corporations assume less and less responsibility for near-epidemic rates of asthma in some communities ... the list goes on and on.

Equally, we could talk about how US foreign policy has relied on an account of reproductive politics. Historically, US development policy relied on an anti-Communist push to reduce "overpopulation" through birth control and sterilization and on loans and tax relief programs designed to promote industrialization that would employ this smaller work force. These are the same loans that ultimately gave way to the Third World debt crisis, as changes in financial policies allowed the cost of this debt to rise exponentially, and the tax relief programs gave rise to US corporate globalization and the offshoring of manufacturing. Or we could look to Cold War militarization and the way the kidnapping of children in Latin America ultimately gave rise to a multi-billion-dollar transnational adoption industry. In fact, my previous books (*Reproducing Empire* and *Somebody's Children*) focused on these very questions.

By way of an epilogue, though, I want to tell one more story about how reproductive politics occupied the center of U.S. public policy fights over the economy: the financial meltdown of 2007–08, specifically housing market speculation by the financial services industry. I will focus on subprime mortgages—the balloon payments, adjustable rates, and introductory teasers—that were offered to "subprime" borrowers instead of the conventional thirty-year, fixed rate mortgages established under the New Deal. What does the economic crisis have to do with reproductive politics? A great deal, as I discovered one night when I walked into a meeting in Springfield, Massachusetts, of No One Leaves, which has protested the foreclosure crisis by keeping people in their homes[4]—about 90 percent of the seats in the room were occupied by Black and Puerto Rican women and their children. The foreclosure crisis was (and still is) disproportionately felt by single mothers and children. It was, in fact, a replay of the welfare and immigration reform debates of the 1990s.

As we have seen, the denigration of some people of color's reproductive labor has been a key piece of conservative strategy in advancing neoliberal ways of thinking about businesses' goal of maximizing profits (through low wages in particular) and shrinking taxes (by shrinking public benefits) since welfare reform. Because we are schooled to think of what happens at home as distinct from the economy, it might seem like a reach to consider the nasty things people say about how people of color raise their kids to be transformative of the economy or politics. But it is. In the early 2000s, women heads of household across the United States became some of the largest consumers of subprime loans. Many of the women who wanted to buy a house were single mothers with children. As journalist Laura Gottesdiener noted, a disproportionate number were also older Black women who owned their homes but were cash-strapped, often having been the financial rock for multiple generations.[5] In 2006, when the bottom started to fall out of the housing market, these loans could not be refinanced; Black and Latinx borrowers, systematically dispossessed of land and assets across generations, were unlikely to have family resources to turn to. However, the early wave of foreclosures did not cause much concern because, as scholar David Harvey noted, "the people affected were low income, mainly African American and immigrant (Hispanics) or women single-headed households."[6] Even earlier, in 1999, Elizabeth Warren noted more broadly that in two decades, the number of women who had declared bankruptcy had grown 600 percent, and among single mothers with children, one in seven had declared bankruptcy.[7]

These were the canaries in the coal mine that might have told policy makers that unregulated financial markets were destroying people's lives; when we look back, we find many unheard voices among activists who cared about racial or gender justice for mortgage reform. But these warnings went unheeded. When, as a result of this sharp rise in foreclosures, the recession began in earnest in 2007 and unregulated financial market losses turned into layoffs and unemployment, still more people were unable to make mortgage payments, and, within months, a death spiral hit the housing market, making it impossible to sell. Single mothers and their children were disproportionately hit by foreclosure. While many were able to double up with relatives or friends, others became homeless.

In 2008, the *New York Times* ran a piece saying as much, looking at Black women homeowners in Baltimore—single mothers for the most part—and showing that bankers had disproportionately targeted them for subprime mortgages.[8] The response was instructive, suggesting how both bankers and op-ed page editors (mis)read these facts in terms of the moral failings of borrowers: a letter from a Baltimore mortgage lender ran the next week, lamenting that these women were losing their homes or borrowing from friends and family to pay extraordinarily mortgage payments, but, he wrote,

> a big part is missing from the media coverage, and it's exactly the reason people took out subprime loans—they had bad credit and posed a big risk to the lenders. Bad credit means missed payments on cars, 30-, 60-, 90-day late payments on credit cards, bankruptcies and so on.... For the most part these people put themselves in a position in which the subprime loan was their only option.[9]

Not mortgage brokers who underwrote discriminatory loans or sought out borrowers they thought unlikely to repay as a way to make a buck, but irresponsible mothers were at fault. As early as 2007, Glenn Beck on Fox News was blaming "illegal immigrant" home buyers, and commentators across Fox were complaining that the Clinton administration had made loans to Blacks and Hispanics, whom they blamed as the morally inferior and financially illiterate cause of the subprime crisis.[10]

The Moynihan report narrative that had animated the welfare reform smears of the 1990s—that the moral failings of Black single mothers were the cause of all the poverty in the Black community, as well as much of what ailed the nation—was more than a way to blame the vulnerable rather than the lenders for the recession. It was, substantially, the cause of the recession. For decades, lenders were trolling for "high risk" borrowers, not content to wait until borrowers shopped for a loan. As one lender admitted, his preferred borrower was an elderly, widowed woman of color living on a fixed income who owned her home and could be persuaded to borrow against it. If she lost her home and could not pay rising interest rates, well, the broker had long since received his fee and the lender who had originated the high-interest loan had already sold it at a profit.[11] For example, consider the case of Flora, whom Elizabeth Warren interviewed in her research on bankruptcy:

> She explained that she and her husband had retired and moved to a small town in the South a few decades earlier to be near family. They bought a modest house. ("That's all we needed.") Flora's husband had passed on, and she was on her own now. Flora said that until recently she had been doing fine, getting by on her Social Security check each month.
>
> Flora explained that she'd gotten a call a few years ago from "a nice man from the bank." She said he'd told her that because interest rates were low, he could give her a mortgage with a lower payment. She'd asked him what would happen to the payment if interest rates went back up. According to Flora, he'd assured her that "the banks know about these things in advance" and that he would "call her and put her back in her old mortgage."
>
> She had taken the deal, and before long, her payments had shot up. She paused, then said quietly, "He never called." The new monthly payment swallowed nearly every penny of her Social Security check. She had tried delaying her payments, borrowing on credit cards, going to a payday lender, but it had all come crashing down.
>
> Next week she would have to leave her home. "I'll be living in my car," she said, "at least for a while."[12]

In a practice activists called "reverse redlining," mortgage lenders sought out Black, Latinx, and female-headed households for mortgages, urging them to considering buying homes, and then "charging them through the roof," as one activist told the *Wall Street Journal*. Subprime industry executives, politicians, and federal regulators fought to keep this high-profit industry expanding, continually easing lending standards.[13] Banking deregulation in the 1980s and '90s incentivized lenders to make loans that were unlikely to be paid back. The lower the borrowers' credit score, the higher the interest rate could go. Securitization meant that mortgage loans and credit card debt could be bundled together and sold, so that no particular bank was responsible if any individual loan was not repaid. Other deregulation measures allowed an ever-expanding array of entities to make loans, so mortgage brokers made increasing profits off origination fees associated with loans, and these too were higher for subprime than conventional loans.[14] "Who was allowed to buy what type of mortgage was so stark," says Laura Gottesdiener in *A Dream Foreclosed,* that the word 'subprime' (the industry's term for predatory loans) became 'a demographic category as much as a financial definition.'"[15] The expectation that these households were morally suspect and unlikely to pay their debts is precisely what had made lenders seek them out for mortgages. In the 1990s, fully one-third of borrowers eligible for conventional loans were steered into subprime loans, because they were much more profitable for brokers and lenders but much more expensive, usually, for borrowers to repay. Win-win for the financial services industry, and when it became clear that government would bail out financial institutions such as AIG that had purchased the bundled high-risk loans (although not Bear Stearns, which was scooped up by J.P. Morgan Chase at bargain-basement rates)—and administrations from Bush to Obama have admitted that all their loan reforms were designed to protect lenders, not homeowners—all the risk devolved onto borrowers, and predatory lenders never paid a price.[16]

Scholars Paula Chakravartty and Denise Ferreira da Silva note that what followed was a wave of condemnation against the "subprime," a category of people "construed as intellectually (illiterate) and morally (greedy), unfit if measured against any existing descriptors of the modern economic subject." Economist Brigitte Young points out, "Mortgage banks targeted women across the board as 'risk borrowers' in relation to men in similarly situated circumstances."[17] Nevertheless, the Black, Latinx, and female subjects of discriminatory treatment in credit markets were taken to be at fault for not paying unpayable loans. After seeking out borrowers based on the bet that these loans couldn't be paid, which drove up the interest rate and origination fees, the lenders could turn around and blame the borrowers for not paying them.

To add insult to injury, it wasn't just those who were behind on their mortgages who were foreclosed on. Lawyers' mortgages earned massive fees, and "foreclosure mill" law firms began to take advantage of judges' inattention and targeted people who should not have been foreclosed on, backdating and falsifying the documents that were supposed to demonstrate what the "subprime" predicted all along: that women and people of color in particular would not pay their bills. Arguably, though, it showed the opposite: like the sharecroppers and agricultural workers who were paid in scrip at the company store and denied access to the ledgers that supposedly showed them in arrears two or three generations ago, societies structured in dominance by geography, race, and gender produced debt bondage, poverty, and homelessness among working folk and single mothers and their kids through fraud and theft. The firm at the epicenter the robo-signing scandal of 2010, David J. Stern, had offices in Miami, San Juan, and Manila, signaling the complicity of massive corruption and sedimented colonialism.[18]

HOW WE GOT HERE

In producing securitized subprime mortgages, mortgage brokers and banks were following the lessons learned in the context of the Third World debt crisis, where unpaid loans yielded more loan products banks can sell, and debts accrued in the 1950s, '60s, and '70s have been repaid over and over, yielding a usurious balance of payments from South to North. Although this process was already under way throughout the era of development, it became embodied in its current, almost surreal form in 1973, when the OPEC oil embargo resulted in a sharp rise in the cost of everything for most nations and currency devaluations in the wake of global inflation that hit Africa and Latin America particularly hard. Meanwhile, OPEC nations deposited massive reserves of petrodollars in New York banks, and as a result, New York was awash in available credit and desperate to be able to make a profit off those extra dollars. As the cost of Latin American and African debt rose on devalued currencies, nations were persuaded to borrow more to pay that debt, albeit at higher rates, given that the loans were more risky. (Indeed, the austerity plans for Third World debt crises—structural adjustment policies that shutter schools and hospitals and raise food prices—are also disproportionately felt by mothers.) Like casinos, New York banks learned to make a fortune off of nothing but risk and money.

Gender and race were explicitly categories through which creditworthiness was understood, and credit markets worked in parallel ways to prevent women of whatever race and people of color of whatever gender from participating in the accumulation of wealth throughout the United States in ways that interlocked with imperial dispossession. But race and gender also acted in ways different from each other. Prior to the Equal Credit Opportunity Act of 1974 and 1976, married women were explicitly barred from personal credit markets—able to get credit cards or loans only in their husbands' name—and redlining prevented people of color from accessing mortgages. Congressional hearings on both demonstrated how local lenders, dependent on loans being repaid, used race and gender as a proxy for reliable financial information about the future (or a crystal ball). For example, a single mom told the following story:

> I was pre-approved for a loan prior to house hunting. The night before I closed on my home the underwriter determined that I was a risk because I was a single mother with two children and two jobs.... There was an attorney involved in one of the homes up the chain and he contacted the underwriter to inform her that he would take my discrimination case pro-bono and she backed down. I got my home, it just took a few extra days. That was 18 years ago. I'm still working 2 jobs. My children are in college and I've never missed a mortgage payment.[19]

Similarly, if a heterosexual couple shopping for a mortgage wanted to count a woman's income toward their creditworthiness, they needed to certify her infertility or sterilization, or, in states where abortion was legal, sign a "baby letter" certifying that they would abort any future pregnancies to allow her to stay in her job. If a woman was divorced, abandoned, or widowed, she lost the credit history developed during her marriage, while her husband kept it. A woman who was single, queer, or, perhaps worst of all, an unmarried mother, rarely had access to either a credit card or a mortgage, and her financial fate was linked to cash wages and rented housing.

Redlining was written into federal housing policy in the 1930s, when the New Deal established the Federal Housing Authority of the Federal Housing Administration (FHA), designed in that earlier depression to combat the evictions that the socialist left was objecting to by stabilizing credit markets. From the FHA, we got thirty-year, low-rate mortgages and explicit racial discrimination. The FHA instructed lenders in redlining, in fact, requiring it: "the valuator should investigate areas surrounding the location to determine whether or not incompatible racial and ethnic groups are present, to that end an intelligent prediction may be made regarding the possibility or probability of the location being invaded by such groups." The 1968 Fair Housing Act rendered this practice illegal, along with refusing to sell or rent to people based on race.[20] In subsequent decades, as the mortgage crisis revealed, banks just hired the shady lenders who had been providing financing in redlined neighborhoods and learned how to get into the loan-shark business themselves, by providing financing at usurious rates to the people they used to refuse to lend to at all.

WHERE WE ARE NOW

The belief that distressed mortgage borrowers were morally suspect also governed the response to calls for the federal government to intervene in the mortgage meltdown. Although many advocates for relief to distressed homeowners made compelling arguments about why it was in the best interest of the nation's economy to help them keep their houses, the hoped-for mortgage bailout never really appeared. Despite pious promises, 5 million families lost their homes from 2007 to 2015, resulting in a 30–40 percent reduction of the wealth of the middle class—concentrated among Black, Latinx, and female-headed households. First TARP—the Troubled Asset Relief Program offered in 2008 under the Bush administration—and then HAMP—the Home

Affordable Modification Program from the Obama administration—failed, by design, to keep people in their homes. Prosecutor Neil Barofsky, the special inspector general for TARP, was so disgusted by that program and how it was used to reward what he called "Wall Street crooks" that he wrote a book entitled *Bailout: How Washington Abandoned Main Street While Rescuing Wall Street.*[21] These programs gave billions to banks, regardless of whether they engaged in wrongdoing, but refused to offer more than a pittance to homeowners.

The key debate was about whether these programs should offer principal reduction to homeowners—about whether, because they bought their homes in a market with inflated prices superheated by predatory mortgage transactions that benefited the banks, the government mortgage authorities could reduce their loans to reflect the sober, morning-after reality of what people's homes were actually worth in the Great Recession. For the most part, Republicans were explicitly against this proposal, while the subsequent Democratic administration hid its opposition behind happy-sounding promises of programs to reduce principal but in practice, many argued, was just another giveaway to the banks. Both, revealingly, couched their reservations in moral terms. Timothy Geithner, Obama's treasury secretary, explained that principal reduction would create incentives for borrowers who were not in trouble to stop paying their mortgages in order to get the principal reduced, which he dubbed a "moral hazard."[22]

CNBC's Rick Santelli, reporting from the Chicago commodity pits, apparently didn't get the word that the Democrats were never going to refinance people's principal and made the conservative case against refinancing mortgages when Obama's bailout was announced in 2009, in what was later billed as the rant that launched the Tea Party: "Government is promoting bad behavior.... Do we really want to subsidize the losers' mortgages? This is America! How many of you people want to pay for your neighbor's mortgage? President Obama, are you listening? How about we all stop paying our mortgages! It's a moral hazard." While the hard-right *National Review* cheered Santelli, Charles Demos at the progressive blog My Direct Democracy (MyDD), called Santelli a racist:

> After watching the [Santelli clip], I first had to check my calendar. Somehow I felt I traveled back in time to the early 1970s to witness first hand Richard Nixon's "northern strategy," his pursuit of white ethnic voters who were so deeply disaffected over Great Society programs ranging from desegregation (remember the Boston busing madness?) to affirmative action among others that they would desert the Democratic Party becoming "Nixon's silent majority" and "Reagan Democrats."
>
>   Rick Santelli is heir to this legacy laced with racist overtones. Note the promo before the rant in the video link at CNBC. CNBC has an upcoming special entitled *The Rise of America's New Black Overclass*. Fear mongering, it's worked before so let's try it again. It's back to the 1970s for the GOP and their rabid white ethnics.[23]

At the same time that Fox News and even the mainstream press were blaming "illegal immigrants" and (subprime) loans to Black and Hispanic borrowers, the Tea Party was born, in part out of the demand that all these unworthy families, many female-headed, be put in the street, that government aid to those conspicuously badly treated by the banks was just another giveaway to unworthy people of color. It was a preview of the Trump electoral strategy.

Perhaps the cruelest cut, though, was HAMP, a 2012 election-year promise to refinance mortgages for distressed borrowers to let them and their children stay in their homes. In fact, as Treasury Secretary Geithner admitted in a meeting that included two of his main critics, Elizabeth Warren (who anchored the progressive wing of the Democratic party under Obama, and often explicitly argued against him) and Neil Barofsky, HAMP was designed to ease foreclosure for the benefit of the banks—to slow rather than stop foreclosures in order to protect the banks from more foreclosures than they could handle at any one time.[24] Barofsky wrote:

> For a good chunk of our allotted meeting time, Elizabeth Warren grilled Geithner about HAMP, barraging him with questions about how the program was going to start helping home owners. In defense of the program, Geithner finally blurted out, "We estimate that they can handle ten million foreclosures, over time," referring to the banks. "This program will help foam the runway for them." A light bulb went on for me. Elizabeth had been challenging Geithner on how the program was going to help homeowners, and he had responded by citing how it would help the *banks*. Geithner apparently looked at HAMP as an aid to the banks, keeping the full flush of foreclosures from hitting the financial system all at the same time. Though they could handle up to "10 million foreclosures" over time, any more than that, or if the foreclosures were too concentrated, and the losses that the banks might suffer on their first and second mortgages could push them into insolvency, requiring yet another round of TARP bailouts. So HAMP would "foam the runway" by stretching out the foreclosures, giving the banks more time to absorb losses while the other parts of the bailouts juiced bank profits that could then fill the capital holes created by housing losses.[25]

Elizabeth Warren wrote after that same meeting, "The Treasury foreclosure program was intended to foam the runway to protect against a crash landing *by the banks*. Millions of people were getting tossed out on the street, but the secretary of the Treasury believes that government's most important job was to provide a soft landing for the tender fannies of the banks. Oh Lord."[26] Fewer than 1 million loans were modified, and many argued that these were low-hanging fruit—loans banks would've agreed to refinance anyway.

In *Bailout*, Barofsky documented rampant and criminal fraud by mortgage servicers in HAMP, as well as two strategies that were perfectly legal but that can be only be called scams by the banks. "One particularly pernicious type of abuse," wrote Barofsky,

> was that servicers would direct borrowers who were current on their mortgages to start skipping payments, telling them that they would allow them to qualify for a HAMP modification. The servicers thereby racked up more late fees, and meanwhile many of the borrowers might have been entitled to participate in HAMP even if they had never missed a payment. Those led to some of the most heartbreaking cases. Homeowners who might have been able to ride out the crisis instead ended up in long trial modifications, after which the servicers would deny them a permanent modification and then send them an enormous "deficiency" bill.[27]

One such homeowner made a video that she put on YouTube that told the story of how she and her son lost their home when their mortgage payment was adjusted after the lender had promised her that she could refinance and keep her lower payments. When she called the bank to find out what had happened, she was told that she would be eligible for an adjusted mortgage, but she should stop making her mortgage payments, which she did, as instructed, for four months. Then the bank put her loan in "forbearance" and began charging new, higher payments, including a $10,000 deficiency payment that she paid for by selling her furniture. She subsequently discovered that "Servicers made more money servicing loans in default than loans that were current, so they encouraged borrowers to default so they could review a modification package. Forbearance payments *do not* go to the loan balance but rather to a suspense account most likely used to pay attorneys and trustees to foreclose." The loan servicers demanded piles of paperwork, and then, after several more months, determined that she was not eligible for a new mortgage. The bank foreclosed.[28]

The second rampant but, again, legal scam was to create a two-track system within the banks, where one side would be negotiating a "trial" mortgage adjustment with the homeowner and the other would be proceeding with a foreclosure. They won both ways: during the "trial" modification period, loan servicers would rack up big fees (because as long as the modification was not final, borrowers were technically "late"—by design—on portions of their mortgage), pocket the partial payments, then deny the modification because of "incomplete" paperwork (homeowners in HAMP modification proceedings reported that banks "lost" their paperwork over and over again, in what many suspected was a deliberate scam—one survey found that homeowners had to submit it an *average* of six times[29]), and then foreclose on the home anyway and resell it. "HAMP was not separate from the bank bailouts," Barofsky wrote, "it was an essential part of them. From that perspective, it didn't matter if the modifications failed after a year or so of trial payments or if struggling borrowers placed into doomed trial modifications end up far worse off."[30] This explained a particularly cruel feature of these modifications: even if you actually got one, in five years the interest rate ballooned, which meant that a borrower would see her payment go up by as much as 23 percent. The same adjustable-rate feature that was criticized as part of sub-prime mortgages was built into HAMP. The only difference was that this one was explicitly given the government's blessing.

If predatory lending had been the norm before 2007, no lending was the order of the day subsequently. Some accused banks of a "credit strike," a refusal to extend credit to consumers until their institutions were offered more favorable terms. Warren explained, "The American people were told that the bailout would make it possible for banks to start lending to small businesses again and to help relieve the foreclosure crisis. But once those no-strings-attached checks were distributed to the big banks, that promise evaporated like a tiny ice cube in the desert."[31] And because the banks operate in an intensely racialized and gendered political economic culture, once again, mothers in particular were looked on as "discreditable" by mortgage underwriters, with recent lawsuits revealing an industry practice of refusing to lend to anyone out on maternity leave. A New York oncologist reported being denied a loan when the lender discovered she was on maternity leave, because the originator concluded she must be out on disability. She wasn't; she was using accrued sick and vacation days and being paid her full salary.[32]

When her story came out in the *New York Times,* others came forward to report similar experiences. One new mother, Carly Neals, was approved for a mortgage by PNC Mortgage, but she was then asked to buy mortgage insurance because of a high loan-to-value ratio. PNC contacted Mortgage Guaranty Insurance Corporation (MGIC) for the insurance, which then requested a verification that she had a two-months reserve in the bank. Neals arranged to have her transaction history faxed from her bank, with a note that her salary had been deposited in two parts because she was on maternity leave. MGIC responded that it couldn't give her mortgage insurance if she was out on maternity. It refused multiple letters from her employer saying that "Carly is an active full-time employee of mine" and required a pay stub. The loan processor at PNC, acting as go-between, wrote Neals that "unfortunately the one showing paternal *[sic]* time off is not going to work." Neals ultimately got the loan and the mortgage insurance—PNC said they had made an "exception" in her case—but she decided that she didn't want to deal with the company any more. She got her mortgage elsewhere and sued them for violations of the Fair Credit Act.[33]

Other women report the return of the "baby letter," where banks ignore a woman's earnings unless she promises not to have a baby or signs a letter saying that she will continue to work after the birth of a child, based on the presumption that a woman of childbearing age cannot be trusted to make rational financial decisions in light of the fact that she can get pregnant (and, though it's never said this way, because many women feel forced to leave the workforce after the birth of a child because good child care options are terribly hard to find, and the ding to the career if you are a mother—though not a father—is substantial and painful.)[34]

No one ever asked a bank to sign a baby letter promising to give all their employees high-quality child care, paid maternity leave, enough sick days to cover the needs of raising a human, or a 40-hour workweek for all to level the playing field. No one ever held them to account for the fact that the unequal distribution of poverty and the consequences of living in a racist society (to randomly pick two well-documented material effects of racism: losing your job because, as a person of color, you can't make bail after the police arrested you for getting a straw with your soda, which they took to be drug paraphernalia, and being judged incompetent just for showing up to work as a person of color[35]), not moral failings, creates strings of failure and stress that make Black and Latinx buyers struggle more to pay loans. Certainly, no one held the banks, securities investors, and mortgage service companies responsible for the moral hazard of the immense misery they created by profiting off of racism and sexism with overt scams that should have been criminal but were perfectly legal, putting millions of people out of their homes and tanking the economy. On the contrary, the government bailed them out.

This book has been arguing that the story about "losers' mortgages" and the "subprime as a demographic category" that made the banks and the financial services industry rich before and after the foreclosure crisis was the rule, not the exception. The massive changes in the economy since the late 1970s—stagnant real wages, shrinking government support for everything from schools to roads to welfare, "personal responsibility" and "moral hazard" as the reasons for vast public policy changes—were driven in significant part through a demonization of the reproductive labor of people understood to be women, particularly women of color, and all people who do care work. These economic changes were first called "neoliberalism" by activists in Cold War Latin America[36] (not in the US American sense of liberal versus conservative but in the economic sense of liberalism as free market fundamentalism), who were identifying an activist program by authoritarian, often military-led governments, characterized by austerity in the public sector and the private enrichment of elites. As Milton Friedman, Ronald Reagan, and Margaret Thatcher brought these economic programs to Latin America as the intensification of World Bank loans and structural adjustment programs, they encountered fierce pushback in the United States (as activist resistance to "Reaganomics"). However, just as Reagan himself campaigned for election by telling a story about "welfare queens" driving Cadillacs and getting rich off the government dole, conservatives in the United States used an account of irresponsible Black and Latinx women and their children to beat back that activism.

BY WAY OF CONCLUSION

As I hope this foreclosure example demonstrates, the politics of reproduction are key to understanding our shared political life in the United States. Reproductive politics and reproductive labor—the work of reproducing the species, from having babies to caring for elders—animate a great deal of what we collectively talk about, from the blogosphere to talk radio to newspapers and books. Its political force is powerful, if not always transparent. We think we are talking about whether immigrants on iffy visas are (all?) rapists, and then, boom, it turns out that most of them are women cleaning our homes and caring for children or elders or disabled folks. We think we are talking about the politics of designer babies and rich ladies who don't want stretch marks, and then it turns out that we are really dealing with the consequences of postponing children until we have earned a college degree and are established in our careers, or the barely acknowledged racial disparities in health and infant death. We listen to folks hating or defending LGBT people through the politics of same-sex marriage, and we realize that a long fight for family rights for many ultimately wound up with marriage rights for a few—and that judges did it "for the children," so that the children of queer folks wouldn't wind up on the public dole. We look back to the end of welfare and the demonization of Black women who supposedly had babies to increase their welfare check, and we realize it was a cover story to force them to work for Walmart or McDonald's for minimum wage and park their kids in substandard day care. We hear conservatives blaming feminists for the work/life time crunch and realize that corporations never changed the expectation that all workers were supposed to be available to work all the time—they just expected mothers (and fathers) to adjust.

Reproductive politics are everywhere. Virtually every demonized figure, everyone that conservative or liberals love to hate, is an emblem of our frustration with the impossibility of both finding enough material resources to support our families and households—wages, a home, reliable transportation, schools—and the huge demands on our time to get these things (if we can find a job, a loan, a pension), such that we don't have time to care for infants, children, elders, and those who are sick or in need of care. We are persuaded to hate irresponsible breeders, welfare mothers, and "illegal" immigrants—or the imaginary figures that stand in for people—because they are compact symbols of the near impossibility of managing the money/time problem, not just for poor folks but now for a huge swath of the middle class as well. While this fear and loathing is not limited to white people, it is overwhelmingly the mobilization of whiteness that turns it into something truly dangerous.

There are clearly things that would help:

- A 40-hour workweek, for example—and not just for the lucky few hourly wageworkers with unionized, benefited jobs.
- Paid parental leave—and not just at a handful of workplaces that are competing fiercely for highly trained workers, such as web workers at Netflix or Adobe, where

individuals are allowed to fend for themselves with maternity leave—if their boss agrees, and they can show that they can still do their work, they can have parental leave (although in reality, it's a perk that few can take advantage of; when the norm is that people who "really" care about their job don't take parental leave, very few do get to go on leave with their new infant).

- An actual social safety net—including food stamps that don't require a day waiting in line, SSI/SSDI that doesn't automatically deny people the first time, a return of AFDC for single mothers with small children and no job—that can support people who are struggling and also take a burden off the extended family network that may be trying, and failing, to support family members who are not making it.
- Less policing and more support for people leaving abusive relationships.
- Schools that don't expel stressed-out kids with disabilities or behavior issues, and high-quality, well-funded public schools.
- Free, high-quality preschool that would take a care burden off families while providing tangible educational benefits for children that last their lifetime.
- An end to discriminatory lending and policing.
- School schedules that match 40-hour workweeks, are compatible with higher education, and give kids real opportunities to run, climb, relax, and build friendships.
- Free higher education.
- Living wages for low-paid workers in McJobs, as represented by the "Fight for $15" campaign.

- Cleaning up toxic environments—psychological and physical—that cause miscarriages, infertility, asthma, cancer, and other chronic diseases.
- Family rights for all households where people provide care and share resources with each other.

These are not expensive fixes, if money is even the right question, in the sense that even major corporations have long since realized that easing work/life burdens improves productivity. The politics of racial division that brought Donald Trump to power (and, before him, Richard Nixon and Ronald Reagan) may make these goals seem out of reach. At the top, in banks for example, race and gender are being deliberately used as a force to manipulate access to things like fair loans, good jobs, and favorable public policies. The withdrawal of support for reproductive labor by business and government (alongside comparable shifts in paid labor, including the offshoring of manufacturing) is also what makes racial resentment available for use as political force to divide working- and middle-class people. The political movements of the middle of the twentieth century got a lot of things right, including especially the importance of a politics of expanding social supports for family, households, and communities. We can't understand the rise of Trump, or combat the forces he represents, without attention to reproductive politics.

NOTES

INTRODUCTION

1. Personal online communication, May 19, 2016.

2. Geduldig v. Aiello, 417 U.S. 484 (1974).

3. Jonathan Rausch, "The No Good, Very Bad Outlook for the Working-Class American Man." *The Atlantic,* December 5, 2012. www.theatlantic.com/business/archive/2012/12/the-no-good-very-bad-outlook-for-the-working-class-american-man/426288/.

4. Joan C. Williams and Heather Boushey, "The Three Faces of Work-Family Conflict: The Poor, the Professionals, and the Missing Middle," Center for New American Progress, January 25, 2010, www.americanprogress.org/issues/labor/report/2010/01/25/7194/the-three-faces-of-work-family-conflict/.

5. "Leisure Time Plummets 20% in 2008—Hits New Low," *HarrisInteractive,* December 4, 2008, www.harrisinteractive.com/vault/Harris-Interactive-Poll-Research-Time-and-Leisure-2008–12.pdf.

6. Victor Fuchs, quoted in Juliet Schor, *The Overworked American: The Unexpected Decline of Leisure* (New York: Basic Books, 2008), 12.

7. Terrance Heath, "Katrina and Conservative Failure, Ten Years Later," *CommonDreams,* August 19, 2015, www.commondreams.org/views/2015/08/19/katrina-and-conservative-failure-ten-years-later.

8. For a discussion of crack and pregnancy, see Wendy Chavkin, "Cocaine and Pregnancy: Time to Look at the Evidence," *Journal of the American Medical Association* 285 (2001): 1626–28.

9. ACLU, "Facts about the Over-Incarceration of Women in the United States," n.d., www.aclu.org/other/facts-about-over-incarceration-women-united-states.

10. Laura Briggs, "'Crack Babies,' Race, and Adoption Reform, 1975–2000," chap. 3 in *Somebody's Children: The Politics of Transracial and Transnational Adoption* (Durham: Duke University Press, 2012).

11. Joseph Stiglitz, "Of the 1%, By the 1%, For the 1%," *Vanity Fair,* May 2011, www.vanityfair.com/news/2011/05/top-one-percent-201105. This article's narrative became a key part of the Occupy Wall Street movement's analysis and powerful slogan, "We are the 99%," when it convened in Zuccotti Park four months later.

12. See W. E. B. DuBois, *Black Reconstruction in America: Toward a History of the Part Which Black Folk Played in the Attempt to Reconstruct Democracy in America, 1860–1880* (New Brunswick, NJ: Transaction Books, 2013 [1935]), especially chap. 16; and George Lipsitz, "The Possessive Investment in Whiteness: Racialized Social Democracy and the 'White' Problem in American Studies," *American Quarterly* 47, no. 3 (1995): 369–87.

13. Maria Shriver, "The Female Face of Poverty," *Atlantic Monthly,* January 18, 2014, www.theatlantic.com/business/archive/2014/01/the-female-face-of-poverty/282892/.

1. "RADICAL FEMINISM'S MISOGYNISTIC CRUSADE" OR THE CONSERVATIVE TAX REVOLT?

1. Daniel Victor and Liam Stack, "Stephen Bannon and Breitbart News, in Their Words," *New York Times,* November 15, 2016, www.nytimes.com/2016/11/15/us/politics/stephen-bannon-breitbart-words.html.

2. Dan Savage, "Do the Santorum," Savage Love (syndicated column), May 29, 2003, http://www.thestranger.com/seattle/SavageLove?oid=14422; Santorum (website), May 27, 2015, www.spreadingsantorum.com.

3. "Santorum's Quotes on the Role of Women," *Washington Post,* February 11, 2012, www.washingtonpost.com/politics/santorums-quotes-on-the-role-of-women/2012/02/10/gIQABbMu4Q_story.html.

4. Jason Howerton, "Fox Guest Leaves Female Commentator Visibly Stunned during Feminism Debate: 'Look, You're Miserable,'" *The Blaze,* May 14, 2015, www.theblaze.com/stories/2015/05/14/fox-guest-leaves-female-commentator-visibly-stunned-during-feminism-debate-look-youre-miserable/.

5. Of the pregnancy discrimination cases filed with the Equal Employment Opportunity Commission, about 60 percent wind up with no finding of reasonable cause. See U.S. Equal Employment Opportunity Commission, "Pregnancy Discrimination Charges FY 2010–FY 2015," n.d., www.eeoc.gov/eeoc/statistics/enforcement/pregnancy_new.cfm.

6. See, for example, K.J. Dell'Antonia, "The Families That Can't Afford Summer," *New York Times,* June 4, 2016, www.nytimes.com/2016/06/05/sunday-review/the-families-that-cant-afford-summer.html.

7. Robert Dreyfuss, "How the DLC Does It," *American Prospect,* December 19, 2001, http://prospect.org/article/how-dlc-does-it.

8. Loretta Ross, "Understanding Reproductive Justice," Trust Black Women: Stand with Us for Reproductive Justice, November 2006 (updated March 2011), www.trustblackwomen.org/our-work/what-is-reproductive-justice/9-what-is-reproductive-justice.

9. Dani McClain, "The Murder of Black Youth Is a Reproductive Justice Issue," *Nation,* August 13, 2013, www.thenation.com/article/murder-black-youth-reproductive-justice-issue/

10. Dorothy Sue Cobble, *The Other Women's Movement* (Princeton, NJ: Princeton University Press, 2004), 120.

11. Carl N. Degler, *At Odds: Women and the Family in America from the Revolution to the Present* (New York: Oxford University Press, 1980).

12. Roy Rozenzweig, *Eight Hours for What We Will: Workers and Leisure in an Industrial City, 1870–1920* (Cambridge, UK: Cambridge University Press, 1985).

13. Cobble, *Other Women's Movement,* 120.

14. Ibid., 2–3.

15. Wolfgang quoted in Cobble, *Other Women's Movement*, 2–3. For example, however, when Friedan was stepping down as president of NOW, which she had helped found four years earlier, she called for a Women's Strike for Equality to mark the fiftieth anniversary of the Nineteenth Amendment granting the vote to women. She wrote about the double role of feminism, to speak to workers and housewives. When the time for the strike came, she said:

> The women who are doing menial chores in the offices as secretaries put the covers on their typewriters and close their notebooks and the telephone operators unplug their switchboards, the waitresses stop waiting, cleaning women stop cleaning and everyone who is doing a job for which a man would be paid more stops. And when it begins to get dark, instead of cooking dinner or making love, we will assemble and we will carry candles alight in every city to converge the visible power of women at city hall…. Women will occupy for the night the political decision-making arena and sacrifice a night of love to make the political meaning clear. (Quoted in Deirdre Carmody, "General Strike by U.S. Women Urged to Mark 19th Amendment; Militant Leader Sees 50th Anniversary of Voting Rights, Aug. 26, as Time for Instant Sexual Revolution," *New York Times*, March 21, 1970, www.nytimes.com)

While NOW, founded not only by Friedan but also Shirley Chisholm and Muriel Fox, was a complicated vehicle for many different feminisms and issues, it was also a target for discontent about the failures of solidarity of middle-class white women on issues of race and class.

16. Daniel Horowitz, *The Making of* The Feminine Mystique: *The American Left, the Cold War, and Modern Feminism* (Amherst: University of Massachusetts Press, 1998).

17. Quoted in ibid., 139.

18. Michael Denning, *The Cultural Front: The Laboring of American Culture in the Twentieth Century* (London: Verso, 1998).

19. Dayo F. Gore, Jeanne Theoharis, and Komozi Woodard, eds., *Want to Start a Revolution? Radical Women in the Black Freedom Struggle* (New York: New York University Press, 2009); Dayo F. Gore, *Radicalism at the Crossroads: African American Women Activists in the Cold War* (New York: New York University Press, 2011); and Benita Roth, *Separate Roads to Feminism: Black, Chicana, and White Feminist Movements in*

America's Second Wave (Cambridge, UK: Cambridge University Press, 2004).

20. See Nancy A. Hewitt, *No Permanent Waves: Recasting Histories of US Feminism* (New Brunswick, NJ: Rutgers University Press, 2010); and Danielle L. McGuire, *At the Dark End of the Street: Black Women, Rape, and Resistance—A New History of the Civil Rights Movement from Rosa Parks to the Rise of Black Power* (New York: Vintage, 2011). Ellen DuBois calls this "left-feminism" in "Eleanor Flexner and the History of American Feminism," *Gender and History* 3 (Spring 1991): 84.

21. Sara M. Evans, *Personal Politics: The Roots of Women's Liberation in the Civil Rights Movement and the New Left* (New York: Vintage, 1980); and Barbara Ransby, *Ella Baker and the Black Freedom Movement: A Radical Democratic Vision* (Chapel Hill: University of North Carolina Press, 2003).

22. For an example of this kind of argument, see Laura Briggs, *Somebody's Children* (Durham, NC: Duke University Press, 2012), 27–58.

23. Ibid., 38–40.

24. Alondra Nelson, *Body and Soul: The Black Panther Party and the Fight against Medical Discrimination* (Minneapolis: University of Minnesota Press, 2011).

25. Raj Patel, "Survival Pending Revolution: What the Black Panthers Can Teach the U.S. Food Movement," in *Food Movements Unite!: Strategies to Transform Our Food System,* ed. Eric Holt-Giménez (Oakland, CA: Food First, 2011), 124–25.

26. For personal reminiscences of COINTELPRO and its effects documented through the Church Commission and other declassified FBI documents, see Mumia Abu Jamal, *We Want Freedom: A Life in the Black Panther Party* (Boston: South End Press, 2004).

27. Nelson, *Body and Soul.*

28. Alexandra Minna Stern, "Sterilized in the Name of Public Health," *American Journal of Public Health* 95, no. 7 (2005): 1128–38, www.ncbi.nlm.nih.gov/pmc/articles/PMC1449330/.

29. Jennifer Nelson, "Abortions under Community Control: Feminism, Nationalism, and the Politics of Reproduction among New York City's Young Lords," *Journal of Women's History* 13, no. 1 (2001): 157–80;

and Laura Briggs, *Reproducing Empire: Race, Sex, Science, and US Imperialism in Puerto Rico* (Berkeley: University of California Press, 2002).

30. See Briggs, *Somebody's Children,* 59–93; and Sally Torpy, "Native American Women and Coerced Sterilization: On the Trail of Tears in the 1970s," *American Indian Culture and Research Journal* 24. no. 2 (2000): 1–22.

31. Alice Kessler-Harris, *Out to Work: A History of Wage-Earning Women in the United States* (New York: Oxford University Press, 1982).

32. Quoted in Christine Stansell, *The Feminist Promise: 1789 to the Present* (New York: Modern Library, 2010).

33. *Parents and the High Cost of Childcare: 2015 Report* (Arlington, VA: ChildCare Aware, 2015), 63–64, http://usa.childcareaware.org/wp-content/uploads/2016/05/Parents-and-the-High-Cost-of-Child-Care-2015-FINAL.pdf.

34. *Wages for Housework: From the Government for All Women* (Brooklyn: New York Wages for Housework Committee, n.d.), http://bcrw.barnard.edu/archive/sexualhealth/WagesForHousework.pdf.

35. Pat Mainardi, "The Politics of Housework," *Redstockings,* 1970, www.cwluherstory.org/the-politics-of-housework.html.

36. Anjani Chandra, Gladys M. Martinez, William D. Mosher, Joyce C. Abma, and Jo Jones, *Fertility, Family Planning, and Reproductive Health of U.S. Women: Data from the 2002 National Survey of Family Growth,* Vital and Health Statistics, series 23, no. 25, DHHS Publication No. (PHS) 2006–1977 (Hyattville, MD: U.S. Department of Health and Social Services, Centers for Disease Control, National Center for Health Statistics, December 2005), www.cdc.gov/nchs/data/series/sr_23/sr23_025.pdf.

37. L.L. Lovshin, "The Tired-Mother Syndrome," *Postgraduate Medicine* 26, no. 1 (1959): 48–54; A.S. Norris, "The Tired Mother," *Journal of the Iowa Medical Society* 54 (1964): 478–81.

38. Evelyn Nakano Glenn, *Forced to Care: Coercion and Caregiving in America* (Cambridge, MA: Harvard University Press, 2010).

39. Arlie Russell Hochschild, *The Second Shift: Working Families and the Revolution at Home* (New York: Penguin Books, 2012).

40. Johnnie Tillmon, "Welfare is a Woman's Issue," *Ms. Magazine* (Spring 1972; first issue), 111–16.

41. Felicia Ann Kornbluh, *The Battle for Welfare Rights: Politics and Poverty in Modern America* (Philadelphia: University of Pennsylvania Press, 2007); Premilla Nadasen, *Welfare Warriors: The Welfare Rights Movement in the United States* (New York: Routledge, 2005); and Annelise Orleck, *Storming Caesars Palace: How Black Mothers Fought Their Own War on Poverty* (Boston: Beacon Press, 2005).

42. Briggs, *Somebody's Children.*

43. Friedrich von Hayek, *The Road to Serfdom* (Chicago: University of Chicago Press, 1944); Milton Friedman, *Capitalism and Freedom* (Chicago: University of Chicago Press, 1962), see especially 87–88. The aphoristic version, that public schools are socialism, was offered in speeches throughout his life in his defense of a school voucher program that he believed would eventually break the public school system. My notion of crisis is indebted to Naomi Klein, *The Shock Doctrine: The Rise of Disaster Capitalism* (New York: Holt, 2007).

44. This account of the rise of neoliberalism is indebted to Robin D.G. Kelley, *Yo' Mama's Disfunktional: Fighting the Culture Wars in Urban America* (Boston: Beacon Press, 1997); Lisa Duggan, *Twilight of Equality? Neoliberalism, Cultural Politics, and the Attack on Democracy* (Boston: Beacon Press, 2012); and David Harvey, *A Short History of Neoliberalism* (New York: Oxford University Press, 1997).

45. Kathleen Gerson and Jerry A. Jacobs, *The Time Divide: Work, Family, and Gender Inequality* (Cambridge, MA: Harvard University Press, 2009).

46. *Parents and the High Cost of Childcare.*

47. Deborah Stone, "Fetal Risks, Women's Rights: Showdown at Johnson Controls," *American Prospect,* December 4, 2000, http://prospect.org/article/fetal-risks-womens-rights-showdown-johnson-controls.

48. Peter T. Kilborn, "Who Decides Who Works at Jobs Imperiling Fetuses?," *New York Times,* September 2, 1990, www.nytimes.com/1990/09/02/us/who-decides-who-works-at-jobs-imperiling-fetuses.html.

49. The union was making this argument because scientists had not been looking for reproductive harm as a male problem. For more on this, see Cynthia R. Daniels, chap. 3 in *At Women's Expense: State*

Power and the Politics of Fetal Rights (Cambridge, MA: Harvard University Press, 2009) for a discussion of the Johnson Controls case; and Cynthia Daniels, *Exposing Men: The Science and Politics of Male Reproduction* (New York: Oxford University Press, 2008).

50. William E. Schmidt, "Risk to Fetus Ruled as Barring Women from Jobs," *New York Times,* October 3, 1989, www.nytimes.com/1989/10/03/us/risk-to-fetus-ruled-as-barring-women-from-jobs.html.

51. Linda Greenhouse, "Court Backs Right of Women to Jobs with Health Risks," *New York Times,* March 21, 1991, www.nytimes.com/1991/03/21/us/court-backs-right-of-women-to-jobs-with-health-risks.html.

52. United Automobile Workers v. Johnson Controls, Inc., 499 U.S. 1196 (1991).

53. George J. Annas, "Fetal Protection and Employment Discrimination—The Johnson Controls Case," *New England Journal of Medicine* 325, no. 10 (1991): 740–43; and Cynthia R. Daniels, "Competing Gender Paradigms: Gender Difference, Fetal Rights and the Case of Johnson Controls," *Policy Studies Review* 10, no. 4 (1991): 51–68.

54. Gillian Thomas, *Because of Sex: One Law, Ten Cases, and Fifty Years That Changed American Women's Lives at Work* (New York: St. Martin's Press, 2016), 148–68.

55. Quoted in Thomas, *Because of Sex,* 168.

2. WELFARE REFORM

1. Angela Willey, *Undoing Monogamy: The Politics of Science and the Possibilities of Biology* (Durham, NC: Duke University Press, 2016), is particularly good at thinking how we privatize wealth and care and then make it seem natural by pretending that the (heterosexual) monogamous couple is produced by biology.

2. Wahneema Lubiano makes this argument—that "welfare queens" functioned as a cover story for the Reagan administration's breaking faith with an economy and public benefits that served people who weren't wealthy—in "Black Ladies, Welfare Queens, and State Minstrels: Ideological War by Narrative Means," in *Race-ing Justice, En-Gendering Power: Essays on Anita Hill, Clarence Thomas, and the*

Construction of Social Reality, ed. Toni Morrison (New York: Pantheon, 1992).

3. "Text of President Clinton's Announcement on Welfare Legislation," *New York Times,* August 1, 1996, www.nytimes.com/1996/08/01/us/text-of-president-clinton-s-announcement-on-welfare-legislation.html.

4. Dorothy Roberts, "Book Review: Welfare and the Problem of Black Citizenship," *Yale Law Review* 105 (1996): 1563–1602.

5. A great many people have written about how the trope of the welfare queen (and before that, the welfare mother) has adhered to Black women; for example, Patricia Hill Collins argues that it is one of a small number of "controlling images" that have long defined Black women to the larger society in "Mammies, Matriarchs, and Other Controlling Images," in *Black Feminist Thought: Knowledge, Consciousness, and the Politics of Empowerment,* 2nd ed. (New York: Routledge, 2000).

6. Eileen Boris and Jennifer Klein, *Caring for America: Home Health Workers in the Shadow of the Welfare State* (New York: Oxford University Press, 2012).

7. In constant 1996 dollars, the minimum wage was $7.21 an hour in 1968 and declined steadily through the 1980s—dropping to $4.24 in 1989. "Federal Minimum Wage Rates, 1955–2014," Infoplease, www.infoplease.com/ipa/A0774473.html. It has, however, gone up since.

8. The most compelling source on this is Barbara Ehrenreich, *Nickel and Dimed: On (Not) Getting By in America* (New York: Metropolitan Books, 2001), an investigative report on low-wage work. Ehrenreich experimented in diverse parts of the country with whether, as a single woman, she could get by on what the market offered. The answer was sometimes yes and sometimes no, but her account makes it very clear that it couldn't be done with a child.

9. Bethany Moreton offers a particularly thoughtful account of what Walmart gets out of a female workforce (and what feminized people get out of Walmart) in *To Serve God and Wal-Mart: The Making of Christian Free Enterprise* (Cambridge, MA: Harvard University Press, 2010).

10. Good Jobs First, a labor group, maintains a website documenting workers' participation in these programs by state and workplace. See "Hidden Taxpayer Costs," updated July 24, 2013, Good Jobs First,

www.goodjobsfirst.org/corporate-subsidy-watch/hidden-taxpayer-costs.

11. Jane Collins and Victoria Mayer, *Both Hands Tied: Welfare Reform and the Race to the Bottom in the Low-Wage Labor Market* (Chicago: University of Chicago Press, 2010).

12. For housing policy, see Peter Dreier, "Reagan's Real Legacy," *Nation,* February 4, 2011, www.thenation.com/article/reagans-real-legacy/; and E. Fuller Torrey, Aaron D. Kennard, Don Eslinger, Richard Lamb, and James Pavle, "More Mentally Ill Persons Are in Jails and Prisons Than Hospitals: A Survey of the States," National Sheriffs Association and Treatment Advocacy Center, May 2010, www.treatmentadvocacycenter.org/storage/documents/final_jails_v_hospitals_study.pdf.

13. Susan J. Douglas and Meredith W. Michaels, *The Mommy Myth: The Idealization of Motherhood and How It Has Undermined All Women* (New York: Free Press, 2005), 178.

14. John Blake, "Return of the 'Welfare Queen,'" January 23, 2012, CNN, www.cnn.com/2012/01/23/politics/weflare-queen/index.html.

15. Josh Levin, "The Welfare Queen," *Slate,* December 9, 2013, www.slate.com/articles/news_and_politics/history/2013/12/linda_taylor_welfare_queen_ronald_reagan_made_her_a_notorious_american_villain.html.

16. Frances Fox Piven and Barbara Ehrenreich, "Workfare Means New Mass Peonage," *New York Times,* May 30, 1987, www.nytimes.com/1987/05/30/opinion/workfare-means-new-mass-peonage.html.

17. "Washington Talk: Q&A: Daniel Patrick Moynihan; Welfare and the Politics of Poverty," *New York Times,* February 19, 1987, www.nytimes.com/1987/02/19/us/washington-talk-q-a-daniel-patrick-moynihan-welfare-and-the-politics-of-poverty.html.

18. "For Welfare Reform, a Strong Economy," Opinion, *New York Times,* September 10, 1987, www.nytimes.com/1987/09/10/opinion/for-welfare-reform-a-strong-economy.html.

19. E. Franklin Frazier, *The Negro Family in the United States* (Chicago: University of Chicago Press, 1939); Daniel Patrick Moynihan, *The Negro Family: The Case for National Action* (Washington, DC: Government Printing Office, 1965); Michael Harrington, *The Other America*

(New York: Simon and Schuster, 1962); Oscar Lewis, *La Vida: A Puerto Rican Family in the Culture of Poverty* (New York: Random House, 1966); Charles Murray, *Losing Ground* (New York: Basic Books, 1984).

20. Charles Murray, "The Coming White Underclass," *Wall Street Journal,* October 29, 1993, A14.

21. Andrew Rosenthal, "Quayle Attacks a 'Cultural Elite,' Saying It Mocks Nation's Values," *New York Times,* June 10, 1992, www.nytimes.com/1992/06/10/us/1992-campaign-quayle-attacks-cultural-elite-saying-it-mocks-nation-s-values.html.

22. See Chris Barcelos, "Distributing Condoms and 'Hope': Race, Sex, and Science in Youth Sexual Health Promotion" (PhD dissertation, University of Massachusetts Amherst, 2016).

23. Melissa Kearney and Phillip Levine, "Why Is the Teen Birth Rate in the United States So High and Why Does It Matter?," *Journal of Economic Perspectives* 26, no. 2 (2012): 141–66; Arline T. Geronimus and Sanders Korenman, *The Socioeconomic Consequences of Teen Childbearing Reconsidered* (Cambridge, MA: National Bureau of Economic Research, 1991); Arline T. Geronimus, "On Teenage Childbearing and Neonatal Mortality in the United States," *Population and Developmental Review* 13 (1987): 245–79; Arline T. Geronimus, "Teenage Childbearing and Personal Responsibility: An Alternative View," *Political Science Quarterly* 112 (1997): 405–30; V. Joseph Hotz, Susan Williams McElroy, and Seth G. Sanders, "The Costs and Consequences of Teenage Childbearing for Mothers," *Chicago Policy Review* 64 (1996), 55–94; Debbie Lawlor, Mary Shaw, and Sarah Johns, "Teenage Pregnancy Is Not a Public Health Problem," *British Medical Journal* 323, no. 7326 (2001): 1428–29; Debbie Lawlor and Mary Shaw, "Too Much Too Young? Teenage Pregnancy Is Not a Public Health Problem," *International Journal of Epidemiology* 31 (2002), 552–53; Kristin Luker, *Dubious Conceptions: The Politics of Teenage Pregnancy* (Cambridge, MA: Harvard University Press, 1996); and Constance A. Nathanson, *Dangerous Passage: The Social Control of Sexuality in Women's Adolescence* (Philadelphia: Temple University Press, 1991). The literature on racial disparities in health is vast, but one particularly accessible recent monograph (that argues against a growing trend in reading that disparity as genetically based) is Dorothy Roberts, *Fatal Invention: How Science, Politics, and Big*

Business Re-create Race in the Twenty-First Century (New York: New Press, 2012).

24. *Welfare and Teen Pregnancy: What Do We Know? What Do We Do?* (Washington, DC: Children's Defense Fund, 1986), http://diglib.lib .utk.edu/cdf/data/0116_000050_000254/0116_000050_000254.pdf.

25. Ellen Goodman, "Welfare Mothers with an Attitude," *Boston Globe*, April 16, 1992, quoted in Lucy Williams, "Race, Rat Bites, and Unfit Mothers: How Media Discourse Informs Welfare Legislation Debate," *Fordham Urban Law Journal* 22, no. 4 (1994): 1159–96.

26. Leon Dash, "Rosa Lee's Story: The Series," *Washington Post*, September 18–25, 1994, www.washingtonpost.com/wp-srv/local/longterm /library/rosalee/backgrnd.htm.

27. Charles M. Sennott, "Finding 4 Generations Sustained by Welfare," *Boston Globe*, February 20, 1994, ProQuest web. Ventura was a sexual abuse survivor struggling with crack addiction, chronic sleep deprivation, and never enough to eat. She had had her children young, after moving to Boston from Puerto Rico as a child, part of a large family typical of the island's agricultural workers. She made the news after she cruelly disciplined her four-year-old son for stealing food from her boyfriend, plunging his hands in boiling water and leaving him alone in their apartment with his siblings for days. A family member called the police, who found the boy, Ernesto Lara, on a mattress with serious injuries, lying in his own blood, urine, and feces. A *Boston Globe* reporter, Charles Sennott, wrote a story in February 1994 claiming that Ventura's family was a case study in the need for welfare reform—virtually all of her thirteen siblings were on welfare, he claimed, and most of her children's cousins as well. But that was a stretch; in fact, only two of her sisters were receiving AFDC. What *was* true was that most of her siblings were disabled by mental illness, and while some worked and others had lost touch with the family (and hence were not included in Sennott's profile), four of her brothers and one sister did receive Social Security Disability Income (SSDI) after working for much of their lives and then becoming disabled. Although again, there is much to be disturbed about in this story, it's not clear that cutting his mother off AFDC after two years would have helped Ernesto—or whether drug treatment and mental health services for

her and her disabled siblings might have been more to the point. And yet limiting AFDC is exactly what Massachusetts governor William Weld called for, holding up the *Boston Herald* front-page photo of the little boy with bandaged hands before the State House while proposing to get his mother off welfare—to take away her grocery money. Charles M. Sennott, "The Boston Globe: Whatever Happened to Claribel? Looking for the Poster Child of the Welfare Reform Movement in Massachusetts, Ten Years Later," *Puerto Rico Herald,* April 11, 2004, www.puertorico-herald.org/issues/2004/vol8n29/WhatClaribel .html.

28. This account of the Chicago case, and the close attention to the *Boston Globe* stories, is significantly indebted to Williams, "Race, Rat Bites, and Unfit Mothers." Nineteen children were found in one squalid apartment when the police busted in in the early morning hours, looking for drugs. They found no drugs, but the media reported that the apartment was filthy, their mothers were out, and trash and dirty diapers were everywhere. According to the families, though, it was the police who trashed the apartment and then blamed the family for the mess. (Given that they were searching for drugs, it certainly seems likely that the police ripped the place apart.) Although the media initially alleged that the children were eating out of the dog bowl, none were found to be malnourished, and the family produced a three-foot-long grocery receipt showing they had bought chicken and rice in bulk days before the children were found. Four families were sharing the apartment, not a happy arrangement by any stretch, but two sisters had moved in with a third and her roommate after a fire put them out of doors. When the dust settled, the charges of child neglect mostly evaporated (and one child, having suffered lifelong from cerebral palsy was released from the hospital, where Department of Family and Youth Services had apparently stuck her for no reason except that she was disabled). What the families were mostly guilty of was being poor, having mothers who had their first child while a teenager, having a landlord who didn't exterminate cockroaches, being on waiting lists for housing, caring for family members, and receiving AFDC; one of the mothers may have also had a drug addiction. If this hadn't been high tide for hating mothers who didn't

have jobs, it's hard to see what about this story deserved national coverage—which it got, from CNN to ABC, from the *Washington Post* to the *Houston Chronicle* to the *Chicago Tribune.*

29. For more on the deviant heterosexuality of welfare queens, see Cathy Cohen, "Punks, Bulldaggers, and Welfare Queens," *GLQ: A Journal of Lesbian and Gay Studies* 3, no. 4 (1997): 437–66.

30. Howie Carr, "Working Moms Do a Job on Whining Welfare Queens," *Boston Herald,* May 23, 1994.

31. Arlie Russell Hochschild, *The Second Shift: Working Families and the Revolution at Home* (New York: Penguin Books, 2012); and Susan J. Shaw, *Governing How We Care: Contesting Community and Defining Difference in U.S. Public Health Programs* (Philadelphia, PA: Temple University Press, 2012).

32. "Washington Talk: Q&A: Daniel Patrick Moynihan."

33. Frances Fox Piven and Barbara Ehrenreich, "Workfare Means New Mass Peonage," *New York Times,* May 30, 1987, www.nytimes .com/1987/05/30/opinion/workfare-means-new-mass-peonage.html.

34. Johnnie Tillmon, "Welfare is a Woman's Issue," *Ms. Magazine* (Spring 1972; first issue), 111–16.

35. Rebecca Blank, "Trends in the Welfare System," in *Welfare, the Family, and Reproductive Behavior: Research Perspectives,* ed. Robert Moffitt (Washington, DC: National Academies Press, 1998), 33–49.

36. See, among others, Dána-Ain Davis, *Battered Black Women and Welfare Reform: Between a Rock and a Hard Place* (Albany: SUNY Press, 2006).

37. Thomas MaCurdy and Jeffrey M. Jones, "Welfare," in *Concise Encyclopedia of Economics,* Library of Economics and Liberty, 2008, www.econlib.org/library/Enc/Welfare.html.

38. R. M. Tolman and J. Raphael, "Review of Research on Welfare and Domestic Violence," *Journal of Social Issues,* 56, no. 4 (2000): 655–82.

39. The same Massachusetts study found that 29 percent of recipients had been hurt in the prior year by a former husband or boyfriend in the context of disputes about child support. Mary Ann Allard, Randy Albelda, Mary Ellen Colten, and Carol Cosenza, *In Harm's Way? Domestic Violence, AFDC Receipt, and Welfare Reform in Massachusetts* (Boston: University of Massachusetts, McCormack Institute, Center

for Survey Research, 1997), https://archive.org/stream/inharmsway-domestoouniv/inharmswaydomestoouniv_djvu.txt.

40. Thanks to Jennifer Nye for this insight. While opponents of mass incarceration have often focused on drug laws, Michelle Alexander makes the point that this is really the tip of the iceberg in terms of how people wind up in prison, and VAWA deserves further interrogation as a site of federal policy with respect to mass incarceration. Michelle Alexander, *The New Jim Crow: Mass Incarceration in the Age of Colorblindness* (New York NY: New Press, 2011).

41. For the long campaign to expand benefits, see, for example, Premilla Nasden, *Welfare Warriors: The Welfare Rights Movement in the United States* (New York: Routledge, 2005); Jill Quadagno, *The Color of Welfare: How Racism Undermined the War on Poverty* (New York: Oxford University Press, 1994); Linda Gordon, *Pitied But Not Entitled: Single Mothers and the History of Welfare* (New York: Free Press, 1994); and Annelise Orleck, *Storming Caesars Palace: How Black Mothers Fought Their Own War on Poverty* (Boston: Beacon Press, 2005).

42. Paul H. Wise, Nina S. Wampler, Wendy Chavkin, and Diana Romero, "Chronic Illness among Poor Children Enrolled in the Temporary Assistance for Needy Families Program," *American Journal of Public Health,* 92 (2002): 1458–61; Michele Adler, "Disability Among Women on AFDC: An Issue Revisited," Office of the Assistant Secretary for Planning and Evaluation, U.S. Department of Health and Human Services, January 1, 1993, http://aspe.hhs.gov/daltcp/reports/afdcwomn.htm.

43. "Program Cost and Size," *Trends in the Social Security and Supplemental Security Income Disability Programs,* Office of Policy, Social Security Administration, 2006, www.ssa.gov/policy/docs/chartbooks/disability_trends/sect01.html.

44. Patricia J. Williams, *The Rooster's Egg* (Cambridge, MA: Harvard University Press, 1995), 5; and Laurie B. Green, *Battling the Plantation Mentality: Memphis and the Black Freedom Struggle* (Chapel Hill: University of North Carolina Press, 2007).

45. LaDonna Pavetti, "Time on Welfare and Welfare Dependency: Testimony before the House Ways and Means Committee, Subcommittee on Human Resources," Urban Institute, May 23, 1996, http://webarchive.urban.org/publications/900288.html.

46. Shaw, *Governing How We Care.*

47. Peter Muennig, Rishi Caleyachetty, Zohn Rosen, and Andrew Korotzer, "More Money, Fewer Lives: The Cost Effectiveness of Welfare Reform in the United States," *American Journal of Public Health* 105, no. 2 (2015): 324–28.

48. Abby J. Cohen, "A Brief History of Federal Financing for Child Care in the United States," *The Future of Children* 6, no. 2, (1996): 26–40; Tommy Thompson, "The Good News about Welfare Reform: Wisconsin's Success Story," Lecture on Welfare and Welfare Spending, Heritage Foundation, March 6, 1997, www.heritage.org/research/lecture /hl593nbsp-the-good-news-about-welfare-reform. For later funding programs, see, for example, Gina Adams and Caroline Heller, *The Child Care and Development Fund and Workforce Development for Low-Income Parents,* Urban Institute, July 16, 2015, www.urban.org/research/publication /child-care-and-development-fund-and-workforce-development-low-income-parents.

49. *Parents and the High Cost of Childcare: 2015 Report* (Arlington, VA: ChildCare Aware, 2015), 63–64, http://usa.childcareaware.org/wp-content /uploads/2016/05/Parents-and-the-High-Cost-of-Child-Care-2015-FI-NAL.pdf; and Gina Adams, Shayne Spaulding, and Caroline Heller, *Bridging the Gap: Exploring the Intersection of Workforce Development and Child Care,* Urban Institute, May 2015, www.urban.org/sites/default/files/alfresco /publication-pdfs/2000225-Bridging-the-Gap.pdf. It was systematically underfunded such that it could never serve all those eligible. For a census study, see Lynda Laughlin, "Who's Minding the Kids? Child Care Arrangements: Spring 2011," P70–135, U.S. Department of Commerce, Economics and Statistics Administration, U.S. Census Bureau, April 2013, www.census.gov/prod/2013pubs/p70–135.pdf.

50. Pamela Loprest, *How Are Families That Left Welfare Doing? A Comparison of Early and Recent Welfare Leavers,* Series B, No. B-36, Assessing the New Federalism Project (Washington, DC: Urban Institute, April 2001; Richard Bavier, "Welfare Reform Data from the Survey of Income and Program Participation," *Monthly Labor Review,* July 2001, 13–24; Maria Cancian, Robert Haveman, Daniel R. Meyer, and Barbara Wolfe, *Before and After TANF: The Economic Well-Being of Women Leaving Welfare,* Special Report no.77, Institute for Research on Poverty,

University of Wisconsin–Madison, May 2000, www.researchgate
.net/publication/245582847_Before_and_After_TANF_The_Economic_
Well-Being_of_Women_Leaving_Welfare; and Jason DeParle, "Welfare Limits Left Poor Adrift as Recession Hit," *New York Times,* April 7,
2012, www.nytimes.com/2012/04/08/us/welfare-limits-left-poor-adrift-
as-recession-hit.html.

51. Laura Briggs, *Somebody's Children* (Durham, NC: Duke University Press, 2012).

52. Cohen, "Brief History of Federal Financing for Child Care in
the United States." For later funding programs, see, for example,
Adams and Heller, *Child Care and Development Fund.*

53. Muennig, Caleyachetty, Rosen, and Korotzer, "More Money,
Fewer Lives."

54. Institute of Medicine and National Research Council, *Transforming the Workforce for Children Birth through Age 8: A Unifying Foundation*
(Washington, DC: National Academies Press, 2015); for recommenda-
tions, see chapter 12, www.nap.edu/read/19401/chapter/21#508.

55. Ellen Galinsky et al., *The Study of Children in Family Child Care
and Relative Care* (New York: Families and Work Institute, 1994);
Suzanne W. Helburn, *Cost, Quality and Child Outcomes in Child Care Centers: Technical Report, Public Report, and Executive Summary,* Colorado University, Denver, Department of Economics, 1995, https://eric.ed.
gov/?id=ED386297; Jonathan Cohn, "The Hell of American Day Care:
An Investigation into the Barely Regulated, Unsafe Business of Looking after Our Children," *New Republic,* April 15, 2013, www.newrepublic
.com/article/112892/hell-american-day-care; Barbara Willer, "Esti-
mating the Full Cost of Quality," in *Reaching the Full Cost of Quality in
Early Childhood Programs,* NAEYC publication no. 317 (Washington, DC:
National Association for the Education of Young Children, 1990),
55–86; and *Parents and the High Cost of Childcare.*

56. Jens Ludwig and Douglas L. Miller, "Does Head Start Improve
Children's Life Chances? Evidence from a Regression Discontinuity
Design," *Quarterly Journal of Economics* 122, no. 1 (2007): 159–208.

57. Laughlin, "Who's Minding the Kids?"

58. Institute of Medicine and National Research Council, *Transforming the Workforce.*

59. Suzanne Helburn and Carollee Howes, "Child Care Cost and Quality," *Future of Children* 6, no. 2 (1996): 62–82.

60. Marcy Whitebook, *Working for Worthy Wages: The Child Care Compensation Movement, 1970–2001* (Berkeley, CA: Institute of Industrial Relations, Center for the Study of Child Care Employment, 2002).

61. Ellen Resse, "But Who Will Care for the Children? Organizing Child Care Providers in the Wake of Welfare Reform," in *Intimate Labors,* ed. Eileen Boris and Rhacel Salazar Parreñas (Stanford, CA: Stanford University Press, 2010), 231–48.

62. *Parents and the High Cost of Childcare.*

63. Jonathan Leonard and Alexandre Mas, "Welfare Reform, Time Limits, and Infant Health," *Journal of Health Economics* 27, no. 6 (2008): 1551–66.

64. Elizabeth T. Wilde, Zohn Rosen, Kenneth Couch, and Peter A. Muennig, "Impact of Welfare Reform on Mortality: An Evaluation of the Connecticut Jobs First Program, a Randomized Controlled Trial," *American Journal of Public Health* 104, no. 3 (2014): 534–38.

65. Sociologist Alice Goffman wrote about this woman, whom she called "Marqueta." Quoted in Thomas Edsall, "Is Poverty a Kind of Robbery?" Campaign Stops: Strong Opinions on the 2012 Election," *New York Times,* September 16, 2012, http://campaignstops.blogs.nytimes .com/2012/09/16/is-poverty-a-kind-of-robbery.

66. Muennig, Caleyachetty, Rosen, and Korotzer, "More Money, Fewer Lives."

67. Lubiano, "Black Ladies, Welfare Queens," 324.

68. Peter Dreier, "Reagan's Legacy: Homelessness in America," *Shelterforce Online* 135 (2004), www.nhi.org/online/issues/135/reagan.html.

69. Quoted in Jason DeParle, "Counter to Trend, a Welfare Program In California Has One Idea: Get a Job!" *New York Times,* May 16, 1993, www.nytimes.com/1993/05/16/us/counter-to-trend-a-welfare-program-in-california-has-one-idea-get-a-job.html.

70. Jana Kasperkevic, "Workers to Protest at McDonald's Stores across US over sexual harassment claims," *Guardian,* October 5, 2016, www.theguardian.com/business/2016/oct/05/workers-protest-mcdonalds-sexual-harassment-claims.

71. The National Organization for Women (NOW), for example, organized civil disobedience, a hunger strike, and lobbying against welfare reform; the American Association of University Women denounced the efforts to end AFDC; and Black feminists and women's historians were particularly outspoken about the critical importance of supporting AFDC. At the same time, the rank-and-file membership of feminist organizations were not equally mobilized by the welfare reform debate; when the NOW Legal Defense and Education Fund did a direct mail piece on welfare reform, not only did the campaign fail to raise money, but it sparked hate mail from some NOW members. Indeed, elected Congresswomen voted for welfare reform and were particularly keen on making men pay child support, which they saw as evening out the inequality of men and women in responsibility for children. The problem with this position is that it (1) required women to answer questions from TANF and the state about their intimate life (who did you sleep with, when, and for how long) and (2) required poor women to stay in financial and hence personal relationships with nonmarital partners, opening them to disputes over custody and sometimes, physical abuse from men they had tried to leave. For this split between feminist leadership and grassroots membership, see Gwendolyn Mink, "Introduction to Disdained Mothers and Despised Others: The Politics and Impact of Welfare Reform," *Social Justice* 25, no. 1 (1998), https://www.socialjusticejournal.org/SJEdits /71Edit.html.

3. OFFSHORING REPRODUCTION

1. The Trump administration gives us fresh evidence that only female appointees get in trouble for hiring undocumented household employees,, telling us something about the gendered, heterosexualized responsibility for reproductive labor even when it is hired out; Trump's proposed labor secretary Andrew Puzder and commerce secretary Wilbur Ross both admitted in the confirmation process that they had hired undocumented household workers. Puzder later withdrew for other reasons, but Ross was confirmed without incident. Mick

Mulvaney, Trump's budget director, admitted during the confirmation process that he failed to pay around $15,000 in taxes for a nanny employed in his household. Alan Rappeport, "Andrew Puzder, Trump's Labor Pick, Admits to Hiring Undocumented Maid," *New York Times,* February 7, 2017, www.nytimes.com/2017/02/07/us/politics /andrew-puzder-labor-trump-undocumented.html.

2. See Mary Romero, *Maid in the U.S.A.* (New York: Routledge, 2002); and Grace Chang, *Disposable Domestics: Immigrant Women Workers in the Global Economy* (Boston: South End Press, 2000) for very smart analysis of these events and the context surrounding them.

3. This figure represents babysitters and other nonrelative care in the child's home as well as nannies. Lynne Casper, Mary Hawkins, and Martin O'Connell, *Who's Minding the Kids? Child Care Arrangements, Fall 1991,* U.S. Bureau of the Census, Current Population Reports, Household Economic Studies P70–36 (Washington, DC: U.S. Government Printing Office, 1994), 7, www.census.gov/sipp/p70-36.pdf

4. Jill Smolowe, "The Zoë Baird Debacle: How It Happened," *Time,* February 1, 1993, www.time.com/time/magazine/article/0,9171, 977610,00.html.

5. Deborah Sontag, "Increasingly, 2-Career Family Means Illegal Immigrant Help," *New York Times,* January 24, 1993, www.nytimes.com /1993/01/24/nyregion/increasingly-2-career-family-means-illegal-immigrant-help.html.

6. Romero, *Maid in the U.S.A.*

7. Here I am thinking of W.E.B. DuBois, *Black Reconstruction in America, 1860–1880* (New York: Free Press, 1997).

8. Deborah Sontag, "Increasingly, 2-Career Family Means Illegal Immigrant Help," *New York Times,* January 24, 1993.

9. Edward Helmore, "'Death Map' of Desert Aims to Save Lives of Desperate Mexican Migrants," *Guardian,* June 1, 2013, www.theguardian .com/world/2013/jun/01/map-us-mexico-migrant-deaths-border.

10. "Bill Clinton's Shameful Legacy on Immigration," *Salon.com,* April 27, 2016, www.salon.com/2016/04/27/bill_clintons_shameful_ legacy_on_immigration_terrible_laws_he_signed_rip_apart_families_ and_authorize_unjust_detention_human_rights_watch_says/; and

Eithne Luibheid, *Entry Denied: Controlling Sexuality at the Border* (Minneapolis: University of Minnesota Press, 2002).

11. Richard Fry, *Gender and Migration,* Pew Research Center, July 5, 2006, www.pewhispanic.org/2006/07/05/gender-and-migration/; and Ana Gonzalez-Barrera and Jens Manuel Krogstad, "What We Know about Illegal Immigration from Mexico," FactTank: News in the Numbers, Pew Research Center, November 20, 2015, www.pewresearch .org/fact-tank/2015/11/20/what-we-know-about-illegal-immigration-from-mexico/.

12. The Bureau of Labor Statistics in 2006 counted 37.2 percent Latino or Hispanic and 19.9 percent African-American "maids or housekeeping workers." It recorded no nannies, but "child care workers" were 17.3 percent Latina and 17 percent Black. Bureau of Labor Statistics, "Employed Persons by Detailed Occupation, Sex, Race and Hispanic Origin" (Washington, DC: Bureau of Labor Statistics, 2007). The BLS has also found this to be the segment of the employed population most likely to be poor. Bureau of Labor Statistics, "A Profile of the Working Poor" (Washington, DC: Department of Labor, 2000).

13. A number of people have made this point; see, for example, Pierrette Hondagneu-Sotelo and Ernestine Avila, "I'm Here, but I'm There: The Meanings of Latina Transnational Motherhood," *Gender and Society* 11, no. 5 (1997); Pierrette Hondagneu-Sotelo, *Doméstica: Immigrant Workers Cleaning and Caring in the Shadows of Affluence* (Berkeley: University of California Press, 2007). Rhacel Salazar Parreñas, *Children of Global Migration: Transnational Families and Gendered Woes* (Stanford, CA: Stanford University Press, 2005).

14. See, for example, Jacqueline Jones, *Labor of Love, Labor of Sorrow: Black Women, Work, and the Family, from Slavery to the Present* (New York: Basic Books, 1985).

15. Shellee Colen, "Like a Mother to Them: Stratified Reproduction and West Indian Childcare Workers and Employers in New York," in *Conceiving the New World Order: The Global Politics of Reproduction,* ed. Faye D. Ginsberg and Rayna Rapp (Berkeley: University of California Press, 1995), 78–102.

16. Linda Burnham and Nik Theodore, *Home Economics: The Invisible and Unregulated World of Domestic Work,* National Domestic Workers Alliance, Center for Urban Economic Development, University of Illinois at Chicago, and DataCenter, 2012, www.domesticworkers.org//sites/default/files/HomeEconomicsEnglish.pdf.

17. Sharon Lerner, "'The Help' Gets Its Due," *Slate,* February 22, 2012, www.slate.com/articles/double_x/doublex/2012/02/domestic_workers_bill_of_rights_and_other_new_laws_protecting_nannies_housekeepers_and_other_in_home_employees_.html.

18. Some of this desire to make domestic labor cheaper was explicit, rather than just part of the general effort to create cheap workers by using immigration enforcement to create a new, less protected, and hence lower-paid workforce. After the Zoë Baird controversy, Congress thoughtfully lowered the taxes employers had to pay for their household employees. See Taunya Lovell Banks, "Toward a Global Critical Feminist Vision: Domestic Work and the Nanny Tax Debate," *Journal of Gender, Race, and Justice* 3 (1999): 1–44.

19. Mae Ngai, *Impossible Subjects: Illegal Aliens and the Making of Modern America* (Princeton, NJ: Princeton University Press, 2004); Alexander Saxton, *The Indispensable Enemy: Labor and the Anti-Chinese Movement in California* (Berkeley: University of California Press, 1975); John Higham, *Strangers in the Land: Patterns of American Nativism, 1860–1925,* 2nd ed. (New Brunswick, NJ: Rutgers University Press, 2002); Gwendolyn Mink, *Old Labor and New Immigrants in American Political Development: Union, Party, and State* (Ithaca, NY: Cornell University Press, 1990); Eithne Lubheid, *Entry Denied,* especially 31–54; and Lisa Lowe, *Immigrant Acts: On Asian American Cultural Politics* (Durham, NC: Duke University Press, 1996). On the longing to have workers without families, see Carmen Whalen, *From Puerto Rico to Philadelphia: Puerto Rican Workers and Postwar Economies* (Philadelphia: Temple University Press, 2001).

20. Alexandra Stern, "Buildings, Boundaries, and Blood: Medicalization and Nation-Building on the U.S.-Mexico Border, 1910–1930," *Hispanic American Historical Review* 79, no. 1 (February 1990): 41–81; Natalia Molina, *Fit to Be Citizens? Public Health and Race in Los Angeles, 1879–1939* (Berkeley: University of California Press, 2006); John Mckiernan-

González, *Fevered Measures: Public Health and Race at the Texas-Mexico Border* (Durham, NC: Duke University Press, 2012); Kelly Lytle Hernandez, *Migra! A History of the U.S. Border Patrol* (Berkeley: University of California Press, 2010); and Monica Muñoz Martinez, "Recuperating Histories of Violence in the Americas: Vernacular History-Making on the U.S.-Mexico Border," *American Quarterly* 66, no. 3 (2014): 661–89.

21. Alicia Schmidt Camacho, *Migrant Imaginaries: Latino Cultural Politics in the U.S.-Mexico Borderlands* (New York: NYU Press, 2008), 62–111; Mireya Loza, *Defiant Braceros: How Migrant Workers Fought for Racial, Sexual, and Political Freedom* (Chapel Hill: University of North Carolina Press, 2016); Deborah Cohen, *Transnational Subjects: Braceros, Nation, and Migration* (Chapel Hill: University of North Carolina Press, 2010); and Ana Rosas, *Abrazando el Espíritu: Bracero Families Confront the U.S.-Mexico Border* (Berkeley: University of California Press, 2014).

22. Joseph Nevins, *Operation Gatekeeper: The Rise of the "Illegal Alien" and the Making of the U.S.-Mexico Boundary* (New York: Routledge, 2002); Timothy Dunn, *The Militarization of the U.S.-Mexico Border, 1978–1992: Low-Intensity Conflict Doctrine Comes Home* (Austin: University of Texas, 1996).

23. Elena R. Gutiérrez, *Fertile Matters: The Politics of Mexican-Origin Women's Reproduction* (Austin: University of Texas Press, 2008).

24. Richard Rayner, "What Immigration Crisis?," *New York Times,* January 7, 1996.

25. Eric Lichtblau, *Bush's Law: The Remaking of American Justice* (New York: Pantheon/Random House, 2008).

26. Bernard Lewis, *What Went Wrong? The Clash Between Islam and Modernity in the Middle East* (New York: Oxford University Press, 2002). It's hard to know what to cite from *Jihad Watch* (www.jihadwatch.org/) or Front Page (www.frontpagemag.com/) because both have become simply anti-Muslim screeds. Suzanne Daley and Alissa Rubin, "French Muslims Say Veil Bans Give Cover to Bias," *New York Times,* May 26, 2015, www.nytimes.com/2015/05/27/world/europe/muslim-frenchwomen-struggle-with-discrimination-as-bans-on-veils-expand.html.

27. Jacqueline Stevens, "Thin ICE," *Nation,* June 5, 2008.

28. Nicholas Riccardi, "Anti-Illegal Immigration Forces Share a Wide Tent," *Los Angeles Times,* May 4, 2006, A1, A12, quoted in Laura

Pulido, "Immigration Politics and Motherhood," *Amerasia Journal* 35, no. 1 (2009): 169–78.

29. Mary Romero, "'Go After the Women': Mothers Against Illegal Aliens' Campaign against Mexican Immigrant Women and Their Children," *Indiana Law Journal* 83, no. 4 (2008): 1355–88, www.repository.law.indiana.edu/ilj/vol83/iss4/8.

30. "Barack Obama, Deporter-in-Chief," *Economist*, February 8, 2014, www.economist.com/news/leaders/21595902-expelling-record-numbers-immigrants-costly-way-make-america-less-dynamic-barack-obama.

31. "Criminal Aliens," Federation for American Immigration Reform, updated August 2015, www.fairus.org/issue/criminal-aliens.

32. Emily Bazelon, "Department of Justification," *New York Times Magazine*, February 28, 2017, www.nytimes.com/2017/02/28/magazine/jeff-sessions-stephen-bannon-justice-department.html.

33. Ginger Thompson, "After Losing Freedom, Some Immigrants Face Loss of Custody of Their Children," *New York Times*, April 22, 2009, www.nytimes.com/2009/04/23/us/23children.html; and Ginger Thompson, "Court Rules for Deportee on Custody," *New York Times*, June 27, 2009, www.nytimes.com/2009/06/28/us/28deport.html.

34. Laura Briggs, *Somebody's Children* (Durham, NC: Duke University Press, 2012), 274.

35. Samantha Schmidt, "DHS is Considering Separating Mothers and Children Who Cross the Border Illegally, *Washington Post*, March 7, 2017.

36. Laura Briggs, "Central American Child Migration: Militarization and Tourism," Special Issue on Militarism and Tourism, *American Quarterly* 68, no. 3 (September 2016): 573–82.

37. Patricia Landolt and Wei Da, "The Spatially Ruptured Practices of Migrant Families: A Comparison of Immigrants from El Salvador and the People's Republic of China," *Current Sociology*, 53, no. 4 (2005): 625–53, doi:10.1177/0011392105052719.

38. Anne-Marie Slaughter, "Why Women Still Can't Have It All," *Atlantic*, July/August 2012, www.theatlantic.com/magazine/archive/2012/07/why-women-still-cant-have-it-all/309020/; and Barbara Ehrenreich

and Arlie Russell Hochschild, *Global Woman: Nannies, Maids, and Sex Workers in the New Economy* (New York: Holt, 2003).

39. Parreñas, *Children of Global Migration*, 128.

40. Ibid., 129.

41. Julia Preston, "Women's Groups Rally for Immigration Reform," *New York Times,* September 12, 2013, sec. U.S. / Politics, www.nytimes.com/2013/09/13/us/politics/womens-groups-rally-for-immigration-reform.html.

4. THE POLITICS AND ECONOMY OF
REPRODUCTIVE TECHNOLOGY AND BLACK
INFANT MORTALITY

1. Alex Kuczynski, "Her Body, My Baby," *New York Times Magazine,* November 28, 2008, www.nytimes.com/2008/11/30/magazine/30Surrogate-t.html.

2. T.J. Matthews and Brady E. Hamilton, "First Births to Older Women Continue to Rise," National Center for Health Statistics, NCHS Data Brief no. 152, May 2014, www.cdc.gov/nchs/data/databriefs/db152.htm.

3. missbhavens, November 26, 2008 (8:59 p.m.), comment on Jessica G., "Writer, Socialite Explains Her 'Mad Desire' for a Baby through Surrogacy," *Jezebel* (blog), November 26, 2008 (3:00 p.m.), http://jezebel.com/5099373/writer-socialite-explains-her-mad-desire-for-a-baby-through-surrogacy.

4. On Alex Kuczynski's "Her Body, My Baby," blog, Northeast Assisted Fertility Group, November 30, 2008. www.assistedfertility.com/blog/2008/11/30/on-alex-kuczynskis-her-body-my-baby/.

5. I'm thinking here of Wendy Chavkin's "body bits." For the broad argument, see Wendy Chavkin and Jane Maree Maher, *The Globalization of Motherhood: Deconstructions and Reconstructions of Biology and Care* (New York: Routledge, 2010). Chavkin uses the phrase in "Globalized Motherhood: Assisted Reproductive Technology in Context," Barnard Center for Research on Women, *Scholar & Feminist Online* 9.1–9.2 (Fall 2010/Spring 2011), http://sfonline.barnard.edu/reprotech/chavkin_01.htm.

6. See Dorothy Roberts, chap. 1 in *Shattered Bonds: The Color of Child Welfare* (New York: Basic Books, 2002) for a careful study of how people lose their children to foster care, evidence echoed in a less comprehensive but consistent way in Laura Briggs, *Somebody's Children* (Durham, NC: Duke University Press, 2012).

7. Roberts, *Shattered Bonds,* ix–x.

8. In addition to Roberts, *Shattered Bonds,* see also Briggs, *Somebody's Children.*

9. Jean Twenge, "'Designer Babies' Are Only for the Rich," *Daily Beast,* July 7, 2014, www.thedailybeast.com/articles/2014/07/07/designer-babies-are-only-for-the-rich.html.

10. On sperm donation regimens, see Rene Almeling, *Sex Cells: The Medical Market for Eggs and Sperm* (Berkeley: University of California, 2011). It appears that at least two egg donors have died of ovarian hyperstimulation syndrome in India. See also Pritha Chatterjee, "Egg Donor's Death," *India Express,* February 9, 2014, http://indianexpress.com/article/india/india-others/egg-donors-death-internal-bleeding-ovaries-severely-enlarged-says-report/; Miriam Zoll, *Cracked Open: Liberty, Fertility, and the Pursuit of High Tech Babies* (Northampton, MA: Interlink, 2013), 73; and Andrew Vorzimer, "17-Year-Old Egg Donor Dies in India," *Spin Doctor,* July 13, 2012, www.eggdonor.com/blog/2012/07/13/17-year-egg-donor-dies-india/.

11. The list is from Müller. Quoted in Banu Subramaniam, *Ghost Stories for Darwin: The Science of Variation and the Politics of Diversity* (Urbana, IL: University of Illinois Press, 2014), 35.

12. Southern Poverty Law Center, "Extremist Files: William Shockley," www.splcenter.org/get-informed/intelligence-files/profiles/William-Shockley.

13. On biocapitalism, see Sarah Franklin and Margaret M. Lock, *Remaking Life and Death: Toward an Anthropology of the Biosciences* (Santa Fe, NM: School of American Research Press, 2003); Kalindi Vora, *Life Support: Biocapital and the New History of Outsourced Labor* (Minneapolis: University of Minnesota Press, 2015); Kaushik Sunder Rajan, *Biocapital: The Constitution of Postgenomic Life* (Durham, NC: Duke University Press, 2006); and Nancy Scheper-Hughes, "Rotten Trade: Millennial

Capitalism, Human Values and Global Justice in Organ Trafficking," *Journal of Human Rights* 2, no. 2 (2003). On surrogacy in India, see Amrita Pande, *Wombs in Labor: Transnational Commercial Surrogacy in India* (New York: Columbia University Press, 2014).

14. Leslie King and Madonna Harrington Meyer, "The Politics of Reproductive Benefits: U.S. Insurance Coverage of Contraceptive and Infertility Treatments," *Gender and Society* 11 (1997): 8–30. For post–Affordable Care Act comparisons, see National Women's Law Center, "Contraceptive Coverage in the Health Care Law: Frequently Asked Questions," January 28, 2015, www.nwlc.org/resource/contraceptive-coverage-health-care-law-frequently-asked-questions.

15. Dána-Ain Davis, "The Politics of Reproduction: The Troubling Case of Nadya Suleman and Assisted Reproductive Technology," *Transforming Anthropology* 17, no. 2 (2009): 105–16.

16. Zoll, *Cracked Open.*

17. If there are increased disabilities, there is a significant debate about whether they are related to IVF, intra-cytoplasmic sperm injection (ICSI), increased rates of twins, or use by people who are either older—and hence at increased risk of age-related problems in the gametes—or infertile—which may signal other kinds of weakness in the gametes. For my argument, it doesn't matter which it is, just that it *is* more common. Michèle Hansen, Carol Bower, Elizabeth Milne, Nicholas de Klerk, and Jennifer J. Kurinczuk, "Assisted Reproductive Technologies and the Risk of Birth Defects—A Systematic Review and Meta-analysis," *Human Reproduction Update* 19, no. 4 (2013): 330–53; B.C. Fauser, P. Devroey, K. Diedrich, B. Balaban, M. Bonduelle, H.A. Delemarre-van de Wall, C. Estella, et al., "Health Outcomes of Children Born after IVF/ICSI," *Reproductive Biomedicine Online* 28, no. 2 (February 2014): 162–82; Catherine Pearson, "IVF, Autism Not Linked, But Study Finds Risk of Intellectual Disabilities," *Huffington Post,* July 2, 2013, www.huffingtonpost.com/2013/07/02/ivf-autism_n_3535435.html; Sven Sandin, Karl-Gösta Nygren, Anastasia Iliadou, Christina M. Hultman, and Abraham Reichenberg, "Autism and Mental Retardation among Offspring Born after In Vitro Fertilization," *Journal of the American Medical Association,* 310, no. 1 (2013): 75–84; Catherine Pearson, "IVF and Birth

Defects Could Be Linked, New Study Finds," *Huffington Post,* October 10, 2012, www.huffingtonpost.com/2012/10/20/ivf-birth-defects_n_1989302. html; and Alexandra Sifferlin, "IVF Linked to More Birth Defects," *Time,* October 22, 2012, http://healthland.time.com/2012/10/22/ivf-linked-to-more-birth-defects/.

18. See, for example, this ad: "Fertility Financing," LightStream, a division of SunTrust Bank, www.lightstream.com/ivf-financing.

19. Rene Almeling, "Selling Genes, Selling Gender: Egg Agencies, Sperm Banks, and the Medical Market in Genetic Material," *American Sociological Review,* 72, no. 3 (2007): 333, quoted in Dorothy Roberts, *Fatal Invention: How Science, Politics, and Big Business Re-create Race in the Twenty-First Century* (New York: New Press, 2012).

20. "SoldierCryo™—Fertility Preservation for Military Personnel," IVF1, www.ivf1.com/soldiercryo-military_fertility_preservation/. Jennifer Terry, "Significant Injury: War, Medicine, and Empire in Claudia's Case," *Women's Studies Quarterly* 37, nos. 1–2 (Spring/Summer 2009): 200–25, is singularly helpful for thinking about injury in the current wars.

21. Marcia Claire Inhorn, *Reproductive Disruptions: Gender, Technology, and Biopolitics in the New Millennium* (New York: Berghahn, 2007); Marcia C. Inhorn, *Cosmopolitan Conceptions: IVF Sojourns in Global Dubai* (Durham, NC: Duke University Press, 2015); and Elizabeth F. S. Roberts, *God's Laboratory: Assisted Reproduction in the Andes* (Berkeley: University of California Press, 2012).

22. Pande, *Wombs in Labor;* and Sharmilla Rudrappa, *Discounted Life: The Price of Global Surrogacy in India* (New York: NYU Press, 2015).

23. Quoted in Jonathan Tobin, "Other People's Babies and American Values," *National Review,* March 17, 2017, www.nationalreview.com /article/445733/steve-king-other-peoples-babies-tweet-undermines-conservative-american-values.

24. Emma Rosenblum, "Later, Baby: Will Freezing Your Eggs Free Your Career?," *Businessweek,* April 17, 2014, www.bloomberg.com/news /articles/2014–04–17/new-egg-freezing-technology-eases-womens-career-family-angst; and Jessica Bennett, "Company-Paid Egg Freezing Will Be the Great Equalizer," *Time,* October 15, 2014, http://time.com/3509930 /company-paid-egg-freezing-will-be-the-great-equalizer/.

25. Danielle Friedman, "Perk Up: Facebook and Apple Now Pay for Women to Freeze Eggs," *NBC News,* October 14, 2014, www .nbcnews.com/news/us-news/perk-fcebook-apple-now-pay-women-freeze-eggs-n225011.

26. Bennett, "Company-Paid Egg Freezing."

27. Shane Ferro, "This Is Why Apple Paying For Egg Freezing Is Great News for Women," *Business Insider,* October 14, 2014, www .businessinsider.com/this-is-why-apple-paying-for-egg-freezing-is-great-for-women-2014–10#ixzz3GEWeEu9J.

28. Rosenblum, "Later, Baby." See also Sarah Elizabeth Richards *Motherhood, Rescheduled: The New Frontier of Egg Freezing and the Women Who Tried It* (New York: Simon and Schuster, 2013).

29. Quoted in Rosenblum, "Later, Baby."

30. Sylvia Ann Hewlett, *Creating a Life: Professional Women and the Quest for Children* (New York, NY: Talk Miramax Books, 2002); and Tanya Selvaratnam, *The Big Lie: Motherhood, Feminism, and the Reality of the Biological Clock* (Amherst, NY: Prometheus Books, 2014), 36.

31. Lori Gottlieb, *Marry Him: The Case for Settling for Mr. Good Enough* (New York, NY: NAL Trade, 2011).

32. Elizabeth Gregory, *Ready: Why Women are Embracing the New Later Motherhood* (New York: Basic Books, 2007); and Sarah Ann Richards, *Motherhood, Rescheduled: The New Frontier in Egg Freezing and the Women Who Tried It* (New York, NY: Simon and Schuster, 2013).

33. See, for example, Micha Cárdenas, "Pregnancy: Reproductive Futures in Trans of Color Feminisms" *Transgender Studies Quarterly* 3, nos. 1–2 (2016) 48–57.

34. Anne-Marie Slaughter, "Why Women Still Can't Have It All," *Atlantic,* July-August 2012, www.theatlantic.com/magazine/archive /2012/07/why-women-still-cant-have-it-all/309020/.

35. Sheryl Sandberg, *Lean In: Women, Work, and the Will to Lead* (New York: Knopf, 2013).

36. Anna Holmes, "Maybe You Should Read the Book: The Sheryl Sandberg Backlash," *New Yorker Blogs,* March 4, 2013, www.newyorker .com/online/blogs/books/2013/03/maybe-you-should-read-the-book-the-sheryl-sandberg-backlash.html.

37. Maureen Dowd, "Pompom Girl for Feminism," *New York Times,* February 23, 2013, www.nytimes.com/2013/02/24/opinion/sunday /dowd-pompom-girl-for-feminism.html.

38. Jodi Kantor, "Sheryl Sandberg, *Lean In* Author, Hopes to Spur Movement," *New York Times,* February 21, 2013, www.nytimes.com /2013/02/22/us/sheryl-sandberg-lean-in-author-hopes-to-spur-move-ment.html; and Anne-Marie Slaughter, "Sheryl Sandberg's *Lean In,*" *New York Times,* March 7, 2013, www.nytimes.com/2013/03/10/books /review/sheryl-sandbergs-lean-in.html.

39. Timothy Egan, "Tapes Show Enron Arranged Plant Shut-down," *New York Times,* February 4, 2005, www.nytimes.com/2005 /02/04/national/04energy.html.

40. Danielle Douglas, "Behind the Mortgage Settlements from the Housing Crisis," *Washington Post,* May 20, 2013, www.washingtonpost .com/business/economy/the-slow-going-process-of-compensating-victims-of-housing-violations/2013/05/19/593b1428-a618-11e2-b029–8fb7e977ef71_story.html.

41. Slaughter's article developed into a book, *Unfinished Business,* which at once goes farther—drawing on the thinking of Ai-Jen Poo and the Domestic Workers Alliance and expanding her policy pre-scriptions to include an "infrastructure of care" for all workers, a higher minimum wage, and high-quality day care for all on a sliding scale—and blunts its edge by describing a happy, bipartisan world where no one is actually opposed to these goals. Anne-Marie Slaughter, *Unfin-ished Business: Women Men Work Family* (New York: Random House, 2015).

42. Rosa Brooks, "Recline! Why 'Leaning In' Is Killing Us," *Foreign Policy,* February 21, 2014, http://foreignpolicy.com/2014/02/21/recline/.

43. "Sheryl Sandberg: Why We Have Too Few Women Leaders," TED Talk, December 2010, www.ted.com/talks/sheryl_sandberg_ why_we_have_too_few_women_leaders.html.

44. Customer reviews, "Lean In: Women, Work, and the Will to Lead," Amazon.com, www.amazon.com/Lean-Women-Work-Will-Lead/dp/0385349947.

45. Lori Moore, "Rep. Todd Akin: The Statement and the Reac-tion," *New York Times,* August 20, 2012, www.nytimes.com/2012/08/21 /us/politics/rep-todd-akin-legitimate-rape-statement-and-reaction.

html; Claire Marshall, "The Spread of Conscience Clause Legislation," *Human Rights Magazine* 39, no. 2 (2014), www.americanbar.org /publications/human_rights_magazine_home/2013_vol_39/january_ 2013_no_2_religious_freedom/the_spread_of_conscience_clause_ legislation.html; and Adam Liptak, "Supreme Court Rejects Contraceptives Mandate for Some Corporations: Justices Rule in Favor of Hobby Lobby," *New York Times*, June 30, 2014, www.nytimes .com/2014/07/01/us/hobby-lobby-case-supreme-court-contraception .html.

46. This position is best exemplified recently by Zoll, *Cracked Open*, but has a long history in the Feminist International Network of Resistance to Reproductive and Genetic Engineering (FINNRAGE) group. As feminist science studies scholar Hilary Rose argues, FINNRAGE did a great deal to get a feminist anti-eugenics politics on the table in opposition to reproductive technology but at the expense of reducing an immensely complicated story into a series of horror stories about brain-dead women being used as incubators, sex-selection abortion being used for "femicide" and a new "brothel model" of reproduction, and the supposed brainwashing of infertile women. See Hilary Rose, *Love, Power, and Knowledge: Towards a Feminist Transformation of the Sciences* (New York: Wiley, 2013).

47. Charis Thompson, *Making Parents: The Ontological Choreography of Reproductive Technologies* (Cambridge, MA: MIT Press, 2005).

48. Ibid.

49. Lynn Morgan and Elizabeth F. S. Roberts, "Reproductive Governance in Latin America," *Anthropology and Medicine* 19, no. 2 (2012): 241–54; and Roberts, *God's Laboratory*.

50. For Centers for Disease Control, see "ART Success Rates," CDC, www.cdc.gov/art/artdata/. Miriam Zoll argues that the failure rate is close to 70 percent when full data is collected in the United States. Zoll, *Cracked Open*, introduction.

51. Rita Arditti, Renate Klein, and Shelley Minden, *Test-Tube Women: What Future for Motherhood?* (London: Pandora Press, 1984); and Gena Corea, *The Mother Machine: Reproductive Technologies from Artificial Insemination to Artificial Wombs* (New York: Harpercollins, 1985).

52. Zoll, *Cracked Open*, introduction.

53. Rickie Solinger, *Wake Up Little Susie: Single Pregnancy and Race before Roe v. Wade* (New York: Routledge, 2013); and Annette Lareau, *Unequal Childhoods: Race, Class and Family Life* (Berkeley: University of California Press, 2003).

54. Arline Geronimus, "Damned If You Do: Culture, Identity, Privilege, and Teenage Childbearing in the United States," *Social Science and Medicine* 57 (2003): 881–93; V. Joseph Hotz, Susan William McElroy, and Seth G. Sanders, "The Costs and Consequences of Teenage Childbearing for Mothers," *Chicago Policy Review* 64 (1996): 85–86. See also Melissa Schettini Kearney and Philip B. Levine, *Why Is the Teen Birth Rate in the United States So High and Why Does It Matter?*, NBER Working Paper no. 17965, National Bureau of Economic Research, March 2012, www.nber.org/papers/w17965, which argues that the economic disadvantages of teen mothers are the function of prior poverty and educational attainment, together with low class mobility.

55. Anjani Chandra, Elizabeth Hervey Stephen, and Rosalind Berkowitz King, "Infertility Service Use among Fertility-Impaired Women in the United States: 1995–2010" (paper, Population Association of America, 2013 Annual Meeting, New Orleans, Louisiana, April 11–13, 2013).

56. Khiara M. Bridges, *Reproducing Race: An Ethnography of Pregnancy as a Site of Racialization* (Berkeley: University of California Press, 2011).

57. Thomas Tafelski and Kathryn E. Boehm, "Contraception in the Adolescent Patient," *Primary Care* 22, no. 1 (March 1995): 145–59. The authors mention suburban residence, white race, and higher education level as good indicators of a patient's ability to comply with a more easily reversible method, the pill. For the black box warning, see "Depo-Provera (medroxyprogesterone acetate injectable suspension)," Safety Alerts for Human Medical Products, U.S. Food and Drug Administration, last updated August 21, 2013, www.fda.gov/Safety/MedWatch/SafetyInformation/SafetyAlertsforHumanMedicalProducts/ucm154784.htm.

58. Kimberly Daniels, William Mosher, and Jo Jones, "Contraceptive Methods Women Have Ever Used: United States, 1982–2010," *National Health Statistics Reports* 62, February 14, 2013, www.cdc.gov/nchs/data/nhsr/nhsr062.pdf.

59. Anjani Chandra, Gladys Martinez, William Mosher, Joyce Abma, and Jo Jones, *Fertility, Family Planning, and Reproductive Health of U.S Women: Data from 2002 National Survey of Family Growth*, series 23, no. 25, Vital and Health Statistics (Hyattsville, MD: National Center For Health Statistics, December 2005), www.cdc.gov/nchs/data/series /sr_23/sr23_025.pdf, 23.

60. Tanzina Vega, "Infertility, Endured through a Prism of Race," *New York Times,* April 25, 2014, www.nytimes.com/2014/04/26/us /infertility-endured-through-a-prism-of-race.html; and Anjani Chandra, Casey Copen, and Elizabeth Hervey Stephen, "Infertility Service Use in the United States: Data from the National Survey of Family Growth, 1982–2010," *National Health Statistics Reports* 73, January 22, 2014, www.cdc.gov/nchs/data/nhsr/nhsr73.pdf.

61. Sudeshna Mukherjee, Digna R. Velez Edwards, Donna D. Baird, David A. Savitz, and Katherine E. Hartmann, "Risk of Miscarriage among Black Women and White Women in a US Prospective Cohort Study," *American Journal of Epidemiology* 177, no. 11 (2013): 1271–78.

62. Carol J. Rowland Hogue and Martha A. Hargraves, "Preterm Birth in the African American Community," *Seminars in Perinatology* 19, no. 4 (1995): 255–62.

63. Wendy Chavkin, "Cocaine and Pregnancy—Time to Look at the Evidence," *Journal of the American Medical Association* 28 (2001): 1626–27. I've written about these issues at length elsewhere; see Ana Ortiz and Laura Briggs, "Crack, Abortion, the Culture of Poverty, and Welfare Cheats: The Making of the 'Healthy White Baby Crisis,'" *Social Text* 76, 21, no. 3 (Fall 2003): 39–57.

64. Estimates for 2016, *CIA World Factbook,* Central Intelligence Agency, 2016, www.cia.gov/library/publications/the-world-factbook /rankorder/2091rank.html

65. "Infant Mortality Rates," Organization for Economic Cooperation and Development, https://data.oecd.org/healthstat/infant-mortality-rates.htm; and T.J. Mathews and Anne Driscoll, *Trends in Infant Mortality in the United States, 2005–2014*, National Centers for Health Statistics Data Brief no. 279, Centers for Disease Control and Prevention, March 2017, www.cdc.gov/nchs/data/databriefs/db279.pdf.

66. *CIA World Factbook,* 2016.

67. Vicky Lovell, "No Time to be Sick: Why Everyone Suffers When Workers Don't Have Paid Sick Leave," Institute for Women's Policy Research, May 2004, http://paidsickdays.nationalpartnership.org/site /DocServer/No_Time_To_Be_Sick.pdf; Jenny Xia, Jeff Hayes, Barbara Gault, and Hailey Nguyen, "Paid Sick Days Access and Usage Rates Vary by Race/Ethnicity, Occupation, and Earnings," Briefing Paper, Institute for Women's Policy Research, February 2016, www .iwpr.org/publications/pubs/paid-sick-days-access-and-usage-rates-vary-by-race-ethnicity-occupation-and-earnings; and Carmen DeNavas-Walt, Bernadette Proctor, and Jessica Smith, *Income, Poverty, and Health Insurance Coverage in the United States: 2012*, Current Population Reports, U.S. Bureau of the Census, September 2013, www.census .gov/prod/2013pubs/p60–245.pdf.

68. See, for example, Sherri Wallace, Sharon Moor, Linda Wilson, and Brenda Hart, "African American Women in the Academy: Quelling the Myth of Presumed Incompetence," in *Presumed Incompetent: The Intersections of Race and Class for Women in Academia*, ed. Gabriella Gutiérrez y Muhs, Yolanda Flores Niemann, Carmen González, and Angela Harris (Boulder: University of Colorado, 2012).

69. Hilary Hansen, "Black Woman Says Flight Attendant Didn't Believe She Was a Real Doctor," *Huffington Post,* October 13, 2016, www .huffingtonpost.com/entry/black-woman-delta-flight-doctor_us_57 ffaefce4b0162c043a745c.

70. Bridges, *Reproducing Race;* and Carol J. Rowland Hogue and Martha A. Hargraves, "Class, Race, and Infant Mortality in the United States," *American Journal of Public Health* 83, no. 1 (January 1993): 9–12.

71. See, for example, Leith Mullings, "Minority Women, Work, and Health," in Wendy Chavkin, ed. *Double Exposure: Women's Health Hazards on the Job and at Home (*New York: Monthly Review Press, 1984), 121–38; or Kamini Maraj Grahame, "'For the Family': Asian Immigrant Women's Triple Day," *Journal of Sociology and Social Welfare* 30, no. 1 (March 2003): 65–90. Still others object to the "double day" framework as positing a private-public dichotomy that never existed for women of color, who saw their work for wages as an extension of work for the family. Evelyn Nakano Glenn, "1994 Split Household, Small Producer and Dual Wage-Earner: An Analysis of Chinese

American Family Strategies," in *American Families: A Multicultural Reader,* 2nd ed., ed. Stephanie Coontz, Maya Parson, and Gabrielle Raley (New York: Routledge, 2008); and Patricia Hill Collins, "Shifting the Center: Race, Class and Feminist Theorizing about Motherhood," chap. 3 in *Mothering: Ideology, Experience, and Agency,* ed. Evelyn Nakano Glenn, Grace Chang, and Linda Rennie Forcey (New York: Routledge, 1994).

72. I'm referring to the *New York Times* piece documenting the effects of welfare "reform" that we saw in chapter 2: Jason DeParle, "Welfare Limits Left Poor Adrift as Recession Hit," *New York Times,* April 7, 2012, www.nytimes.com/2012/04/08/us/welfare-limits-left-poor-adrift-as-recession-hit.html.

73. See Valerie Wilson and William M. Rodgers III, *Black-White Wage Gaps Expand with Rising Wage Inequality* (Washington, DC: Economic Policy Institute, September 2016), www.epi.org/publication/black-white-wage-gaps-expand-with-rising-wage-inequality.

74. T.J. Mathews and Marian McDorman, "Infant Mortality Statistics from the 2010 Period: Linked Birth/Infant Death Data Set," *National Vital Statistics Reports* 62, no. 8 (December 18, 2013), www.cdc.gov/nchs/data/nvsr/nvsr62/nvsr62_08.pdf.

75. See Roberts, *Fatal Invention,* for an excellent exploration of the it-must-be-genes argument with respect to many different health questions.

76. Tyan Parker Dominguez, Emily Ficklin Strong, Nancy Krieger, Matthew W. Gillman, and Janet W. Rich-Edwards, "Differences in the Self-Reported Racism Experiences of US-Born and Foreign-Born Black Pregnant Women," *Social Science and Medicine* 69, no. 2 (July 2009): 258–65; and T.J. Mathews, Marian F. MacDorman, and Marie E. Thoma, "Infant Mortality Statistics from the 2013 Period Linked Birth/Infant Death Data Set," *National Vital Statistics Reports* 64, no. 9 (August 6, 2015), www.cdc.gov/nchs/data/nvsr/nvsr64/nvsr64_09.pdf.

77. See especially the introduction to the JAMA special issue: Chavkin, "Cocaine and Pregnancy." I've written about these issues at length elsewhere. See Ortiz and Briggs, "Crack, Abortion, the Culture of Poverty"; and Briggs, *Somebody's Children.*

78. Bridges, *Reproducing Race*; Kenneth C. Schoendorf, Carol J.R. Hogue, Joel C. Kleinman, and Diane Rowley, "Mortality among Infants of Black as Compared with White College-Educated Parents," *New England Journal of Medicine* 4, 326, no. 23 (June 1992): 1522–56.

79. Tyan Parker Dominguez, "Adverse Birth Outcomes in African American Women: The Context of Persistent Reproductive Disadvantage," *Social Work in Public Heath* 26 (2011): 3–16; Cheryl Giscombe and Marci Lobel, "Explaining Disproportionately High Rates of Adverse Birth Outcomes among African Americans: The Impact of Stress, Racism, and Related Factors in Pregnancy," *Psychological Bulletin* 131, no. 5 (2005): 662–83; Michael Lu, Milton Kotelchuck, Vijaya Hogan, Loretta Jones, Kynna Wright, and Neal Halfon, "Closing the Black-White Gap in Birth Outcomes: A Life-Course Approach," *Ethnicity and Disease* 20 (Winter 2010); Amani Nuru-Jeter, Tyan Dominguez, Wizdom Hammond, Janxin Leu, Marilyn Skaff, Susan Egerter, Camara Jones, and Paula Braveman, "It's the Skin You're In: African American Women Talk About their Experiences of Racism: An Exploratory Study to Develop Measures of Racism for Birth Outcome Studies," *Maternal and Child Health Journal* 13, no. 1 (January 2009): 29–39; Nancy Krieger, "Does Racism Harm Health? Did Child Abuse Exist before 1962? On Explicit Questions, Critical Science, and Current Controversies: An Ecosocial Perspective," *American Journal of Public Health* 93 (2003): 194–199; Sherman A. James, "Confronting the Moral Economy of US Racial/Ethnic Health Disparities," *American Journal of Public Health* 93, no. 2 (2003): 189; Schoendorf et al., "Mortality among Infants"; Diane L. Rowley and Vijaya Hogan, "Disparities in Infant Mortality and Effective, Equitable Care: Are Infants Suffering from Benign Neglect?," *Annual Review of Public Health* 33 (April 2012):75–87; Janell Ross, "Racism Linked to Infant Mortality and Learning Disabilities," *The Root,* December 11, 2013, www.theroot.com/articles/culture/2013/12/racism_linked_to_premature_births/; Halimah Abdullah, "Racism May Affect Infant Mortality Rates," *McClatchy DC,* September 28, 2007, www.mcclatchydc.com/news/article24470281 .html; Nancy Dole, David A. Savitz, Irva Hertz-Picciotto, Anna Maria Siega-Riz, M.J. McMahon, and Pierre Buekens, "Maternal Stress and Preterm Birth," *American Journal of Epidemiology* 157, no. 1 (January

2003): 14–24; and Lisa Rosenthal and Marci Lobel, "Explaining Racial Disparities in Adverse Birth Outcomes: Unique Sources of Stress for Black American Women," *Social Science and Medicine* 72 (March 2011): 977–83.

80. Jiyoun Kim, Andrew C. Merry, Jean A. Nemzek, Gerry L. Bolgos, Javed Siddiqui, and Daniel G. Remick, "Eotaxin Represents the Principal Eosinophil Chemoattractant in a Novel Murine Asthma Model Induced by House Dust Containing Cockroach Allergens," *Journal of Immunology* 167, no. 5 (September 1, 2001): 2808–15, quoted in Roberts, *Fatal Invention,* 109.

81. I wanted to say "pregnant woman or trans man" here, to acknowledge the sometimes isolating and invisible experiences of pregnant trans men, but there are no instances I am aware of where the medical and newspaper articles I am reading here admit to the existence of pregnant trans men.

82. Centers for Disease Control and Prevention, "Ten Great Public Health Achievements—United States, 1900–1999," *Morbidity and Mortality Weekly Report* 48, no. 50 (December 24, 1999): 1141–43, www.cdc.gov/mmwr/preview/mmwrhtml/mm4850bx.htm.

83. Rick Gladstone, "'Tale of Two Cities' Widens Worldwide for Children, Study Shows," *New York Times,* May 5, 2015, www.nytimes.com/2015/05/05/world/africa/tale-of-two-cities-widens-worldwide-for-children-study-shows.html.

84. Ada Calhoun, "The Criminalization of Bad Mothers," *New York Times,* April 25, 2012, www.nytimes.com/2012/04/29/magazine/the-criminalization-of-badmothers.html; Lynn Paltrow, "Roe v. Wade and the New Jane Crow: Reproductive Rights in the Age of Mass Incarceration" *American Journal of Public Health* 103, no. 1 (January 2013): 17–21; and Dorothy Roberts, "Destroying Black Families in the Name of Child Protection," part 1 in *Shattered Bonds,* 2–100.

85. Annie Menzel, *The Political Life of Black Infant Mortality* (PhD dissertation, University of Washington, 2014), https://digital.lib.washington.edu/researchworks/bitstream/handle/1773/26159/Menzel_washington_0250E_13773.pdf.

86. Monica Casper and Lisa Jean Moore, *Missing Bodies: The Politics of Visibility* (New York: NYU Press, 2009).

87. Schoendorf, Hogue, Kleinman, and Rowley, "Mortality among Infants of Black as Compared with White College-Educated Parents"; and Munroe Proctor, Selma Taffel, Kenneth Keppel; et al., "Correspondence: Infant Mortality among Blacks and Whites," *New England Journal of Medicine* 327 (October 22, 1992): 1243–44.

88. Bridges, *Race and Reproduction.*

89. Menzel, *Political Life of Black Infant Mortality.*

90. Monica Casper and William Paul Simmons, "Accounting for Death: Infant Mortality, the MDGs, and Women's (Dis) Empowerment," in *Counting on Marilyn Waring: New Advances in Feminist Economics,* ed. Margunn Bjørnholt and Ailsa McKay (Bradford, ON: Demeter Press, 2014): 91–105.

91. Ruth Wilson Gilmore, *Golden Gulag: Prisons, Surplus, Crisis, and Opposition in Globalizing California* (Berkeley: University of California Press, 2007), 28.

92. See chart produced by the Centers for Disease Control, "Infant Mortality and Low Birth Weight among Black and White Infants— United States, 1980–2000," *Morbidity and Mortality Weekly Report* 51, no. 27 (July 12, 2002): 589–92. We can produce the additional data from Mathews, MacDorman, and Thoma, "Infant Mortality Statistics From the 2013 Period"; and T.J. Mathews and Marian MacDorman, "Infant Mortality Statistics from the 2005 Period Linked Birth/Infant Death Data Set," *National Vital Statistics Reports* 57, no. 2 (July 30, 2008), www.cdc.gov/nchs/data/nvsr/nvsr57/nvsr57_02.pdf.

93. Nathan James, "The Federal Prison Population Buildup: Options for Congress," Congressional Research Service, CRS Report R42937, May 20, 2016, www.fas.org/sgp/crs/misc/R42937.pdf.

94. Leith Mullings and Alaka Wali, *Stress and Resilience: The Social Context of Reproduction in Central Harlem* (New York: Kluwer Academic, 2001).

95. Ibid., chap. 6.

96. Sherman James, "John Henryism and the Health of African-Americans," *Culture, Medicine, and Psychiatry* 18, no. 2 (June 1994): 163–82.

97. Quoted in Mullings and Wali, *Stress and Resilience,* 163. There are other versions of this speech, but all agree on the broad outlines and

that it moved its listeners strongly. See Nell Irving Painter, *Sojourner Truth: A Life, A Symbol* (New York: Norton, 1997), 164–78.

98. Mullings and Wali, *Stress and Resilience,* 193–264.

99. Videotaped deposition of David B. Goerlitz in Steven R. Arch et al. vs. the American Tobacco Company et al., quoted in Sandra Lane, *Why Are Our Babies Dying? Pregnancy, Birth and Death in America* (Boulder, CO: Paradigm, 95.

100. Leith Mullings, "Resistance and Resilience: The Sojourner Syndrome and the Social Context of Reproduction in Central Harlem," *Transforming Anthropology* 13 (2008): 79–91.

101. Arlene T. Geronimus, "The Weathering Hypothesis and the Health of African-American Women and Infants: Evidence and Speculations," *Ethnicity and Disease* 2, no. 3 (1991): 207–21.

5. GAY MARRIED, WITH CHILDREN

1. On gay people and children, see Laura Briggs, *Somebody's Children* (Durham, NC: Duke University Press, 2012), 245–50. On bar communities, see Elizabeth Lapovsky Kennedy and Madeline D. Davis, *Boots of Leather, Slippers of Gold: The History of a Lesbian Community* (New York: Routledge, 1993); and David Ruben, *Everything You Always Wanted to Know About Sex but Were Afraid to Ask* (New York, Bantam Books, 1971), especially 176–82. On the social transformations of gay genes, see Suzanna Danuta Walters, *The Tolerance Trap: How God, Genes, and Good Intentions Are Sabotaging Gay Equality* (New York: NYU Press, 2004). On trays at the ends of hallways, see, for example, Leslie Scism and Mary Flannery, "Two Patients Quietly Enter AIDS Unit," *Philadelphia Daily News,* February 12, 1987, http://articles.philly.com/1987–02–12/news/26176523_1_aids-unit-aids-patients-groups-for-aids-victims. As many of us remember, the practice was not at all limited to Philadelphia.

2. Priya Kandaswamy, "State Austerity and the Racial Politics of Same-Sex Marriage in the US," *Sexualities* 11, no. 6 (2008): 706–25; Gwendolyn Mink, *Welfare's End* (Ithaca, NY: Cornell University Press, 1998); Lisa Duggan, "Holy Matrimony!" *Nation* 278, no. 10 (2004): 14–19; Kerry Abrams, "Polygamy, Prostitution, and the Federalization of Immigration Law," *Columbia Law Review* 105, no. 3 (April 2005): 641–716.

Martha Ertman argues that even for Mormons, threatened with war against Utah over polygamy, their "wrong" marriages were perceived as race treason, as a crime against whiteness. Martha M. Ertman, "Race Treason: The Untold Story of America's Ban on Polygamy," *Columbia Journal of Gender and Law* 19, no. 2 (2010): 287–366.

3. In identifying the Moynihan report's characterization of Black families as "dysfunctional," I mean to evoke Robin D. G. Kelley's brilliant book *Your Mama's DisFUNKtional! Fighting the Culture Wars in Urban America* (Boston: Beacon Press, 1997).

4. Federal Interagency Forum on Child and Family Statistics, "Family and Social Environment: Family Structure and Children's Living Arrangements" in *America's Children: Key National Indicators of Well-Being, 2015* (Washington, DC: U.S. Government Printing Office, 2015), www.childstats.gov/americaschildren15/family1.asp.

5. Briggs, *Somebody's Children;* Daniel Winunwe Rivers, *Radical Relations: Lesbian Mothers, Gay Fathers, and Their Children in the United States since World War II* (Chapel Hill, NC: University of North Carolina Press, 2013).

6. Rivers, *Radical Relations,* 135–36.

7. Minnie Bruce Pratt, "Down the Little Cahaba" in *Crime Against Nature* (Ithaca, NY: Firebrand Books, 1990).

8. Carl Wittman, "A Gay Manifesto," in *Out of the Closets: Voices of Gay Liberation,* ed. Karla Jay and Allen Young (New York: Douglas Book Corporation, 1972), 333–34.

9. Heather Murray, *Not in This Family: Gays and the Meaning of Kinship in Postwar North America* (Philadelphia: University of Pennsylvania Press, 2010).

10. Kath Weston gave her book on lesbian gay kinship this title: *Families We Choose: Lesbians, Gays, Kinship* (New York: Columbia University Press, 1991).

11. Stephen Vider, "'The Ultimate Extension of Gay Community': Communal Living and Gay Liberation in the 1970s," *Gender and History* 27, no. 3 (2015).

12. Emily K. Hobson, *Lavender and Red: Liberation and Solidarity in the Gay and Lesbian Left* (Berkeley, CA: University of California Press, 2016), 50.

13. As Saidiya Hartman wrote, "Slavery is the ghost in the machine of kinship," in *Lose Your Mother: A Journey Along the Atlantic Slave Route* (New York: Farrar, Straus and Giroux, 2008); or, as Judith Butler asked, "Is kinship always already heterosexual?" in "Is Kinship Always Already Heterosexual?," *Differences: A Journal of Feminist Cultural Studies* 13, no. 1 (2002): 14–44.

14. Rivers, *Radical Relations*, 99.

15. Chris Bull and John Gallagher, *Perfect Enemies: The Religious Right, the Gay Movement, and the Politics of the 1990s* (New York: Crown, 1996).

16. Rivers, *Radical Relations*, 169–180.

17. Cindy Rizzo, "A National Voice for Lesbian Mothers," *Gay Community News* 16, no. 44 (May 28–June 3, 1989): 5.

18. Laura Mamo, *Queering Reproduction: Achieving Pregnancy in the Age of Technoscience* (Durham, NC: Duke University Press, 2007).

19. Tamar Lewin, "Disabled Woman's Care Given to Lesbian Partner," *New York Times,* December 18, 1991, www.nytimes.com/1991/12/18/us/disabled-woman-s-care-given-to-lesbian-partner.html; Karen Thompson and Julie Andrzejewski, *Why Can't Sharon Kowalski Come Home?* (San Francisco: Spinsters/Aunt Lute, 1988); Nan Hunter, "Sexual Dissent and the Family: The Sharon Kowalski Case," in *Sex Wars: Sexual Dissent and Political Culture,* ed. Lisa Duggan and Nan D. Hunter (New York: Routledge, 2006), 101–6; and Joan Griscom, "The Case of Sharon Kowalski and Karen Thompson: Ableism, Heterosexism, and Sexism," in *Race, Class, and Gender in the United States: An Integrated Study,* ed. Paula S. Rothenberg (New York: St. Martin's, 1998), 346–56.

20. Rivers, *Radical Relations*, 135.

21. Rod Sorge, "Gay Couples Defined as 'Family'; In a Precedent-Setting Case, the New York State Supreme Court Expands the Definition of What Constitutes a Family to include Gay Men, Lesbians and Unmarried Heterosexuals," *Gay Community News,* July 16–22, 1989, 1; and Carlos Ball, *From the Closet to the Courtroom: Five LGBT Rights Lawsuits That Have Changed Our Nation* (Boston: Beacon, 2010), 22–66.

22. Ball, *From the Closet to the Courtroom.*

23. Tom Stoddard, "Why Gay People Should Seek the Right to Marry," *Outlook* (Fall 1989): 12.

24. Linda Greenhouse, "Wedding Bells," Opinionator Blog, *New York Times*, March 20, 2013, http://opinionator.blogs.nytimes.com /2013/03/20/wedding-bells/.

25. Tamar Lewin, "Disabled Woman's Care Given to Lesbian Partner," *New York Times*, December 18, 1991, www.nytimes.com/1991/12/18 /us/disabled-woman-s-care-given-to-lesbian-partner.html.

26. Ball, *From the Closet to the Courtroom*, 57.

27. Positively Revolting, "On Lesbian and Gay Weddings and the Urge to Smash Blenders," *Gay Community News* 15, no. 10 (September 20–26, 1987): 5.

28. Walter Wheeler and Carey Junkin, "It Is Time for the Wedding," *Gay Community News* 15, no. 10 (September 20–26, 1987): 5; also Jay Deacon, "The Wedding: Duplicating Het Marriage, or Celebrating Community?," *Gay Community News* 15, no. 12 (October 4–10, 1987): 7.

29. Michael Botkin, "A Gay Affair; The Wedding Comes Off, amid Criticism, but to the Delight of Thousands," *Gay Community News* 15, no. 14 (October 18–24, 1987): 16.

30. Paula Ettelbrick, "Since When Is Marriage a Path to Liberation?," *Out/Look: National Lesbian and Gay Quarterly* 6 (Fall 1989): 9, 14–17.

31. Tom Stoddard, "Why Gay People Should Seek the Right to Marry," *Out/Look: National Lesbian and Gay Quarterly* 6 (1989): 9–13.

32. Andrew Sullivan, "Here Comes the Groom: A (Conservative) Case for Gay Marriage," *New Republic*, August 27, 1989, https:// newrepublic.com/article/79054/here-comes-the-groom.

33. William Seltzer and Margo Anderson, "The Dark Side of Numbers: The Role of Population Data Systems in Human Rights Abuses," *Social Research* 68, no. 2 (Summer 2001): 481–513.

34. Lisa Duggan, *The Twilight of Equality? Neoliberalism, Cultural Politics, and the Attack on Equality* (Boston: Beacon, 2004), 50.

35. Katherine Franke, *Wedlocked: The Perils of Marriage Equality* (New York: NYU Press, 2015); see also Duggan, *Twilight of Equality*.

36. I'm thinking, of course, of the lead plaintiff, pastor Oliver Brown, and his daughter Linda and the way the NAACP—and the court, in its decision—prominently featured the research of Kenneth Clark and Mamie Phipps Clark, whose "doll test" found that Black children liked white dolls better than Black ones—that they were a

nicer color and they liked to play with them better and struggled to identify themselves with the Black doll. "Kenneth Clark, 90; His Studies Influenced Ban on Segregation," *Los Angeles Times,* May 3, 2005, http://articles.latimes.com/2005/may/03/local/me-clark3. On the difference between the NAACP and gay movement lawyers, see Jennifer Nye, "Gay Marriage in Utah and Oklahoma? Social Movements, Social Change, and the Law in the Postwar United States" (lecture, University of Massachusetts Amherst, History Department, January 29, 2014). Much of this and the subsequent discussion of how these weren't "movement cases" comes from here.

37. Ariel Levy, "The Perfect Wife: How Edie Windsor Fell in Love, Got Married, and Won a Landmark Case for Gay Rights," *New Yorker,* September 30, 2013, www.newyorker.com/magazine/2013/09/30/the-perfect-wife.

38. "Hawaii Horror Story! Hawaii's ACLU Takes Public Opinion Poll to Determine if They Will Support Gay Civil Rights," *Gay Community News* (Hawaii), July 1990: 1, quoted in Bill Rubenstein, "Divided We Litigate: Addressing Disputes among Group Members and Lawyers in Civil Rights Campaigns," *Yale Law Journal* 106, no. 6 (1997): 1623–81.

39. ACLU, Gay and Lesbian Advocates and Defenders, Lambda Legal, National Center for Lesbian Rights, Equality Federation, Freedom to Marry, Gay and Lesbian Alliance Against Defamation, Human Rights Campaign, and National Gay and Lesbian Task Force, "Make Change, Not Lawsuits," May 2009, www.aclu.org/files/pdfs/lgbt/make_change_20090527.pdf.

40. "Justicia reafirma validez de matrimonio igualitario en Puerto Rico," *El Mundo,* March 10, 2016, http://elmundo.pr/3067/180085/a/justicia-reafirma-validez-de-matrimonio-igualitario-en-puerto-rico

41. Movement Advancement Project, Family Equality Council, and Center for American Progress, *All Children Matter: How Legal and Social Inequalities Hurt LGBT Families (Full Report),* October 2011, www.lgbtmap.org/file/all-children-matter-full-report.pdf.

42. "Straight Couples Pivotal in Gay Marriage Fight," *Arizona Republic,* November 9, 2006, http://tucsoncitizen.com/morgue/2006/11/09/32052-straight-couples-pivotal-in-gay-marriage-fight/.

43. Tara Parker-Pope, "Kept from a Dying Partner's Bedside," *New York Times,* May 8, 2009), www.nytimes.com/2009/05/19/health/19well .html.

44. Goodridge v. Department of Public Health, 440 Mass. 309 (March 4, 2003–November 18, 2003): 309–94, 317.

45. Ibid., 331.

46. Ibid., 334.

47. Ibid.

48. See *Goodridge* at 358–359, 798 NE2d at 979–980 [Sosman, J., dissenting].

49. Hernandez v. Robles, 855 NE2d 1 (NY 2006).

50. In re Marriage Cases 43 Cal.4th 757 (2008) [76 Cal.Rptr.3d 683, 183 P.3d 384], 57 (pdf file), http://scocal.stanford.edu/opinion/re-marriage-cases-33178.

51. *In re Marriage Cases,* footnote 38. See also Mary Anne Glendon, *The Transformation of Family Law* (Chicago: University of Chicago Press, 1989), 306.

52. Beyond Marriage, "Beyond Same-Sex Marriage: A New Strategic Vision for All Our Families and Relationships," July 1, 2006, https://mronline.org/2006/08/08/beyond-same-sex-marriage-a-new-strategic-vision-for-all-our-families-relationships/.

53. United States v. Windsor, 570 U.S. ____ 133 S.Ct. 2675, 186, 23. Kennedy further pointed out that "DOMA also brings financial harm to children of same-sex couples. It raises the cost of health care for families by taxing health benefits provided by employers to their same-sex spouses" (24).

54. Katherine Franke, "The Politics of Same-Sex Marriage Politics," *Columbia Journal of Gender and Law* 15, no. 1 (2006): 236–48, argues that lesbian and gay activists had a "Moynihan moment" in all their arguments about how children need marriage, pointing to a 2003 Human Rights Campaign pamphlet on the advantages of same-sex marriage for the children of gay couples. I think that's not quite right. The Human Rights Campaign paper by Lisa Bennett and Gary Gates, *The Cost of Marriage Inequality to Children of Same-Sex Parents,* points to the concrete material and practical disadvantages that the children of gay couples suffer: taxation of domestic partners' health insurance;

legal obstacles and greater expense of second-parent adoption; barriers to second parents' ability to seek medical care for the child, visit the child in the hospital, enroll the child in school, retain custody and/or visitation in the event of divorce, and so forth. While it is reasonable to argue about whether these advantages that should be limited to married parents, it is not Moynihanesque to point out that they are; the neo-con and Moynihan argument is that social ills such as unemployment, delinquency, and criminality that might otherwise be attributed to the pernicious effects of poverty and the activities of the police in poor communities can be laid at the door of single mothers. Lisa Bennett and Gary J. Gates, *The Cost of Marriage Inequality to Children of Same-Sex Parents: A Human Rights Campaign Foundation Report* 13 [2004], http://freemarry.3cdn.net/17c4bf167576a9b74c_7dm6bxloy.pdf.

55. See, for example, J. Robert Brown Jr., Catherine E. Smith, Kyle C. Velte, Susannah William Pollvogt, and Tanya Washington, "Brief for Amici Curiae Scholars of the Constitutional Rights of Children in Support of Respondent Edith Windsor Addressing the Merits and Supporting Affirmance," http://digitalcommons.du.edu/cgi/viewcontent.cgi?article=1028&context=law_facpub.

56. See, for example, Brad Sears and M. V. Lee Badgett, "Same-Sex Couples and Same-Sex Couples Raising Children in California: Data from Census 2000," May 2004, 2, www.law.ucla.edu/williamsproj/publications/CaliforniaCouplesReport.pdf.

57. Kitchen v. Herbert, 961 F.Supp.2d 1181 (D. Utah 2013), 27, www.freedomtomarry.org/page/-/files/pdfs/UtahKitchenHerbertRuling.pdf.

58. Bostic v. Shafer, 760 F.3d 352 (4th Cir. 2014), 28–29, www.freedomtomarry.org/page/-/files/pdfs/Bostic-Decision.pdf.

59. De León v. Perry, Case 5:13-cv-00982-OLG, 25, http://web.stanford.edu/~mrosenfe/US_DeLeon_v_Perry.pdf. See also Nancy Polikoff, *Beyond (Straight and) Gay Marriage* (blog), http://beyond-straightandgaymarriage.blogspot.com/2014/11/its-children-stupid-or-why-ryanne-nolan.html.

60. Obergefell v. Hodges, 576 U.S. ___ (2015), 4, 15, www.supremecourt.gov/opinions/14pdf/14-556_3204.pdf.

61. Ibid., 15.

62. Nan Hunter, "The Undetermined Legacy: 'Obergefell v. Hodges,' *Nation,* June 29, 2015, https://www.thenation.com/article/the-undetermined-legacy-of-obergefell-v-hodges/.

63. The sentence is Lisa Duggan's, from many talks: for example, "The Miseries of Marriage: What Do Queers Lose When We 'Win'?," (panel, Annual Meeting of the American Studies Association, October 8–11, 2015, Toronto, ON).

EPILOGUE

1. "Parents' Guide to Student Success," National PTA, 2013, https://s3.amazonaws.com/rdcms-pta/files/production/public/Common%20Core%20State%20Standards%20Resources/2013%20Guide%20Bundle_082213.pdf.

2. *Collateral Costs: Incarceration's Effect on Economic Mobility* (Washington, DC: Pew Charitable Trusts, 2010), www.pewtrusts.org/~/media/legacy/uploadedfiles/pcs_assets/2010/collateralcosts1pdf.pdf; "Women in Prison Fact Sheet," Women in Prison Project, Correctional Association of New York, April 2009, www.correctionalassociation.org/wp-content/uploads/2012/05/Wome_in_Prison_Fact_Sheet_2009_FINAL.pdf; and "Children of Incarcerated Parents Fact Sheet," New York Initiative for Children of Incarcerated Parents, Osborne Association, n.d., www.osborneny.org/images/uploads/printMedia/Initiative%20CIP%20Stats_Fact%20Sheet.pdf.

3. *Death by a Thousand Cuts: Voices from America's Affected Communities of Color* Journey for Justice Alliance, May 2014, www.j4jalliance.com/wp-content/uploads/2014/02/J4JReport-final_05_12_14.pdf; and "Data Snapshot: School Discipline," Civil Rights Data Collection, Issue Brief no. 1, U.S. Department of Education Office for Civil Rights, March2014,http://ocrdata.ed.gov/Downloads/CRDC-School-Discipline-Snapshot.pdf.

4. See "Who We Are," About, Springfield No One Leaves, www.springfieldnooneleaves.org/about/who-we-are/; Nicolas Hartigan, "No One Leaves: Community Mobilization as a Response to the Foreclosure Crisis in Massachusetts," *Harvard Civil Rights–Civil Liberties Law Review* 45, no. 1 (Winter 2010): 181–204; Sara Abramsky, "Fighting

Foreclosure in Boston," *Nation,* June 15, 2011, www.thenation.com /article/fighting-foreclosure-boston/; and look also to the work of Occupy Our Homes, Neighborhood Organizing for Change, Chicago Anti-Eviction Campaign, and the Colorado Foreclosure Resistance Coalition.

5. Laura Gottesdiener, *A Dream Foreclosed: Black America and the Fight for a Place to Call Home* (New York Zuccotti Park Press, 2013), 63–65.

6. David Harvey, *The Enigma of Capital* (London: Profile Books, 2010), 1.

7. Elizabeth Warren and Amelia Warren Tyagi, *The Two-Income Trap: Why Middle-Class Parents Are Going Broke* (New York: Basic Books, 2003), 5, 9.

8. John Leland, "Baltimore Finds Subprime Crisis Snags Women," *New York Times,* January 15, 2008, www.nytimes.com/2008/01/15/us /15mortgage.html.

9. James Biagioli, "The Subprime Crisis," *New York Times,* January 22, 2008, www.nytimes.com/2008/01/22/opinion/l22subprime.html.

10. Catherine Squires, "Bursting the Bubble: A Case Study of Counter-Framing in the Editorial Pages," *Critical Studies in Media and Communications* 28, no. 1 (2011): 28–47; Jillian Báez and Mari Castañeda, "Two Sides of the Same Story: Media Images of Latinos and Subprime Mortgage Crisis," *Critical Studies in Media Communication* 31, no. 1 (2014): 27–41.

11. Gottesdiener, *A Dream Foreclosed,* 63.

12. Elizabeth Warren, *A Fighting Chance* (New York: Metropolitan Books/Holt, 2014): 86.

13. Susan Schmidt and Maurice Tamman, "Housing Push for Hispanics Spawns Wave of Foreclosures," *Wall Street Journal,* January 5, 2009, www.wsj.com/articles/SB123111072368352309.

14. Neil Fligstein and Adam Goldstein, "The Anatomy of the Mortgage Securitization Crisis," in *Markets on Trial: The Economic Sociology of the U.S. Financial Crisis,* ed. Michael Lounsbury and Paul M. Hirsch (Bingley, UK: Emerald, 2010), 27–68.

15. Gottesdiener, *A Dream Foreclosed.* See also Miranda Joseph, *Debt to Society: Accounting for Life Under Capitalism* (Minneapolis: University of Minnesota Press, 2014).

16. David Dayan, "Obama's Foreclosure Relief Plan Was Designed to Help Bankers, Not Homeowners," *American Prospect* (Winter 2015), http://billmoyers.com/2015/02/14/needless-default/.

17. Paula Chakravartty and Denise Ferreira Da Silva, "Accumulation, Dispossession, and Debt: The Racial Logic of Global Capitalism—An Introduction," *American Quarterly* 64, no. 3 (2012): 361–85; and Brigitte Young, "Gender, Debt, and the Housing/Financial Crisis," chap. 23 in *Handbook of Research on Gender and Economic Life* (Cheltenham, Gloucestershire, UK, and Northampton, MA: Edward Elgar, 2013), 384.

18. Andy Kroll, "Florida AG Unveils Foreclosure Mills Probe," *Mother Jones,* August 10, 2010, www.motherjones.com/mojo/2010/08/florida-ag-probing-foreclosure-mills; Andy Kroll, "Fannie and Freddie's Foreclosure Barons," *Mother Jones,* August 4, 2010, www.motherjones.com/politics/2010/07/david-j-stern-djsp-foreclosure-fannie-freddie.

19. "MomsRising Lauds Settlement in Case Involving Pregnancy Discrimination in Mortgage Lending" (press release), MomsRising, June 1, 2011, www.momsrising.org/page/moms/momsrising-lauds-settlement-in-caseinvolving-pregnancy-discrimination-in-mortgage-lending.

20. Amy Castro Baker, "Eroding the Wealth of Women: Gender and the Subprime Foreclosure Crisis," *Social Service Review* 88, no. 1 (March 2014): 59–91.

21. Neil Barofsky, *Bailout: How Washington Abandoned Main Street While Rescuing Wall Street* (New York: Simon and Schuster, 2013).

22. Quoted in Office for the Special Inspector General for the Troubled Asset Relief Program, *Quarterly Report to Congress* (SIGTARP: Washington DC, July 21, 2010), 175–76, www.sigtarp.gov/Quarterly%20Reports/July2010_Quarterly_Report_to_Congress.pdf.

23. Quoted in Eric Etheridge, "Rick Santelli: Tea Party Time," Opinionator, *New York Times,* February 20, 2009, http://opinionator.blogs.nytimes.com/2009/02/20/rick-santelli-tea-party-time.

24. David Dayan, "This Man Made Millions Suffer: Tim Geithner's Sorry Legacy on Housing," *Salon,* May 14, 2014, www.salon.com/2014/05/14/this_man_made_millions_suffer_tim_geithners_sorry_legacy_on_housing/. See also Barofsky, *Bailout.*

25. Barofsky, *Bailout*, 156–57.

26. Warren, *A Fighting Chance*. 118.

27. Barofsky, *Bailout*, chap. 8.

28. ForclosureMom, "Mom Raps about Foreclosure," October 14, 2010, https://youtu.be/GPPRaKIO-jA. At first I was put off by the white woman in gangsta garb, but it occurred to me finally that she was both expressing how she was shamed and impoverished and claiming her authority in ways that positioned her with Black and Latinx communities.

29. Paul Kiel, "Disorganization at Banks Causing Mistaken Foreclosures," *ProPublica,*May 4, 2010, www.propublica.org/article/disorganization-at-banks-causing-mistaken-foreclosures-050410, quoted in Barofsky, *Bailout*, 152.

30. Barofsky, *Bailout,* 157.

31. Warren, *Fighting Chance,* 111.

32. Tara Siegel Bernard, "Need a Mortgage? Don't Get Pregnant," *New York Times,* July 19, 2010, www.nytimes.com/2010/07/20/your-money/mortgages/20mortgage.html.

33. Maureen R. St. Cyr, "Gender, Maternity Leave, and Home Financing: A Critical Analysis of Mortgage Lending Discrimination against Pregnant Women," *University of Pennsylvania Journal of Law and Social Change* 15, no. 109 (2011): 116–17, http://scholarship.law.upenn.edu/jlasc/vol15/iss1/6/.

34. Ibid.

35. Joan Brasher, "Black Academics Expected to 'Entertain' When Presenting, New Study Says," *Research News @ Vanderbilt,* August 17, 2015, http://news.vanderbilt.edu/2015/08/black-academics-expected-to-entertain-when-presenting-new-study-says/#.VdL_ivO6BAw.facebook; and Nick Pinto, "The Bail Trap," *New York Times Magazine,* August 16, 2015, www.nytimes.com/2015/08/16/magazine/the-bail-trap.html.

36. Laura Briggs, "Activisms and Epistemologies: Problems for Transnationalisms," *Social Text* 97, no. 26: 4 (Winter 2008): 79–96.

INDEX

abortion: abortion/birth control rights, 29, 30, 121–122; eugenics and, 243n46; fetal protection policies and, 42–43; mortgage creditworthiness and, 199; public funding for/regulation of, 4, 22, 121–122, 123, 124

adoption: Black women and, 105; immigrants and, 93–94; Native women and, 13, 29; second parent adoption, 160–161, 166, 176–177, 184–185, 256n54; transnational adoption, 111, 191

A Dream Foreclosed (Gottesdiener), 192–193, 196

age: age at first pregnancy, 55–56, 112, 116, 122, 126–127, 239n17; delayed childbearing, 16, 105–106, 111–112, 115–116, 126, 141, 144, 147–148. *See also* teenage pregnancy/mothers

AIDS. *See* HIV/AIDS

Aid to Dependent Children (ADC), 31

Aid to Families with Dependent Children (AFDC): Black feminists and, 47, 231n71; dependency narrative, 53–54, 56, 58; development of, 31, 63–65; drug use and, 57; hyperfertility and, 57; marriage and, 53–55; people with disabilities and, 58–59, 64–65; race and, 35–36, 58; single mothers and, 12, 53–55; SSI/SSDI and, 63–65; stigma and, 35; TANF and, 65–70, 231n71; tax revenue and, 8–9; teenage pregnancy/mothers and, 58, 70–71; use demographics, 56–57; welfare reform and, 65–70, 132, 224n27, 225n28, 231n71; white mothers and, 12, 56–57; workfare, 51–53, 63. *See also* welfare programs

Alexander, Michelle, 227n40

American Society for Reproductive Medicine, 114, 115, 124–125

debt/credit markets *(continued)*
policy and, 196–197, 199–200;
poverty discourse and, 9, 194;
racial discrimination and, 72,
198–199, 200; student loan debt,
7, 56, 125–126; Third World debt,
39, 81, 82, 83, 110–111, 191, 198,
208–209; unmarried mothers
and, 199. *See also* foreclosure
crisis
Defense of Marriage Act, 182–183,
256n53
Defense of Marriage Act
(DOMA), 176, 182–184, 256n53.
See also *United States v. Windsor*
De León v. Perry (2015), 183–184
Demos, Charles, 202
dependent care: child custody and,
163, 168; disability custody
agreements, 163; family rights
and, 185–186; kinship relationships and, 175; privatization of,
9, 41–46; Sharon Kowalski case,
162–163, 166, 168, 170, 185. *See also*
care work
discrimination: foreclosure crisis
and, 72, 198–199, 206–208;
lesbians and gay men and, 153,
156–157, 170; pregnancy/
pregnancy-related discrimination, 4–5, 42, 206–208, 215n5; sex
discrimination, 5, 24, 41–42. *See
also* racial discrimination
domestic labor: Asian workers, 84,
95–96; Black workers, 233n12;
care deficit and, 95–96; child
care and, 32, 33; collective
households and, 154–155; day
care *vs.*, 76, 82–83, 98; domestic
worker rights, 84, 242n41;
employer costs and, 234n18;
housing and, 77–78; immigrant

workers and, 77–78, 80, 99;
Latinx workers, 80, 84, 233n12;
legal rights of, 84; leisure time
vs., 7, 21, 31–33; maids/house-
keeping workers, 233n12; middle
class households and, 76–78,
82–83; migration status and, 84;
nannies *vs.* day care/child care,
76, 82–83, 98; Nannygate, 75–77,
78–79, 100; offshoring reproductive labor, 80, 95–96, 97; sexual
harassment and, 84; stratified
reproduction and, 83–84; unfree
women and, 33; wages and
working conditions, 83–84, 94,
97; Wages for Housework
movement and, 22, 30–36. *See also*
care work; household labor
domestic violence: care work and,
99; mass incarceration and, 64,
99, 227n40; out of status
immigrants and, 99; sexual
harassment, 73, 84; welfare
recipients and, 64, 226n39, 231n71
Domestic Workers Alliance,
242n41
Dowd, Maureen, 117
drug use: infant mortality and, 12,
129, 134–135, 214n8, 245n63;
pregnancy and, 12, 214n8, 245n63
DuBois, Ellen, 217n20
Duggan, Lisa, 171–172, 185, 258n61
Dykes with Tykes, 156

early childhood education: day
care and, 22, 28–29, 67–69, 73;
free breakfast programs, 28;
Head Start, 28, 67–68; people
with disabilities and, 67; welfare
programs and, 65–69
economic status: bank/mortgage
company predation and, 17–18;

76–78, 98; Native women and,
33; public support for reproductive labor, 190; time famine, 190;
welfare rights movement and,
34–36
housing: Braschi case, 164–166, 171,
176–177, 185; domestic workers
and, 77–78; housing subsidies,
50, 54, 71–72; immigrant workers
and, 77–78, 87–88; kinship
relationships and, 164–167;
redlining, 72, 143, 193–194,
195–196, 199–200; substandard
housing, 87–88, 136, 138, 143, 146;
welfare programs and, 50, 54,
58–59, 70–71, 224n27, 225n28. *See
also* foreclosure crisis
Human Rights Campaign, 256n54
Hunter, Nan D., 174, 185
Hurricane Katrina, 9

immigrants/immigration:
adoption and, 93–94; amnesty,
87; Arab women, 89–91; Asian
women, 86, 89–91, 150; birthright
citizenship, 89; bracero
program, 87–88; care crisis in
home country, 80–81; care work,
77–78, 81–84, 99, 100; Central
Americans and, 86–89, 94;
Chinese women and, 86;
Cordero case, 78–79, 80;
criminalization of violations, 89;
day care/child care and, 15, 99;
detention and deportation, 79,
81, 84, 85, 88–89, 90, 92–94;
domestic labor/nannying and,
15, 99; domestic violence and, 99;
exploitation of, 77, 87; feminism
and, 98–99; foreclosure crisis
and, 194, 202; foster care and,
93–94; free trade agreements

and, 8–9, 88–89, 189; globalization and, 15, 80, 83, 98; historical
development of, 85–89; as
household workers, 15, 33, 76–78,
98; housing and, 77–78, 77–79;
immigrant fathers and, 96, 97;
immigration reform, 78–79, 80;
long-distance motherhood,
94–97, 233n13; low-wage work
and, 234n18; Mexicans and,
86–87; migratory workforce
and, 15, 75–76, 80–81; mothers
and, 91–94; Nannygate and,
75–77, 78–79, 100; offshoring of
reproductive labor and, 15,
80–81, 98, 100, 212; Operation
Gatekeeper, 79, 88–89; out of
status workers, 84; racial
restrictions of, 85–89; refugee
policy and, 93–94; reproductive
politics and, 100; sexual
harassment and, 84; stratified
reproduction and, 81–84;
structural adjustment programs
and, 81, 82, 83, 191, 198, 208–209;
terrorism and, 79, 91–94; US
Border Patrol, 79, 87, 91;
whiteness and, 85–86; young
children and, 93–94
Immigration Reform and Control
Act (IRCA), 78–79
impoverished/low-income women
and households: assisted
reproductive technologies and,
108–109; birth control and,
108–109, 121–122, 123; child care
workers and, 233n12; class
mobility and, 18, 55–56, 72–73,
244n54; culture of poverty
discourse and, 53–55, 56, 112;
debt/credit markets and, 9, 194;
early pregnancy start, 111, 112;

lesbians/queer women *(continued)*
gay parenting; same-sex
marriage
Levin, Josh, 51
low-wage work: child care workers
and, 31, 83–84, 233n12; female
work force and, 221n9; immigration enforcement and, 234n18;
labor organizing and, 22, 221n10,
242n41; maids/housekeeping
workers, 233n12; McJob employers, 3, 48–49, 66, 73, 211; migration
status and, 84; minimum wage
rates, 49, 83–84, 221n7, 242n41;
single women and, 221n8; tax
policy and, 49; Walmart, 48–49,
73, 122, 210, 221n9; Walmart and,
48–49, 73, 210, 221n9. *See also*
impoverished/low-income
women and households
Lubiano, Wahneema, 47–48, 71,
220n2
Luis, Martha, 93

Madrigal v. Quillian, 29
Mainardi, Pat, 31–32, 33, 34
Mamo, Laura, 161
March on Washington for Lesbian
and Gay Rights, 153, 169
marriage: adoption and, 160–161, 166,
176–177, 184–185, 256n54; Chinese
women and, 85–86; Defense of
Marriage Act, 182–183, 256n53;
defense of marriage acts, 176,
182–183, 256n53; family rights and,
185–186; feminist marriage
critiques, 155–156, 168–169;
financial services industry
discrimination, 199; immigrants
and, 150–151; impact on children,
256n54; kinship relationships
and, 182–186; moral harm

discourse of unmarried parents,
182–186; Native people and,
150–151; as oppressive, 154–156;
privatization and, 150–151, 1
85–187; race and, 251n2; right to
contraceptive use and, 170–171;
settler colonialism and, 150–151;
as social safety net erosion and,
175, 182; *United States v. Windsor,*
182–185, 256n53. *See also* same-sex
marriage
Marxism, 10–11, 20
mass incarceration, 64, 191, 227n40
McConnell, James, 167
McConnell v. Anderson, 167–168
McInnes, Gavin, 20
Menzel, Annie, 137–138
Mexican women/households:
anti-immigrant sentiments,
91–94; bracero program, 87–88;
immigration policies and,
86–89; as terrorists, 91–93. *See
also* Latinx women/households
middle class women/households:
career sacrifice discourse,
112–114, 115–121; care gap and,
99–100; crisis of care work,
116–121; day care *vs.* nannies, 76,
82–83; Nannygate, 75–77, 78–79,
100; stratified reproduction and,
81–84; stress storms and, 60, 73;
structural infertility and, 16,
105–106, 111–112, 141, 144, 147–148;
work-life balance, 116–121
miscarriage/stillbirth, 128–129, 130,
144–145, 146
Moore, Lisa Jean, 138
Moreton, Bethany, 221n9
Mothers Against Illegal Aliens,
91–92
mothers/motherhood: use of term,
4–5; age at birth, 115–116;

birthright citizenship, 89; class mobility and, 55–56; culture of poverty and, 53–55, 56; delayed childbearing, 16, 105–106, 111–112, 115–116, 126, 141, 144, 147–148; globalization of, 83, 98; immigrant girls and women, 92–93, 233n113; long-distance motherhood, 94–97; maternity leave, 24–25, 34, 99–100, 206–208, 211; nonworking *vs.* working mothers, 59–63; parental incarceration and, 191; stay-at-home moms and, 17, 19–21, 24, 62, 116–121; stratified reproduction and, 81–84; structural infertility and, 11–112, 16, 105–106, 141, 144, 147–148; transnational motherhood, 233n113; wages-for-motherhood welfare rights movement, 34–36; welfare reform, 50–63

Moynihan, Daniel Patrick, 52–53, 61–62, 172, 194–195, 252n3, 256n54

Müller, Hermann, 107–108, 238n11

Muller v. Oregon, 44–45

Mullings, Leith, 141–144

Mulvaney, Mick, 231n1

Murray, Charles, 53–55, 56

Muslim women/households, 90–91, 150

NAACP (National Association for the Advancement of Colored People), 173–174, 254n36

nannies. *See* domestic labor

Nannygate, 75–77, 78–79, 100

National Coalition of Black Gays, 152–153

National Gay Task Force, 152

National Organization for Women, 43, 99, 216n15, 231n71

National Organization for Women (NOW), 216n15

National Welfare Rights Organization (NWRO), 35

Native women/households: adoption and, 13, 29; care work and, 48; foster care and, 13, 36; household labor and, 33; Indian boarding schools, 13, 29, 33; Indian Child Welfare Act and, 13; infant mortality rates, 134; involuntary sterilization, 29; racialized and gender marriage discourse, 150; reproductive labor and, 12–13; reproductive politics and, 29–30; welfare programs and, 11, 12

neoliberalism: use of term, 8; biocapitalism, 108, 238n13; development and rise of, 36–41; feminism and, 40–41, 45–46; free market fundamentalism and, 8, 36, 38, 39–40, 44, 82, 124, 208; globalization and, 8 , 189; impact on workforce labor, 36–41; offshoring reproductive labor, 15, 80–81, 98, 100, 212; personal responsibility and, 14; privatization and, 8; racism and, 188–191; redistribution of wealth and, 21, 23, 39, 40–41, 72–74, 189; shrinking government spending, 8–9, 11–12, 98–100, 139, 189, 192–193, 208–209; social safety net and, 131; Trump administration and, 188–190; unions and, 37–38; welfare programs and, 9, 131; workforce and, 40–41. *See also* privatization

Nixon administration, 30–31, 51, 202

No One Leaves (MA), 192

Nye, Jennifer, 227n40

148. *See also* teenage pregnancy/
mothers
privatization: ARTs and, 16, 112,
123–125; of care, 8, 47–49, 73–74,
146, 188–189; of care through
marriage, 185–187; conservative
movements and, 22; of day care/
child care, 8; of dependency, 9,
41–46, 180–183, 187; gay marriage
and, 16–17, 149–151, 171–172,
180–183, 186–187; of household
labor, 97–100; Johnson Controls
case, 41–45, 219n49; neoliberalism and, 8–10, 17; of reproductive labor, 22–23, 105. *See also*
neoliberalism; public policy
public policy: culture of poverty
and, 53–55, 56; Fair Housing
Act, 199–200; free trade
agreements, 8–9, 88–89, 189;
impact of Walmart on, 48–49,
73, 210, 221n9; mortgage bailout,
200–209; Nannygate and, 75–77,
78–79, 100; privatization of
household labor, 97–100;
redistribution of wealth, 21, 23,
39, 40–41, 72–74, 189; redlining,
199–200; structural adjustment
programs, 81, 82, 83, 191, 198,
208–209. *See also* neoliberalism;
privatization; social safety net
Puzder, Andrew, 231n1

Quayle, Dan, 54–55
queer people/households: ARTs
and, 16, 116; collective households, 154–155; as families, 16–17;
financial services industry
discrimination and, 199; gayby
boom and, 158–161; HIV/AIDS
care work and, 150, 163–167, 168;
homonormativity and, 171–172;

impact on children, 256n54;
privatization and, 17; respectability politics, 155–156, 164,
168–170, 173–174, 181; same
sex-marriage and, 256n54;
sodomy laws and, 124, 153, 169,
174, 181. *See also* family forma-
tions; kinship relationships;
same-sex marriage

race dynamics: feminism and, 23,
27–30, 169; impoverished
households and, 104–105; racial
equality efforts, 39; welfare and,
34–36
racial discrimination: controlling
images and, 47–48, 221n5; cover
stories, 71, 220n2; debt/credit
markets and, 72, 198–199;
foreclosure crisis and, 72,
198–199, 200; foster care and, 105;
reproductive coercion, 105
racial disparities: of assisted
reproductive technologies,
106–108, 111–112; *Brown v. Board of
Education,* 28, 173–174, 254n36;
Clarke doll test research and,
173–174, 254n36; compensatory
function of whiteness, 13–14;
credit markets and, 198–199; doll
test, 254n36; eugenics and, 15–16,
107–109, 243n46; fertility/
infertility and, 127–129, 146–148;
foster care and, 104–105, 238n6;
as genetically based, 134, 223n23;
infant mortality and, 10, 16,
105–106, 129–144, 131–136, 146,
209; miscarriage and, 106–107,
128–129, 130, 144–145, 146; moral
harm discourse of unmarried
parents, 182–185; neoliberalism
and, 188–191; property taxes and,

Troubled Asset Relief Program (TARP), 200–203

Trump administration: anti-immigrant white nativism, 3, 92–93; globalization and, 8, 189; immigration policy, 92–93, 100; neoliberalism and, 188–190; racial resentment politics of, 14, 188–190, 212; reproductive labor and, 19–21; undocumented household labor and, 231n1

Tyler, Robin, 170

unions: Johnson Control case and, 41–46, 219n49; labor feminism and, 23–27, 98–99; neoliberalism and, 37–38; Reagan administration and, 39–40; trade agreements and, 77; United Electrical, Radio, and Machine Workers Union, 26; women in the workforce and, 23–24. *See also* labor organizing

United Automobile Workers v. Johnson Controls, Inc., 41–45, 219n49

United Electrical, Radio, and Machine Workers Union (UE), 26

United States v. Windsor (2013), 182–185, 256n53

unmarried mothers: Aid to Families with Dependent Children and, 12, 53–55; Black women and, 182–183; class mobility and, 55–56; debt/credit markets and, 199; family rights and, 185–186; fertility and, 83, 126–127; financial services industry and, 199; gay and lesbian parents and, 182–186; kinship relationships and, 150; moral harm discourse of unmarried parents, 182–186;

same-sex marriage and, 150, 182–183; stratified reproduction and, 83–84; subprime mortgages and, 4, 17–18, 192–194; welfare programs and, 12, 53–55, 61–62, 66, 83, 150, 182–183, 185–186; white women and, 54–55

Ventura, Claribel Rivera, 58–59, 224n27

Vider, Stephen, 155

Violence Against Women Act (VAWA), 64, 99, 227n40

Voeller, Bruce, 152

Volcker, Paul, 38–39

Wages for Housework movement, 30–36

wages/income: day care/child care, 31, 48–49, 69; double day framework and, 20, 36–37, 63, 73, 83, 132, 169–170, 186–187, 246n71; family wage, 8, 38–39, 60; minimum wage rates, 49, 83–84, 221n7, 242n41; of nannies, 83–84; rates of decline, 6; stratified reproduction and, 83–84; welfare rights and, 34–36. *See also* debt/credit markets; low-wage work

Wali, Alaka, 141–144

Walmart, 48–49, 73, 210, 221n9

Warren, Elizabeth, 193, 195, 203–204, 206

wealthy women/households: class mobility and, 18; redistribution of wealth and, 21, 23, 39, 40–41, 72–74, 189; stratified reproduction and, 81–84; war on women and, 21

Wedding, the (1987), 169, 170, 173

Weld, William, 224n27